CRITICAL CHEERS

P9-APA-262

"Each of his essays builds swiftly, tapping home its point with sharp little blows . . . Rooney makes us care."

Washington Post

"Rooney hasn't lost his touch turning the ordinary into something special with rueful wit, a sense of the ridiculous and the down-to-earth notion that we are fellow sufferers."

Publishers Weekly

"His humor continues to pour forth like a perfect martini. It is crisp, dry and goes straight to the point."

Atlanta Journal-Constitution

"More varied and much meatier than his previous works . . . This is the best work yet."

Library Journal

"You'll be thrilled with *Pieces of My Mind* . . . Rooney can make absolutely anything interesting—and he does."

Mademoiselle

"Rooney at his best!"

AP

"Hilarious essays . . . His articles make me laugh, sometimes out loud."

Boston Herald

"Immensely enjoyable . . . always a pleasure."

Chattanooga Times

"Curmudgeonly, funny, entertaining"

San Francisco Chronicle

"He's upbeat with a sense of humor . . . his writing is overlaid with wit."

Philadelphia Inquirer

"For a good time, invite Rooney . . . Even more enjoyable than his earlier books."

Cedar Rapids Gazette

PIECES OF MY MIND

ANDREW A. ROONEY

AVON
PUBLISHERS OF BARD, CAMELOT, DISCUS AND FLARE BOOKS

AVON BOOKS
A division of
The Hearst Corporation
1790 Broadway
New York, New York 10019

The Atheneum edition contains the following Library of Congress Cataloging
in Publication Data:

Rooney, Andrew A.
  Pieces of my mind.
  Essays taken from the author's syndicated newspaper columns.
  I. American wit and humor. I. Title.
PN6162.R633   1984   814'.54   84-45038

First Avon Printing, October 1985

Jane Bradford and Neil Nyren had
a lot to do with the editing and
organization of this book
and I thank them for it.   A.R.

Preface

WRITERS are repeatedly asked to explain where they get their ideas. People want their secret. The truth is there is no secret and writers don't have many new ideas. At least, they don't have many ideas that a comic strip artist would illustrate with a light bulb over their heads.

New ideas are one of the most overrated concepts of our time. Most of the important ideas that we live with aren't new at all. If we're grown up, we've had our personal, political, economic, religious, and philosophical ideas for a long time. They evolved out of some experience we had or they came from someone we were exposed to before we were twenty-five. How many of us have changed our opinion about anything important after we were twenty-five because of some new idea?

Like almost everything else that gets popular, new ideas and the concept of creativity have been trivialized. People are passing off novelty for invention. Not many products have been improved with a new idea compared to the number whose quality has been diminished by inferior workmanship and the use of inferior materials. The shortage we face in this country is not new ideas, it's quality work.

Much of the progress of the world has come through genuine creativity but we've cheapened the whole concept by treating creativity as if it were a commodity that could be bought and sold by the pound.

Colleges teach courses in "creative writing" as if a course in just plain writing weren't enough. Trying to teach someone to be creative is as silly as a mother trying to teach her child to be a genius.

I don't know where we all got the thought that ideas come in a blinding flash or that we can learn how to be struck with creative new ideas. Not many ideas come that way. The best ideas are the result of the same slow, selective, cognitive process that produces the sum of a column of figures. Anyone who waits to be struck with a good idea has a long wait coming. If I have a deadline for a column or a television script, I sit down at the typewriter and damn well decide to *have* an idea. There's nothing magical about the process, no flashing lights.

Creativity is a by-product of hard work. If I never have another really new idea, it won't matter. Enough writers are already exploring the new, the far-out, and the obscure. We don't understand the old ideas yet. I'm satisfied trying to quantify the obvious.

We have our ideas. What we need now are more people who can do something good with them.

Contents

VI: **FAMILIAR THINGS**

VII: **OPINIONS**

I:

IT'S ONLY A PLATE

It's Only a Plate

Do I grieve for an icebox? I do.

We're about to buy a new refrigerator—which I still tend to call "the icebox"—and I feel good and bad about it. We need a new one and it's going to be more convenient but I hate getting rid of the old one. It's been such a dependable friend in time of need to eat. I just know nothing good is going to come to it when the dealer delivers the new one and takes the old one away. He'll probably take a few parts off it and just dump the rest of it somewhere. It seems so ungrateful of me.

I was sitting in the kitchen last night, looking around. It's changing gradually from the kitchen it was when the kids were growing up. The table I made that we all ate at thousands of times has been replaced. I hated to see that go, too. It's the kind of progress I don't appreciate. Now the kitchen is in for another big change when that icebox goes. I'll bet the new one won't have as satisfying a sound when you open and close it. New refrigerators have more of a sneaky sound when they open and close. I like a refrigerator door that closes with a solid, reassuring bang. I like the sound this old one has because I associate it with all the good food that came out of it.

But I didn't set out here to write of iceboxes. The question in my mind is whether or not we should be sentimental about inanimate objects. I am incurably so. I feel terrible when I trade in a car I've liked. I even hate to throw out a comfortable old pair of pajamas that are ripped or buttonless or in some other way too disreputable to wear even in the privacy of bed.

Being sentimental about a car or a pair of pajamas or a refrigerator is ridiculous and I know it but I can't help myself. I have this irrational notion that the refrigerator has feelings and will be hurt when I cast it aside after it's given me seventeen years of good service. It will want to know what it's done wrong to deserve ending up in the dump. The car I drive for 91,000 miles before I trade it in will be heartbroken at being turned over to a new owner who will abuse it.

Some inanimate objects don't get me at all. That's lucky. For instance, I retired a television set from the living room about a year ago and felt nothing for it. It was ten years old and we'd watched a lot of good and bad shows on it, but somehow it never earned my affection. It was just a piece of equipment.

My mother came to grips with this and she licked any tendency she had to be sentimental about *things*. She knew that over a lifetime, it was just too sad. Losing people was all the sadness she needed.

I remember one night in our house a guest was trying to help with the dishes. As the guest was rinsing a small, old platter under running water, she hit the platter against the faucet and it cracked cleanly in two. While my mother was dismissing the broken platter as being of no importance at all, in order to make the guest feel better about having broken it, I quietly put the pieces on a shelf. I always think I can mend a plate.

Later, after the guest had gone, I saw mother looking at the two pieces and I asked her about it.

"Yes," Mother said, "Bessie gave that plate to your Dad and me when we were married. I've had it forty-five years." She paused for just one brief, sad beat, I thought, and then she threw both pieces in the wastebasket and said, "But it's only a plate."

I hope I'm not around the house when the men come to take the old refrigerator away, though. I don't think I could stand it, and the truckers would think it was pretty strange to see a grown man standing around with tears in his eyes as they carried out a tired, seventeen-year-old icebox.

A New Kitchen

FOR several years now I've tried to keep my wife from talking about buying a new house by heaping unnecessarily lavish praise on her for something like the new curtains she bought for the living room or the wallpaper in the front hall.

The praise I gave her for the new carpet she had put down in the twins' room apparently wasn't excessive enough, because within just a few days she started talking about moving or having the kitchen done over.

While I hate to encourage her by giving in every time in these negotiating procedures, I am pleased to announce we are having the kitchen done over.

My wife ways we don't have enough cupboard space in the kitchen but I know for sure this is an illusion. Whether a kitchen cupboard, a file cabinet or a clothes closet overflows, depends more on the person putting things into it than on its size. But "Yes, Dear" we'll get new cabinets . . . anything but move.

So they're going to tear out the old cabinets and replace the stove, which they call "the range." They're going to rearrange the lighting, do over the electrical wiring and, of course, put down a new floor. The floor isn't level enough to put one down, though, so first they'll have to take the old one up. I figure if I'm lucky, this new kitchen isn't going to cost me much more than twice what the house cost in the first place. If the President was doing as much for the unemployed as my wife is, the country would be a lot better off.

Last weekend we spent both Saturday and Sunday taking everything out of the kitchen. I don't mean *almost* everything. I mean *everything*. We spent twelve hours each day arguing about what to keep and what to throw out. I lost my last argument at eleven P.M. Sunday night, when I wanted to keep ten of those little pink birthday cake candleholders that I found drifting around in the back of a drawer.

You don't realize how much stuff piles up in those drawers, cabinets and closets in the kitchen. Some of the work of emptying them out and finding places to put the stuff temporarily was useful and satisfying. When you discover that you have three bottles of vinegar, each partly used, it's a great feeling to consolidate the vinegar into two bottles and throw out the empty one. We threw out dozens of bottles, cans and jars emptied through the process of consolidation.

I made several decisions that would have shocked any good cook and didn't even tell my wife what I was doing. For instance, I poured a quarter of a bottle of relatively inexpensive corn oil into a bottle of expensive virgin olive oil that was more than half full. I mixed a small amount of marmalade in with some apricot jam.

My wife kept saying I wouldn't throw anything out but she was wrong. I threw out a bottle that had more than two inches of ketchup in it because we seldom use ketchup. And she says I won't throw anything out.

It wasn't one of the outstanding experiences of our married life but we know now that we have fourteen cans of tuna fish, three half-used boxes of soap pads, a bag of potatoes behind the sink that have begun to sprout and more frozen leftovers in the freezer, which will shortly be disconnected, than we'll ever be able to identify, let alone consume.

For the time being at least, I think I've bought myself another few months before the subject of moving comes up again.

Casting Out Books

IN the futile attempts we all make to tidy up our lives and our surroundings, nothing is more difficult than throwing out a book. I can't even bring myself to throw out a terrible book. I have all I can do to throw out a magazine. It has to be done, though, and I'm trying to develop some plan.

At about age forty, each of us should resolve to throw away or give away one book for each new book we acquire. There are books we will never part with and shouldn't. If you've read and liked a book and taken a little of it into your life, you should keep it forever. It doesn't take up much room, it's attractive on the bookshelf, it doesn't take much dusting and it provides evidence to visitors in your house that you're literate. Even though you may never actually take it down and read it again, the presence of its title staring out at you every day is a reminder of its contents.

The books we should throw out are the junk books we acquire and the books that were good in their time but which have no lasting value. This includes most popular novels. No one reads a novel twice and most of them are read as entertainment and diversion. Nothing that is merely entertaining and diverting is worth saving.

There are some serious problems when you get right down to what to throw out. We have some big, expensive, arty picture books that we never look at. They don't fit on our shelves and we never look at them, but they cost so much I can't bring myself to ditch them and they're hard to give away. No one *else* wants them either. Most of them were gifts in the first place.

Volumes of old books, gilt-edged or bound in leather, are a problem. They look good on your shelves but you've never read the collected works of Dickens and never will. They were left to you by someone in the family who never read them. As a matter of fact, none of the eight volumes has ever been read by anyone and probably ought to be given to a worthy cause, although I doubt if a worthy cause would read them either.

I'm looking at my bookshelves as I write. There's *Catch-22* up there. It's a good book but I won't be reading it again.

There's *Dr. Zhivago.* I wouldn't want Boris Pasternak to know but I never got through the whole thing. Sorry, Boris, but I think you'll have to make room for someone else.

Here's a thin hardcover book I've just taken down. It's published by the U.S. Chamber of Commerce and it's called *America's Outstanding Young Men, 1938-1966.*

Now, this is the kind of book I keep. It's dated but the names in it bring back ideas and memories that might otherwise be lost to me forever. They pick ten outstanding young men every year. Look at this! In 1938 Howard Hughes was thirty-four and they thought he showed promise. Rudy Vallee's on the list and so is Elmer Layden, the Norte Dame football coach. Orson Welles is here. He was twenty-three in 1938 and considered a genius. It seems to me it's been all downhill for Orson since he turned twenty-four. Geniuses do not make their living doing television commercials. Anyway, I'm certainly not going to throw out this little book. It'll always remind me how short life is and that I'd better keep moving.

If I had to make a few rules for which books to throw out, I'd say throw out:

1—Books of advice on how to make money, lose weight or have a happy marriage.

2—Any book whose jacket says that it's "a torrid romance."

3—Any novel whose title brings to your mind no memory whatsoever of plot or character.

4—Any book whose title begins, *The Anatomy of . . .*, *A Treasury of . . .* or *The Changing Face of . . . .*

5—All the books that have been made into movies you've seen.

This should make room for some new books on your shelves.

Old Appliances

THERE'S nothing older than an old electrical appliance. An old piece of furniture may qualify as an antique and an old piece of clothing may make a good rag, but an old electrical appliance is junk. We've got to face that fact in America.

It's not easy to accept the idea that an appliance has a defined life span. Usually the appliance is so new, so shiny, so magic and so expensive when we buy it that its mortality is no more questioned by us than our own.

In our house today, pushed to the rear of upper shelves in the kitchen, hidden behind pots in the lower cabinets and stashed away in cellar, attic and garage are dozens of dead pieces of electrical equipment. We have several electric coffee percolators that I'd never think of using again, old irons so full of sediment from the water that they no longer steam, two or three nonworking radios, several food mixers, nine hair dryers, a record player and a black-and-white television set.

Perhaps what we need is some kind of friendly mortician who would console us on the loss of our electrical loved ones and promise to dispose of them in a dignified manner. Just tossing a Mixmaster into the trash seems so uncivilized.

The absolutely worst thing you can do with an old appliance is give it to a friend or another family member as if you were doing them a favor. This not only puts the burden of throwing it away on them but they're further burdened with the fear that you'll show up at the house and ask where it is.

We really haven't had electrical appliances for all that long, in terms of the history of the world or even the history of the United States. The first ones are just getting to the age when they're absolutely no good at all but there's a whole generation of appliances that came along in the forties, fifties, sixties and seventies that would be on Social Security now if they were people.

While people are lasting longer than they used to, appliances aren't lasting as long, so there are more people alive today and more appliances that ought to be tossed out.

The whole problem first dawned on me when a quarter-inch drill I owned stopped working. It still looked okay but it just wouldn't work. Naturally, I decided to have it fixed. Well, as we all know, *deciding* to have an appliance fixed and actually *getting* it fixed are two different things. Most modern appliances were not designed to be fixed. They were designed to be used until they broke down and then thrown away.

Anyway, I set the drill aside to be fixed at a later date and went out and bought a new one. I can use two, I thought to myself.

That was eleven years ago tomorrow and the drill that won't work is still right where I left it, waiting to be fixed. I realize now that I should have thrown it out the day it broke. There were still a lot of parts that were not broken, I suppose, but if you don't know which are and which aren't, that does you no good at all.

In the year 3000 I suppose there might be some museum value to my son's first record player but, as things stand today, it's just one more piece of junk taking up space in the room he used to occupy, and next Saturday morning I'm going to start with that. Out it goes.

The Red Badge of Character

IF it weren't for the fact that new things are so satisfying to buy, it would be depressing how soon they start to deteriorate after you acquire them.

When I buy a new car, which isn't often, I always wait with a feeling of dread for the day I put the first scratch or dent in it. Sooner or later it has to come. Once I scraped the side of the car on the green paint of the garage door when I was putting it away in a hurry during a rainstorm. Another new car I had, got its first dent in the parking lot of a supermarket. Some fellow parked too close to me and the edge of his door banged into mine when he opened it. It wasn't much of a dent but it doesn't take much to change your attitude toward a new car. Once it happens, even if it's within the first few weeks after you bought it, the car seems used and you begin thinking of your next one, pristine and undented.

We bought a new carpet for the living room eight years ago. On the third night after we got it, I took a cup of coffee into the living room after dinner to drink while I watched television. I drank most of it but by the time I got to the last half-inch it was cold and I put the cup on the little table next to my chair. Half an hour later I reached for the second section of the newspaper and dumped the cup on the floor, spilling the cold coffee. For an instant I was pleased that the cup hadn't broken but then I saw the spot on the rug. I ran to the kitchen for damp cloths and tried to remember whether it was lemon juice or club soda you use on coffee spots (I know it's tomato juice you put on a dog that gets into a skunk). Nothing took the coffee stain out, though, and from its third day that new carpet has been just another old rug with a spot on it, that I'd like to get rid of.

When I was twelve, my mother bought me a corduroy suit. It must have been the first real suit with matching pants and jacket that I ever had. It even had a vest.

That Sunday we went to my uncle's house for dinner and I wore my new suit. I was very proud of it, especially the vest. We came home late that afternoon and our English bulldog, Spike, had been locked in the house most of the day so I took him out in the backyard to play. For some reason, I didn't bother to change my clothes first.

Spike loved to pull on a heavy leather strap we had

and I started to play tug-of-war with him. He weighed almost as much as I did and it was always a close contest. Somehow he got me over by the fence at the side of the yard. He gave me a hard tug and I caught my new corduroy pants on a nail sticking out of the fencepost. It tore a jagged hole in the pants just above the knee.

As you can imagine, that was not one of the best days in my life. I felt terrible about tearing my pants and even worse about how mad my mother was. My mother sewed them up and I wore them for several years but never with any pleasure. As a matter of fact, that experience gave me a complex about new suits. Whenever I buy a new one, I'm nervous every time I wear it during its first six months. I can still see that jagged tear in the knee.

Fortunately, there are characteristics that possessions have, or acquire, that we sometimes prefer to brand-newness. If we keep a car long enough, we lose the feeling that it's a new car we banged up and start thinking of it as a somewhat battered but lovable old friend.

It's a good thing we can take as much pleasure from oldness as newness because, for the most part, we have to live with more oldness. When we buy something new, we're looking for something, unlike ourselves and our other possessions, perfect. It never stays that way for long and it's this period of disillusion and disappointment that we find so hard to live with. As the possession acquires more of the character of the owner, the owner feels easier about its defects. I wouldn't recognize my old Ford station wagon without those dents in the front fender and the missing piece of decorative stripping on the door on the driver's side. They're part of the car now and I like it, but I recall how upset I was about them for the first few years.

Sartorial Shortcomings

From time to time it is brought to my attention that I'm not the best-dressed man in the world. Someone wrote once that I looked as though I slept in Grand Central Station every night. I have four grown children who unfortunately aren't afraid of me and they've never hesitated to point out my sartorial shortcomings, either. The least they could do is lie a little if they really love me.

I'm relatively unaware of how I look in clothes. I usually look once in the mirror when I dress in the morning but that only shows me myself from the chest up.

I don't know where I go wrong. I buy pretty good clothes but one of us is usually the wrong shape.

Maintaining clothes in good condition is as hard as keeping a house painted and in working order. For example, it's inevitable that you're going to get a spot on a necktie or the lapel of a coat once in a while. I keep all kinds of spot remover at home and in the office and I've never had any success with any of them. That spray can, with the powder in it, just plain doesn't work for me. I've used it a dozen times on grease spots and the same thing always happens. The grease spot is gone and I'm left with a big, plainly visible splotch of white chalk imbedded in the fabric. Nothing takes that out, ever.

Most brands of spot cleaner use carbon tetrachloride. I've tried to remove a thousand spots from a thousand neckties with carbon tet. All I get is a ring bigger and more obvious than the original spot.

I've seen women remove spots successfully. They say you just have to keep rubbing in circles. I've rubbed spots in circles with carbon tet until I was blue in the face from the fumes and I still get nothing but a big ring and a smelly tie.

In the morning I often take a pair of pants, a shirt or a coat into the back room where we have an iron set up. My intentions are good. I don't want to burden my wife with my problems and I want to look neat. I don't want to embarrass my friends or my family.

I have yet to iron a pair of pants that end up with fewer than two creases down the front of each leg. I'd like to have one of those machines the dry cleaners have. They just lay a pair of pants on there any which way, they pull down that handle, there's a big whoosh of steam and presto! the pants are perfect.

Shirts? Who can iron a shirt? I've never ironed a shirt yet that didn't look worse when I finished with it than it did when I started.

Neckties are smaller but they're at least as hard to iron as a shirt. You'd think they'd be easy but if you press down on a tie, you get the imprint of the lumpy lining on the front of the tie. As a result, many of my ties look like my pants.

During the summer I often carry a tie in my pocket instead of wearing it. Many of them never recover during the winter.

It's a good thing socks don't show much because if my kids think my pants and jackets look bad, they should see my socks. I've given up trying to put them on right side out because at least half the time I don't even have a pair. I just look for two socks in the drawer that are somewhere near the same color. I haven't had pairs of socks in years.

The funny thing is that I have a clear idea in my mind what someone well dressed looks like. I know what I want to look like and sometimes I realize I'm unconsciously thinking that's what I *do* look like. Obviously I'm dreaming.

I had several friends in school who were always well dressed, and I can go around for days thinking I look more or less the way they looked. Marshall always looked just right. Then someone will casually tell me I look like an unmade bed and I'm brought back down to earth.

The only thing for me to do is take the position that clothes don't make the man.

Buying Clothes

IF I had known for sure, when I bought the clothes I own, that I was going to like them and wear them, I could have saved myself a fortune. The clothing business would be in big trouble if all of us liked everything we bought when we got it home, because we wouldn't be traipsing back to the store in a few weeks to buy something to replace it. My average is slightly below fifty percent. I like and wear less than fifty percent of everything I buy once I get it home. My clothes closets are filled with pants, jackets, shirts and shoes that seemed attractive and practical to me in the store when I bought them but haven't worked out at all.

To make up for those, I have four or five suits I've owned for ten years that I've worn and worn. I wouldn't part with them for anything. I reach for the same old things year after year. Toward the middle of spring when the weather starts to turn hot, I put away th clothes I've worn all winter and think to myself that some of those old favorites have seen their last season.

I cannot quite bring myself to throw out the old favorites, though, and I decide to give them one last summer vacation in the back of my closet.

In September, when the first nip is in the air, I reach for something warmer. I take out that old favorite, look it over and put it on. It looks fresher and better than it did at the end of last year. I can get away with it for another year, I think to myself. And another. And another.

One of the great disappointments to me about clothing is how consistently I find that the most expensive clothes I buy are the best. This doesn't seem fair or biblical. When I pay more for an all-wool suit or an all-cotton shirt by a good maker, it looks better, fits better and wears longer. When I buy a snappy-looking synthetic jacket or a pair of pants that are supposed to do everything but walk to the washing machine by themselves, I'm usually disappointed. I wear the jacket a few times and then it begins to drift to the unused end of the clothespole in my closet.

A second disappointment to me when it comes to

buying clothes is that you can never repeat anything. If you buy something you like and wear it for a year and decide you'd like another similar to it, you can never get one. They don't make them that way any longer. Clothing manufacturers are a restless bunch. They don't stick with a good thing when they have it. They try something else and it's usually worse. That's fashion.

I have a pair of light brown corduroy pants that are a little thin at the knees and ragged around the pockets. I still like them and wear them Saturdays but I'd like a new pair so my wife wouldn't be embarrassed when we go to the supermarket together. I can't find those corduroy pants anywhere. They're all bell-bottomed and without belt loops this year.

In America we treat clothes the way we treat food. We spend more for food than is necessary to nourish ourselves and more for clothes than is necessary to cover ourselves. We have fun with these luxuries and I have no objection to them but I wish the manufacturers would spend a little more time thinking about quality and a little less on style.

The fact is that most of us don't wear most of the clothes or shoes we own. We just *have* them.

Dave Garroway used to have his clothes closet divided into sections by size. He was always going from 180 to 230 and back down again so in the morning he'd weigh himself to see which size suit he should wear. My weight goes up and down, too, but I don't have my clothes separated by size. When my weight is up, my clothes fit tight. When my weight is down, they hang on me.

I think it might be a good idea if we set aside one

night a year when we took everything we own out of the closet and every shirt, sock and set of underwear out of our dresser drawers and tried them each on in front of a mirror.

Next to the mirror there should be a huge wastebasket.

Underwear

You have to look for good in people wherever you can find it. A very nice thing about most people is that they wear their best underwear when they get dressed up to go to a party, even though it isn't going to show. There's something basically honest about that.

One of the pleasures of a vacation is being able to wear your old underwear. I have a lot of it that's too good to throw away but not good enough to wear out in the world. On a normal, nonvacation day, there's always that thought that some emergency might arise that would cause to be revealed what you're wearing underneath. Maybe you'll be hit by a bicycle and taken to a doctor's office where you'll be told to undress. (It is quite possible that one of the reasons doctors charge so much is that they see the good underwear people are wearing and conclude they must be rich.)

The pleasure of wearing old clothes on vacation isn't limited to underwear. Another good part of my vacation is being able to wear the shirts I own that are frayed at the collar after several years of regular duty. At the beginning of my vacation, I go through my dresser drawers and remove the shirts that have seen their best days. I get a pair of scissors and cut the sleeves off just above the elbow.

I can't tell you the satisfaction I get from wearing these old friends on vacation. It gives me the feeling that I'm saving money but I also like the idea of getting everything there is out of something. Wearing a comfortable old shirt with a frayed collar on vacation is conservation at its best.

Some old clothes don't adapt themselves to being worn on vacation. I own several gray business suits that are beginning to look seedy. The pants fit and they're comfortable but I wouldn't think of wearing them to hang around in on vacation.

Most dress shoes don't take kindly to this kind of retirement, either. I have a few old pairs that I keep to hack around in but shoes that were meant to be shined never look right with paint on them. I've bought myself a pair of work shoes for vacation and I alternate between them and old sneakers that were once tennis shoes.

Vacation clothes have to be clothes that are loved. It's not a time for wearing rejects that don't fit or clothes that you've hated since you got them home from the store. Sometime last winter I bought a package of three undershirts. The label said they were "100 percent cotton."

The undershirts were good in all regards, except I noticed that when I wore them, my shoulders itched. A writer can't write if his shoulders itch so I removed my outer shirt and looked for one of those scratchy labels they often put in the neck. There was none. I put the shirt back on but my shoulders still itched.

When I undressed for bed that night, I inspected the stitches in the top of the shoulder straps of my new underwear. Aha! There were the offending threads, and I question whether or not they were cotton.

Now what do I do? I can't take the underwear back to the store and demand my money back because they make my shoulders itch. This doesn't sound like a reasonable complaint, so I put the three undershirts in the bottom of my drawer until last week. Foolishly I decided that while the undershirts weren't good enough to wear to work in the city, they'd be just the thing to wear on vacation in the country. This was a mistake. I don't want my shoulders to itch on vacation any more than I want them to itch when I'm at work.

I've put those three undershirts back in the bottom of a dresser drawer. Someday maybe I'll take them to a textile laboratory and find out whether or not the shirts are really "100 percent cotton," including those threads in the shoulders.

Clothes Make the Woman

MEN and women are doing more things the same way in our society but there's still a huge difference in their attitudes toward clothes and the way they dress. You never know what a woman's going to wear. You have a pretty good idea what a man's going to have on.

"What'll I wear?" isn't a question a man asks very often because he doesn't have that many choices.

A woman may wear a skirt one day and pants the

next. You wouldn't find a man wearing pants one day and a skirt the next.

I'm not complaining. This is just a comment. I admire women's ability to adjust to this kind of change every day but I wonder if it doesn't slow them down in a hundred little ways. If I wore different kinds of clothes every day, I'd always be slipping things in a pocket that wasn't there. I become as familiar with the clothes I wear as I am with being right-handed and if I dressed differently every day, it would certainly delay me. For instance, I usually leave things in my pants pockets overnight. It saves time knowing I'm going to wear them again tomorrow.

Women have a vastly greater array of underwear than men. I don't come in contact with a lot of women's underwear but I do read the ads in the Sunday papers like everyone else and I'm amazed at the variety. I don't wonder it takes longer for the average woman to dress than for the average man. Just for a woman to decide which underwear to take out of the drawer would use up several minutes. I could have my shirt and pants on by that time.

Years ago it was just a question of whether a woman's slip showed or not. Underwear for women has come a long way since then. It ranges all the way from none to lash-ups that rival an astronaut's space suit.

I hope women understand I'm just being friendly. I just want to help. Most men have four or five pairs of shoes. A man has a couple of pairs of dress shoes, usually one black pair and one brown. He has a pair of work shoes, a pair of sneaks or running shoes and maybe a pair of heavy boots.

There are lots of women who own twenty-five or thirty pairs of shoes. These are not rich women. They may be working women or housewives who aren't fancy dressers but anyone looking in their closets at the shoes on the floor might guess they were in show business. Most women could wear a different pair of shoes every day for a month and still have some left over.

Women own more belts than men. Women have more belts than shoes. Half the dresses they own take a belt and no two dresses take the same one. A man has a couple of belts to hold up his pants. They are not considered decorator items. Some men have just two belts. They have one for when they weigh 164 pounds and another for when they weigh 187. Men don't have drawers filled with belts nor do belts drip from hooks in their closets. Having so many belts to choose from is not going to help women get ahead in the world.

There's one good thing that women and men agree on. Neither wears a hat much anymore. Hats are just for fun or special occasions now. When I was growing up, my mother didn't leave the house without a hat on and neither did my father. My father wore a fedora, one of the silliest, least efficient pieces of clothing ever designed. My mother had a selection of hats she wore, depending on the occasion and the clothes she was wearing.

I like attractively dressed women but I do have a nervous feeling that women should buy fewer clothes. If women didn't have so many decisions to make when they open their closet doors in the morning, they'd be off to a better start.

Shoes

THE single biggest step women have taken toward equality with men, since they acquired the right to vote in 1920, is in the shoes they're wearing. Fewer women are tottering around on high, spindly heels and there is no doubt that the change in footwear is going to help them stay even or get ahead of men. Up until now it's taken women longer to do everything because in the shoes they were wearing, they couldn't get anywhere as fast as men.

One of the most encouraging things I see every day is women walking to work in New York City. New York, more than almost anyplace else in the country, is a walking city. Hundreds of thousands of people walk twenty or thirty blocks from where they live uptown or downtown, into midtown where they work. Thousands of women are hustling along in good, rubber-soled sneakers. Sneakers have become so sophisticated that no one calls them that anymore but I'm sure you know what I mean. The women either carry a bag with the shoes they plan to wear in the office or they have left shoes at the office. They change into those when they get there. In most cases even their dress shoes have heels that are low compared to those women wore in the past.

I don't know how women ever got trapped into wearing spike heels. Spike heels are only slightly less arcane than the bindings Chinese women used to use to make their feet small. I say I don't know but I suppose I do know. Women's legs look sexier in high heels than in sneakers. What I really don't know is why this is so.

For some obscure reason men have got themselves thinking that a woman's leg, from the knee down, is more attractive if the calf is quite full but tapering off sharply into a thin, bony ankle. If the heel is propped up on a platform, it tends to make a lump of the calf muscle. That's the look we like.

The answer is for men to reeducate themselves about what looks attractive about a woman's leg. That shouldn't be hard. I've just about got myself to the place where a woman's leg looks better to me in a pair of sneakers than in shoes with heels.

There hasn't been much progress made in what men wear on their feet. The average man is wearing shoes that don't really come close to approximating the outline of his feet. He buys a pair of shoes that are about an inch longer than his feet so they won't pinch his toes and then he starts breaking them in. Breaking in a pair of shoes means stretching them by wearing them until they're close enough to the shape of your feet so they don't hurt much when you walk in them.

If you look at a man's foot in his shoes, you can tell the shoes don't really fit. The widest part of his foot almost always stretches the leather so that the upper part of the shoe hangs over the sole.

For years now they've been molding ski boots to fit your foot precisely and I'm waiting for that to happen with the ordinary shoes we wear. I confidently expect the time isn't far off when both men and women will be able to walk into a shoe store and have shoes made for them that exactly conform to the shape of their feet.

Molded shoes can be bought now but they are made mostly for people with orthopedic problems and they're very expensive. Even people with normal feet look funny in molded shoes because the shoes *are* the shape of their feet and we're not used to that. We're used to pretending that our feet are the shape of our shoes and they're not, of course.

Feet have gotten a dirty deal over the years. We haven't paid half as much attention to them as we've paid to our hands. Feet are what Howard Cosell would call the unsung heroes of our bodies. We ought to give them a better break and the women walking to work in sneakers or running shoes are taking a big step in that direction. If I wore a hat, I'd take it off to them.

Change the Oil and the Glove Compartment, Please

A NEW car manual tells you to have the oil changed at least every season, but it never gives you any advice about the glove compartment. The things in the glove compartment need changing at least as often as the oil in the crankcase.

I've read about states applying for national disaster relief that weren't in as bad shape as the glove compartment of my car. Yesterday I was looking for a pencil when I was in the car in a supermarket parking lot.

Pencils are one of the most difficult things to keep in a glove compartment because they drift to the bottom of it and way back. Finally I took everything out of the glove compartment, put it on the passenger seat and started through it methodically.

Following is the list of contents:

—Three badly folded maps of New York State, one of Ohio and a Hertz map of the San Francisco Bay Area.

—Various envelopes pertaining to new or old car registrations.

—A parking ticket from Washington, D.C., dated March 9, 1979.

—Three screws, a small stainless steel bolt and a wavy kind of washer. These have all fallen off some interior part of the car during its lifetime but I don't know where they fell from.

—The manual of operation for the car. It says on the cover: "Instructions: Read carefully before operating." I've had the car since 1977 but I haven't read it yet.

—Three pennies and a Canadian quarter.

—Half a roll of assorted Life Savers.

—One pair of sunglasses with the earpiece broken off.

—Several old grocery lists, some envelopes and bits of paper with things written on them, all of which must have been important at one time.

There were no gloves in the glove compartment and I never did find a pencil. I quickly shoved everything back in and slammed the door shut.

The most valuable thing about many old cars is the stuff in the glove compartment and what lies behind the cushions of the front seat. If you've owned a car for five years, it's likely that at least ten dollars' worth of small change and other valuables will have slipped down there. The change mixes with old Kleenex, rubber bands, lost keys, combs, important papers and pencils. That's where the pencils go in a car, down behind the front seat where you can't get at them. Some day a car manufacturer is going to make a car with a glass-bottomed front seat so you can look down and see all the money.

The trunk of a car has many of the same kind of items in it that the glove compartment has, only bigger. One of the great things about buying a new car used to be the tool kit they gave you with it. New cars don't come with tool kits anymore but there are plenty of other things that fill the trunk.

I happen to know that at this very moment the trunk of my car contains two boards, a plastic bag of clothes I've been meaning to take to the Goodwill or the Salvation Army, a snow shovel, a bundle of old *National Geographics* and a partridge in a pear tree.

What I'd like, when I start packing the trunk to go somewhere, is a car equipped with one of those compactors like they have on garbage trucks. I could open the trunk, press the button and have the trunk lid come down, slowly and with great force. It would compact everything already in the trunk. That would make plenty of room for me to dump the suitcases in there and take off.

For the time being, I guess I'll just have the oil changed.

Directions

EARLY next year I'm going to take a week off and read the directions for all the things I've bought that came with the warning READ DIRECTIONS CAREFULLY BEFORE OPERATING.

There's no sense reading directions to something before you understand a little bit about it, because they don't mean anything to you. You have to know enough about something to be confused before directions help. Once I've pressed some wrong buttons or tried to open something by pressing on it when I should have been pulling on it or sliding it sideways, then I can understand the directions.

I have a whole box of directions I've never read. Many of them are still in their plastic wrappers. When Christmas comes again, I'll probably be getting more. Last Christmas my kids gave me a new camera. I've shot ten rolls of film with it and I've made about all the mistakes there are to be made. It will be fun now to see if the directions have any good suggestions.

It is always surprising to me to see how many issues divide our population almost in half. For example, I think it's safe to say that we are about evenly divided between people who read directions before operating, as they're warned to do under threat of death, and people who don't ever read the directions. The same people who don't read the maps in the glove compartments of their cars are the ones who don't pore over the instructions for operating their new washing machine or video cassette player.

My wife drives a Saab and during the three years we've had it, I've used it a dozen times. For the life of me I can't figure out how the heater works. I almost froze last winter driving into the city one day. This summer I drove in with it on a hot day and fussed with the controls the whole hour trying to get the air conditioning to work. That night I complained to my wife about how complicated the controls were. I said I was going to read the directions about how to work the air conditioning.

"Forget it," she said. "It doesn't have air conditioning."

In spite of some bad experiences, I'm a firm believer in the trial and error method of learning. If I were asked to take the space shuttle into outer space, I'd first want to climb on board and start fooling with the controls before I read anything about it. If I do read the directions about something before I know a single thing about it, I get so discouraged I give up. If, on the other hand, I bumble along making mistakes, confident that I can always look at the directions if I have to, then I usually find out how to do it the hard way.

Direction writers have improved over the years. Even the directions that come with a piece of Japanese electronic equipment are written in better English than they used to be.

You'd think it might be dangerous to ignore written directions but usually those little red tags say something like DANGER: UNDER NO CIRCUMSTANCES SHOULD THIS BE PUT IN A BATHTUB FULL OF WATER! They warn you against some very obvious things.

Most of us know by now that you don't put a toaster in the dishwasher and that you shouldn't drop the television set when you're bringing it in the house. On the other hand, it has been my experience that FRAGILE THIS SIDE UP can usually be ignored with no ill effects. Unless you've bought a cut-glass crystal pitcher that comes filled with champagne, there aren't many things you can't carry upside down.

I'm going to look through my box of directions for the ones about my camera but usually if I really want the directions for one specific piece of equipment, those are the directions I threw out.

Wastebaskets

WHAT would you say are the ten greatest inventions of all time?

The wheel would have to be high on the list and so would the engine, steam or gasoline. The printing press, radio, airplane, the plow, telephone, cement, the spinning wheel, the automobile and now I guess you'd have to include the computer. How many's that?

You can make your own list but don't count discoveries. Discoveries are different from inventions. Nuclear energy, for instance, isn't so much an invention as it is a discovery, like electricity or fire.

The propeller to drive a boat is a good invention although you wouldn't put it in the top ten. Someone just suggested the zipper. I reject the zipper. It's a handy gadget but it's a gadget.

One of the things you never see mentioned in the schoolbooks when they talk about inventions is, in my mind, one of the greatest developments of all time. It is the wastebasket. I could live without laser beams, the phonograph record or the cotton gin, but I couldn't do without a wastebasket.

If some historian wishes to make a substantial contribution to the history of mankind, he or she might find out who invented the wastebasket. It is time we had a National Wastebasket Day in that person's honor.

There are four important wastebaskets in my life although we have nine altogether in our house. The four are in the bedroom, the kitchen, the room in which I write at home and my office away from home.

Day in and day out, I can't think of anything that gives me more service and satisfaction than those wastebaskets.

I begin using a wastebasket early in the morning. When I'm getting dressed and I get ready to put the stuff on top of my dresser back in my pants pocket, I go through it and sort out the meaningless bits of paper I've written meaningless notes on. Those I throw in the wastebasket in order to give my pockets a clean start for the day. I make room for new meaningless bits of paper.

In my writing room, nothing is more important to me than my wastebasket. This essay takes only three pieces of paper, typed and double-spaced when it's completed. You might not think so from some of the things you read in it but I seldom finish an essay in fewer than ten pages. You get three and the wastebasket gets seven.

The kitchen wastebasket is the only controversial one. Margie and I don't always agree on what goes into it. There's a fine line between what goes into the garbage can and what goes into the wastebasket.

The young people of today have television but one of the things they're missing is the experience of burning the papers in the backyard. It was a very good thing to do because it was fun, and while you were doing it you got credit for working.

Most towns have ordinances prohibiting the burning of papers now. I approve of the law but I sure miss burning the papers. Taking the wastebaskets downstairs and out into the garage to dump them into the big trash container that the garbage man picks up, is not nearly so satisfying a way of disposing of their contents as burning them used to be.

In recent years there's been an unfortunate tendency to make wastebaskets more complicated and fancier than is necessary. Many of the good department stores and fancy boutiques have made them into gifts. A wastebasket is not a proper gift item. Many wastebaskets in these places have been decorated with flowers or clever things painted on them. A wastebasket doesn't want to be clever and it doesn't want to be so cute or gussied up that it calls attention to itself, either. Wastebaskets should be inconspicuous.

You can make your own list of the ten greatest inventions of all time but leave a place for the wastebasket.

Stop, Thief!

MORE people than ever are stealing things and many of those things are being taken from me.

Crime rate statistics by government agencies are impersonal numbers, but when crime hits home, it hurts. Just since I sat down at my typewriter ten minutes ago, several things have disappeared. The thieves in my life are getting so good at taking things that I didn't even notice anyone come in this room. The door is closed, the windows are down but obviously someone got in. They've taken a pen I had right here next to me, for example.

Not three minutes ago I had a pad of paper on which I'd made some notes and now that's gone. It just disappeared. Why would a thief want my notebook?

I happen to know I put that notebook right next to . . . wait a minute. Okay, my notebook is here. I'm sorry about that. I did think it had been stolen. In this one case I may have been wrong but I know that pen I had was lifted by some light-fingered person who . . . hold it. Here's the pen in my shirt pocket. Maybe that wasn't really stolen either but there are plenty of things missing around here and someone must be taking them.

I wear glasses for reading or writing and a day seldom goes by that some low-down thief doesn't steal a pair from me. The thief must be afraid because I really get mad when I can't find my glasses. Obviously he gets worried about being caught red-handed and puts them back where he knows I'll find them at a later time. My glasses will sometimes show up in a coat pocket two days later or under the Sunday newspapers on the coffee table in the living room where he's planted them. Three or four times a year the thief makes off with them for good and I have to buy new ones. I don't know why anyone would want to steal my glasses all the time.

The funny thing about all this stealing is that they don't seem to go after anything of real value. How much could a burglar get from a fence for a few pieces of leftover steak I know for sure I put way back on the middle shelf of the refrigerator the other day? Obviously someone came into the kitchen in the middle of the night and stole the steak. If he's so hungry he has to take stuff out of our icebox, I guess I can't get too mad at him. He must be really hard up, because half the time when I go look for something in the refrigerator I can't find it.

There are many times when things seem to be taken more to irritate me than for any other reason. I can understand someone stealing a car but why would anyone take just the car keys? They're always disappearing. What do thieves do with car keys?

In my shop it seems to be the little things that are always missing, too. Yesterday I was looking for a five-eighths set wrench to tighten a bolt on the lawn mower. Every other size was right there in the box where I keep them but the one I needed had been stolen. It seems like that's always the way.

My wristwatch is often taken and one day last winter I was going home on the train with a briefcase full of papers and that was stolen. I can't account for what happened any other way. I know I put the briefcase on the overhead rack before I sat down but when I got home, the briefcase was gone. I didn't have it with me. The papers were all valuable to me but apparently they weren't to the guy who took it because several days later I stopped at the lost-and-found office at the railroad station and the briefcase was there. He must have stolen it and then turned it in.

Every politician who runs for office talks about getting tough with criminals. When it comes to the thieves who are taking my personal possessions all the time, I'd like to lock them up and throw the key away. I probably wouldn't even have to throw it away. If I put it on top of my dresser for a few days, the key would disappear.

The Jeep

WHY is it when the manufacturers of an appliance or a piece of machinery decide to make a new, improved model of it, they often destroy the qualities it had that we liked?

There have been very few pieces of machinery so loved as the Jeep. Its invention was a bit of American genius. It was a simple, rugged and versatile little vehicle that did a thousand jobs, all of them well.

The Jeep was most loved by Americans who fought in World War II, but affection for it wasn't limited to those people. Everyone got to know and love the Jeep . . . and then they started improving it.

The Jeep they ended up making for the civilian trade was big, comfortable, automatic and expensive. It was everything the original Jeep was not. There's a time to live and a time to die, I know, but the Jeep died an unnecessarily premature death. If there were brand new Jeeps for sale today that were built with the same design and quality of the original I suspect there would be several hundred thousand people who'd want one.

A story out of Washington recently reported that a new vehicle designed to replace the Jeep isn't working out very well. The vehicle is nicknamed "The Hummer," a contrived abbreviation of its official designation, "High Mobility Multipurpose Wheeled Vehicle."

Even that name, "The Hummer," isn't as good as the name "Jeep." "Jeep" came about naturally, as a nickname should. Its official designation as a vehicle was "General Purpose." This was abbreviated as "GP" and thus, "Jeep."

The Pentagon tested The Hummer and announced that "Reliability was very low." No one ever said that about a Jeep.

The Army had ordered 55,000 of these new, unreliable vehicles at a cost of $20,000 each.

I checked back and found that on July 3, 1941, the Army signed a contract for the original Jeep. The price was $738.74 each.

How would you like to get yourself a brand new WWII Jeep for $738.74 today? Come to think of it, I'll take two. That would be two solid little vehicles that work for a total of $1,477.48. Ten would cost me $7,387.40.

There are hundreds of pieces of equipment I've

owned and liked over the years. Invariably when I've set out to replace them, I've been disappointed with the new model. Within the past year I've had this experience with a kitchen blender, a clock radio I dropped and a watch I lost. In each case the replacement—same brand—was less satisfactory than the original.

How does a company set out to change a product for the worse? The first thing it does is have a board of directors meeting. The board decides to satisfy its stockholders by raising the margin of profit on its most successful item.

In order to accomplish this, the board can do one of two things. It can cheapen the product or it can charge more for it.

The board decides to do both. They cheapen the product *and* charge more for it.

Within a year, sales begin to drop off and the board of directors is puzzled. They blame it on the economy or interference from Washington.

At the next board meeting they take drastic steps. They decide to paint their product a different color, put it in a bigger box and make it out of plastic instead of metal.

When all this fails to improve sales, they take one last, desperate measure. They authorize the president to spend three million dollars on a huge new ad campaign featuring the once-famous Hollywood star, now looking for work, Smith Barney.

The last thing they seem to think of doing to improve sales is to go back to making the good product they had in the first place.

The Big Fix

How would it be if we picked some year in the near future and didn't buy anything new at all that year? We'd spend the entire 365 days fixing things we already have. It's gotten so everyone's throwing it away and buying a new one instead of having the old one fixed, and that seems wrong.

Wouldn't it do just as much for the economy and more for the ecology if I spent $2,500 having my old car done over instead of spending $10,000 for a new one?

There's going to be some job relocation necessary but it wouldn't do any harm at all if those people in Detroit who make cars spent a year fixing them. They might be more careful when they went back to the assembly line.

It's hard to believe our economy has to depend on selling us things we don't need. There must be another way. There are a thousand things I keep buying that I don't need. I've got four electric shavers but three of them don't work. I have three quarter-inch drills but only one is operational. There are two ice-cream freezers in the garage but the motors on both of them need work. We have two retired toasters and a closet full of gadgets that just barely don't work anymore. I don't need new models. I need someone who'll fix my old models.

I'd start not buying from the ground up. I'd have all

the old shoes I own soled and heeled and I'd put new shoelaces in them. Then I'd shine them and wear them. I wouldn't buy any new ones.

I'd go through my closet, bring out the clothes that need work and take them to the tailor or sew on a few buttons myself. The art of turning a frayed collar might be revived.

I don't think we need any new houses for a year, either. The building industry will howl but there's plenty of work for them to do. Like Detroit, they could learn a little about building new ones by fixing the old ones they put up ten or twenty-five years ago.

Everywhere I go I see perfectly good houses that have been abandoned. Why couldn't the building industry, and the people who want houses, rebuild those instead of building new ones?

Why cut down more trees when we have wooden houses rotting for want of a little care and a coat of paint?

Why dig up more iron ore to turn into cars and farm machinery when we have cars and farm machinery rusting away that only need mechanical repair and some grease?

It would be a year in which no new books would be published. Each of us would read the books we bought in past years and never read. The writers are writing faster than the readers are reading. The readers need time to catch up and I speak with firsthand knowledge when I say that it wouldn't hurt if the writers spent a little more time with their work.

No new games at Christmas! Sorry, Atari. Sorry, Trivial Pursuit! We have enough games in our closets. We'll dust off our chess, our checkers and mah-jongg sets and bring out the Monopoly and the Scrabble boards. Maybe we'll play Michigan.

In the back room, attic, garage or basement, there must be a lot of old Hula Hoops, roller skates, bongo boards and wagons for the kids to play with. Maybe there are even some stilts, a pogo stick, a Flexible Flyer and a yo-yo.

If no one is selling anything new, this could hurt television and newspapers which depend on advertising revenue. Newspapers might have to charge what it costs to produce them. Network television would have to find some other way to collect from us. How much would a newspaper cost if we had to pay for it directly? For all we consumers know, it might be cheaper in the long run to pay for both directly.

Well, I'm dreaming, of course. We're not going to stop buying new things but I sense something basically wrong. It's wrong to be using up the earth's resources and throwing them away as fast as possible so we can make new ones just because our economy depends on sales.

II:

HOUSE BEAUTIFUL

A Nest to Come Home to

EVERYONE should have a nest to come home to when the public part of the day is over. Having a little room with a comfortable chair to settle into is important. You should be surrounded by familiar things. You can talk or read or watch television or doze off but you're in your basic place. You're home and you don't have to watch yourself.

I'm not sure the furniture stores and the room designers are in tune with what most Americans want. We've never had a designer design anything in our house. It's all happened by accident. I like our house a lot better than I like those rooms I see in magazines that have been put together by designers. They look more like the rooms they have just outside the men's room or the ladies' room on the ballroom floor of an expensive hotel. There isn't a decorator who ever lived who could surround me with the things I like to have around me in my living room.

Decorators go for fuzzy white rugs that show the dirt, glass-topped tables you can't put your feet on and gilt-edged mirrors that only Napoleon wearing his uniform would look good in.

I like to have the windows covered so the neighbors can't see in and I agree you shouldn't just cover them with newspaper but it's very easy to carry curtains too far. When strangers come into your living room and say right away how nice the curtains are, then you know you've gone too far with the curtains. Friends who come to your house once in a while should not be able to remember what the curtains look like.

It must be difficult to sell furniture. No one in a store would sell you a chair in which the springs were beginning to sag but most chairs aren't very comfortable until that begins to happen. No one wants to pay a lot of money for a secondhand piece of furniture and yet furniture looks better when it has a well-worn look.

My green leather chair is eighteen years old now and the rest of the family complains about what it looks like but I notice they take every chance they get to sit in it. I don't take that chair when I come into the room because I'm the husband or the father. I sit in that chair because it's *my* chair. It's as much mine as my shoes. If they want one like it they can have one but I like a chair I can call my own. Familiar things are a great comfort to us all.

When the Christmas catalogs begin to come in and there's a noticeable increase in the amount of mail coming into the house, I usually make a decorating change of my own. I move another little table over by my chair so I have a table on either side of me. It's a temporary thing for one time of year. When the Christmas cards start coming, I have a better way of separating the cards from the bills and the junk mail from the personal letters. If you keep the newspaper, the mail, a letter opener, a glass, scissors, three elastic bands, some paper clips, some loose change, the television guide, two books and a magazine next to you, one table next to your chair isn't enough at Christmas.

When I sit down in my chair at night, it's the one place in the world I have no complaint with. It's just the way I like it. I'm wearing comfortable clothes, my feet are up and I'm surrounded by things that are there because I choose to have them there.

I was telling my wife how quickly and how well American soldiers make a nest for themselves, no matter what their circumstances are. They can be out in a field somewhere but first thing you know they've dug a foxhole and invented some conveniences for themselves out of empty coffee cans and cardboard containers. They've made that one little spot in the world their own. It's true but I never should have told my wife.

"That's what this place looks like," she said, "a foxhole."

My Dream House

IF you had all the time and all the money you needed to build yourself the perfect house, what would it be like? I have some ideas for my dream house.

First, it would have a big, handsome, wooden front door that everyone used. No one would come in the back way or through the kitchen door as a regular thing. Most houses are designed so that the front door isn't really convenient and is only used occasionally by guests who come to dinner Saturday night or by Jehovah's Witnesses wanting to give you literature. There is no reason why a front door couldn't be put in a convenient place.

There would be a four-car garage for our two cars. This would allow space for the things we presently have in our two-car garage instead of our two cars.

There would be both a living room and what we used to call the parlor in my grandmother's house. I don't actually like parlors but they're convenient for some occasions. They provide a place to keep chairs that aren't comfortable enough to sit on, walls on which to hang gilded mirrors and pictures you don't like, and shelves on which to put knickknacks and various pieces of homely but expensive china. The bookshelves in the parlor would hold the books we never read.

The dining room would be elegant, spacious, wood-paneled and quietly lit. It would have a huge and beautiful oval table that would expand to seat twenty or contract to be comfortable for four. The extra chairs would recede into the floor at the push of a button.

The living room or family room would be small and cozy with several comfortable, worn leather chairs, a mushy couch long enough to sleep on stretched out, and a television set too big for the size of the room. It would also have a stereo record player, although we never use the one we have. It would have small windows and could be entered through only one door. More than one door ruins any room.

The kitchen would have a fireplace, an alcove with a comfortable breakfast table, at which we'd usually eat dinner, and a lot of indestructible butcher block counter tops. It would have a big, professional range with eight burners, two ovens and an open flame grill. There would be a walk-in refrigerator like the ones they have in meat markets. I'd never bend over to get something out of the bottom of the refrigerator again.

In one corner of the kitchen would be a dumbwaiter that would take things from the kitchen to the rooms upstairs and to the basement downstairs.

The cellar or basement would be divided into four parts. One part would have the furnace, washer, dryer and a bin of replacement parts for every appliance in the house. A second room would have all my woodworking equipment and would be hermetically and acoustically sealed so that neither dust nor noise could drift out of it into the rest of the house. There have been some complaints about that in our present house.

In the back, running the full length of the house, I'd have a swimming pool fifty yards long and four yards wide. I don't want to play in a pool, I just want to do laps.

The fourth part of the basement would be a small, nicely equipped gym in which I'd regularly lose weight.

Upstairs there would be five bedrooms with ten adjoining bathrooms. When there are two people in a bedroom, one bathroom per bedroom is not enough. It would be nice when all the kids are home.

Each of the many huge clothes closets would be equipped with a Disposal down which could be dumped old shoes, worn or unattractive shirts, socks with holes in them and spotted neckties.

These are some of the things I'd like in my dream house.

House Beautiful

Y EARS ago, when I was making a living the hard way, writing for magazines, I sold an article to *House Beautiful*. Every once in a while I look through the magazine to see what their writers are writing today. The magazine is attractive but I can't relate to much that's in it. The articles and the advertisements are either for things I don't buy or they're so elaborate they scare me off. If this is House Beautiful, I live in House Homely.

Here's a two-page ad for a Jacuzzi whirlpool bath. There's an attractive woman lying on a pillow on the tile floor. The tub itself is sunk into the floor and she, I judge, is about to get in. Behind the woman on the bathroom floor, there's a sink, a toilet, a bidet and a fireplace with burning logs. Overhead is a crystal chandelier.

I don't like to discourage attractive advertising like this but Jacuzzi ought to know that my attention is more attracted to the barely clad woman on the floor and to the fireplace behind her than it is to the whirlpool bath they're trying to sell. My mind wanders away from commerce in the presence of nudity. I'm wondering whether she'll climb in facing the fire or with her back to it. Will she lie back, up to her pretty neck in suds, and gaze at the crystal chandelier?

Here's another good-looking ad in *House Beautiful* for "The 100 Greatest Books Ever Written." They're bound in genuine leather and cost thirty-five dollars each. Among the books shown are *The Mill on the Floss*, *The Scarlet Letter* and *Faust* by Goethe. I had to read *The Mill on the Floss* when I was sixteen and it is my opinion that it isn't even one of the 10,000 best books ever written. A book in leather is an awful burden to lay on someone anyway. Generation after generation has to take those leather-bound books with them whenever they move and no one ever reads them. A book should live or die by what's inside it, not what's outside.

It takes a while to get to the articles in a magazine like *House Beautiful* these days if you start from the beginning. If you like ads, of course, that doesn't matter. There are 178 pages in this issue and of those, about 100 are ads.

One of the articles is about a doctor and his wife in New Orleans who like to entertain.

"Once a year," the article says, "the Ochsners give a buffet reception for 200 . . ." There are wonderful pictures of the Ochsners' attractive home all fixed up ready for a party, but it's difficult for me to translate their party in terms of one we could give in our house.

The Ochsners put dining tables everywhere to handle the crowd. They put one table out by the pool, for instance. We don't even have a pool if you can imagine anyone that poor. They put tables on the patio. We don't have a patio, either. I suspect that if *House Beautiful* ever saw our house they wouldn't want to have anything to do with me. They'd certainly be embarrassed to find their magazine on the coffee table in our living room.

One problem Mrs. Ochsner says she has when there are 200 people for dinner is finding enough silver forks for all of them. I can sympathize with Mrs. Ochsner here. We'd have that trouble, too. My wife's family left us twelve but one went out with the garbage, and and another was mangled in the Disposal so we'd be 190 silver forks short.

Just to prove all their houses aren't filled with frou-frou, *House Beautiful* has an article about what they call "A Magnificient Hand-Hewn Log Cabin." It is magnificent, too. The picture of the living room shows a fireplace like the one in the bathroom in the Jacuzzi ad and a bookshelf. I can't read the titles in the book-shelf but I imagine that somewhere up there is a com-plete set of "The 100 Greatest Books Ever Written," bound in leather.

Things to Do Today

FOR a while after I got in bed, I couldn't think where the day had gone. Then it started coming back to me, slowly but clearly.

I definitely remember starting to make a list that morning after I'd read the paper and had a second cup of coffee. "TTDT" I'd put at the top of the page of a blank sheet of paper. It stands for "Things to Do To-day." I always put that at the top of the page. It's a little joke I have with myself. I remember most of the items on the list:

—Clean leaves out of gutter.

—Put storm door on back door.

—Rake leaves out of ivy at front.

—Clean out garage so we can get both cars in when the snow comes.

—Split logs brought down from the country so they'll fit into small wood stove in kitchen.

—Cover ventilating fan in attic.

—Take air conditioner out of kitchen window.

—Take lawn mower that hasn't worked in three years to dump.

—Put tools where they belong.

Sitting there at the breakfast table Saturday morning I felt very contented with my list. Just putting down the things I ought to do gave me some of the same kind of satisfaction that actually doing them would have. Nothing is too much for me to do Saturday morning at the breakfast table when I'm planning my day. It isn't until I get started that I run into trouble.

Last Saturday I got so little done on my list that I lay in bed that night trying to reconstruct my day and as I did I realized where I went wrong. I picked the wrong job to do first. I had picked the fifth item on my TTDT list, "Split Logs."

I had gone to the garden shed to get an axe, a light sledgehammer and a wedge. I set the first heavy log on my chopping block and felt the blade of the axe. It needed sharpening. I do that on a small belt sander I have in the basement so I went there with the axe in my hand.

It would have taken no more than five minutes except that I had removed a worn sandpaper belt from the machine and had to replace it with another. In loosening a screw on the sander, I dropped a critical washer on the floor and it rolled under my worktable along with quite a bit of debris. It was forty-five minutes before I got back out in the yard to the chopping block.

Now my axe was sharp, I was sharp and the first log was ready to be split asunder. I arched back with the axe dropped low behind my back. Holding it at the end of the handle like a baseball bat, I brought the axe over my head and down with all the might I could muster. Thuck! That was the noise the axe made as it buried itself no more than an inch into the log. I had assumed it would cleave it with one mighty swipe.

What I had forgotten was that the log was elm and elm is susceptible to the dread disease that has killed almost all the trees but it's highly resistant to being split with an axe.

An hour later I had the axe, the wedge, a good wood chisel, two screwdrivers and a small crowbar buried in that log. They were trapped and I was no closer to splitting it than when I started.

It was almost noon before I got everything free and by that time I was hungry again. I put the tools away, went in and made myself a grilled cheese sandwich.

I looked at the rest of my TTDT list. Nothing I couldn't do next Saturday, I thought to myself, so I watched some football on television, took a little nap and then went to the store and bought a new suitcase.

That's where last Saturday went.

Lifting

MEN enjoy lifting things. They don't like carrying them anywhere once they've lifted them but it's satisfying for them to pick up a heavy object. Last weekend was very satisfying for me. I was helping someone move out of an apartment and there was a lot of lifting to be done.

There's something macho about lifting. Men like the idea of being able to lift heavier objects than women can. It seems like a harmless thing to feel superior about. We can't have babies. It's little enough to leave us.

I can't think why else men would enjoy lifting things if it isn't to prove that they can lift more than women. Once they've lifted something, men often don't know what to do with it. Women have a better idea of where to put something down once it's been lifted.

There are a dozen heavy objects around our house that I've been lifting for twenty-five years and it's going to be interesting to see how old I am before I can no longer pick them up. Once a year, for example, I put an air conditioner in the kitchen window and another in our bedroom window. Once a year I take them out, so I lift each one twice a year. I don't know how much they weigh but it's plenty. My gauge for weight is a bag of cement which is about 100 pounds. The air conditioners are at least that heavy and very cumbersome. There's no place to hang on as you lift. The one in the kitchen is toughest because the windowsill is chest-high and I have to get it up to that. I've seen these champion weight lifters put barbells over their heads but they have it easy. I'd like to see them put my kitchen air conditioner over their heads. They wouldn't know where to grab hold of it and lifting it chest-high is only part of it. It doesn't fit into the window neatly so I have to jockey it into position while I'm lifting. Let's see them make air-conditioner lifting an Olympic event.

I'm worried now about next year. We were having some work done around the house last month, so my wife had two men put the air conditioners in. I hate to get out of shape by missing a year like that. I remember the cowboy theory that if you lift a calf on the day it's born and continue to lift it every day, you'll still be able to lift the animal when it's full-grown. My air conditioners aren't getting any bigger, but I am.

Big television sets are in the same category as air conditioners. They often put a handle on top and call them "portable" but they aren't really. Television sets share a common fault with a lot of other objects in a house that you occasionally have to move to another room. They are almost always about the same width as the door you have to take them through. This means that there's no room for your hands if you go through the door straight and if you turn sideways, you have to get yourself and the television set through the door at the same time.

When I'm carrying something heavy and bulky down a pair of stairs in the house, my wife is always properly solicitous of my welfare. She keeps saying things like "Be careful." I suspect I'm sharing her concern with the object I'm carrying. She may not want me to hurt myself but she doesn't want me to drop what I'm carrying, either.

To tell you the truth, I've never found that the advice "Don't hurt yourself" has helped me as far as getting hurt is concerned. Either I do or I don't. I don't mind if someone says things like that to me but what I do object to is when they try to help. I'll have something heavy delicately balanced on my shoulder and I'll start walking with it. My wife decides it's too heavy. She wants to help so she lifts the back end of it.

There are some things I don't enjoy lifting. Bringing the groceries in from the car is no fun. They aren't heavy enough to be challenging and there's no place to put them down when you get inside.

Putting the garbage out is another lifting job I don't get much of a kick out of. A full garbage can, one of those big ones, is hard to lift because it's awkward. There's nothing to do but lean over and grab the handles on either side. I bet the move accounts for half the back problems in America.

I've seen all these books advising women on how to get along with a man. My advice would be for them to flatter men at least once a month by saying, "Dear, will you please lift this for me?"

A Trip to the Dump

THE President says this country is in desperate need of a moral revival. He isn't the first one to say it, either. Almost anyone who says anything has been saying it for years. The trouble is, no one knows how to revive us morally.

I have a simple idea that might just do the trick. I say we should all take our own garbage to the dump. Every able-bodied person in the country would set aside an hour twice a week to dispose of trash and garbage. There would be no exceptions. The President would pack up whatever waste was produced in the private rooms of the White House and take it to the dump just like the rest of us. A President should keep in touch with reality, too.

Going to the dump is a real and exhilarating experience. It is both satisfying and educational. It makes you acutely aware of what you have used in your home and what you have wasted. There's no faking it with garbage.

In a family, dump duty would be divided up. The kids would take their turns going to the dump with the adults. A kid can get to be voting age without knowing that the wastebasket or the garbage pail isn't the end of the line if he or she has never been to the dump. Children too young to drive would, of course, be accompanied by an adult to the dump.

The first thing you realize when you go to the dump

is that we should be a lot more careful in separating what professional garbage collectors call "wet garbage" and just trash. All garbage is not the same. Trash is cans, bottles, papers, cardboard boxes and broken electrical appliances. "Wet garbage" comes from the kitchen.

Next, you have to get over that natural feeling of revulsion that garbage tends to induce. Keep in mind that coffee grounds, watermelon rinds, potato peels and corncobs were not revolting before we made them what they are today and mixed them together in our garbage pail. Think of them separately and in their original state and make a little game of breaking down the odor into its component parts.

It is possible to be overcome by a sense of your place in history at the dump. You are, at that moment, a part of the future of the universe. You are helping to rearrange the planet Earth. Man has always considered himself separate from Nature but a trip to the garbage dump can make him aware that he is not. In the millions and millions of years Earth has existed, there have been constant changes taking place. You probably live in a city that was once a lake or an ocean. The mountains you see may have had their cliffs sheared clean by a glacier when it moved relentlessly through your area an eon ago, dropping rich, loamy topsoil in the valley when it melted. Now, like the glaciers, you are doing your part to rearrange the location of the elements on Earth.

Little by little, we are taking up material from the ground in large amounts in one place, making something of it, shipping it across the country to other places, using the things, turning them into trash or garbage and burying them in ten thousand separate little piles called dumps in other places. In the process, we often ruin both places, of course, but that's another story.

If being in on this cosmic kind of cosmetics doesn't interest you to think about the dump, there are other pleasures. There is a cathartic pleasure to be enjoyed from getting rid of stuff at the dump and there is a camaraderie among neighbors there that doesn't exist at the supermarket. Everyone at the dump feels he is doing a good and honest thing and it gives him a warm sense of fellow feeling to know that others, many with more expensive cars, are doing the same grubby, down-to-earth job.

Nowhere is morality higher in America than at the dump Saturday morning and I recommend a trip there as a possible cure for what so many people think ails America, morally.

The Real Homecoming

AFTER a vacation it's traditional to tell your friends "It's great to be home." It may be great to *be* home but *coming* home is no fun at all. Most of us take a summer vacation and some weekend trips and ever since I was a kid I've hated that part where you arrive home at ten o'clock Sunday night.

It doesn't matter what time of year you take a vacation, coming back to your house is a miserable experience. If it's in the winter, the house is cold and dank. If it's in the summer, the house is hot and dank.

Out front the mail has piled up and wet newspapers are scattered all over the lawn. You've probably left a light on to convince the burglars there's someone there, but that one lonely light burning every night might as well be a neon sign flashing "NOT HOME! NOT HOME! NOT HOME!" Burglars may be dishonest but they aren't dumb.

In the driveway there are fliers from the local grocery chains telling you about this week's specials which, by this time, are two weeks old. There are weeds everywhere and the place looks as if it hasn't been lived in for six months. You've been gone two weeks and you've got a ghost house on your hands.

All I ever want to do when I get home from vacation is sit down and rest or go to bed but I never can because there are too many things to do. I expect magic when I open the door but I never find it. I always expect things to be perfect. It seems to me the house should have corrected itself while we were away. It should look the way I'd like it to look, not the way we left it.

If you left in a hurry, which you probably did, there are clothes scattered around the area where you packed. There are things you forgot or decided at the last minute not to take.

If you had a quick breakfast or just a cup of coffee before you pulled out, the chances are the dirty dishes and cups are still in the sink. Even if burglars came while you were away, they wouldn't have taken the dirty dishes.

We had a particularly nasty shock coming home

after our first weekend away this summer. Last year I installed one of those big exhaust fans in the roof. It's been good for cooling down the upstairs rooms by bringing the outside air in through an opened downstairs window. The trouble came because this winter we put a small wood-burning stove in our kitchen fireplace. The attic fan goes on automatically at a certain temperature whether we're home or not and when we're away with all the doors and windows closed, the fan has only one place from which to draw air. It draws it down the chimney and through the wood stove. Anyway, when we returned home this time, the whole house smelled as if it had burned down several weeks ago. It was permeated with the smell of the wood stove and the chimney.

One the ten worst jobs in life is emptying the trunk of the car after a trip. There's trash that should be thrown out. There are suitcases, paper bags and loose packages of things you bought while you were away. There may be fruits and vegetables that seemed attractive when you bought them at the country stand but seem unnecessary now.

Things in the trunk of a car have a way of intermingling with the handle of the jack or they get trapped back up in there with the light wires and they're hard to reach. It often takes me five trips to empty the car and there are still things left in it.

I'll bet the President doesn't have to empty the trunk of his car when he gets back to the White House after a trip. No wonder people want to be President.

When the car is mostly empty, I take the suitcases upstairs and that's another unpleasant experience, unpacking a suitcase you've been living out of for a week. It's mostly dirty underwear, socks and shirts and mine smells of the cheap perfume that comes from the little bars of soap I take when I leave a hotel.

Once I've got things cleared away enough to go to bed, I usually decide to take a shower. I get undressed, turn on the shower and then remember that I turned off the hot water heater before we left. Now I have to put on some clothes, go down to the cellar, turn on the oil burner and wait twenty minutes for hot water.

Sometimes coming home is such a pain in the neck I wonder whether going away is worth it.

Showered with Perfection

So many things in life are bent, broken, empty, leaking, worn-out or otherwise unsatisfactory that it's always a pleasure to report something that's perfect the way it is.

Things are going very well in the shower of our house this year. We've finally got things the way we want them.

Next to falling into your own warm bed on a cold night when you're dog-tired, the most comforting thing to do is to take a long, hot shower.

A hot shower is like eating peanuts. You can't stop. I have to use a lot of willpower every morning to get myself out of the shower and into my clothes.

About three years ago we took the tub out of the

upstairs bathroom and had a tilë shower installed. It's big enough to turn around in comfortably and there are two little shelves high in the back corner where the spray doesn't hit. An assortment of shampoos, brushes and some miscellaneous junk is kept on the shelves. There are some items up there I don't understand but who knows what anyone else does in the shower?

The new shower wasn't completely satisfactory at first. It wasn't the shower's fault. For a while the thermostat on the heater in the basement wasn't working properly. Halfway though my shower, the water would turn tepid, then cool and finally cold. There's nothing worse than getting lathered up and then having the hot water give out.

The first shower head the plumber put on wouldn't adjust the way I wanted it to, either. I was never happy with it. I like heavy streams of water with a fairly small radius. I don't like pinpoint needles of water that hit me in the head and the feet at the same time. I like to be able to control which part of me is getting hit with water.

We replaced the first shower head and this one is just right. It's almost too good. It's costing me a few minutes' sleep every day because the shower's so nice now I'm staying in it longer and I have to get up earlier in order to catch my train.

The biggest improvement the new shower has over the old one in the bathtub is the glass door. It doesn't let any water leak out onto the floor and it ends the necessity for a shower curtain. The curtain was the worst thing about our old shower. Water was always getting on the floor and if you didn't leave the curtain pulled all the way open when you finished, it got moldy where it was folded against itself.

The best new development in my shower-taking life is a tiny electric heater I've put in the bathroom. It has a small fan behind the coils and does a good job of heating the room. But wait, don't go away! Here's the best part. I've got it on a timer.

The timer in the bathroom is set to start the little heater five minutes before my radio alarm goes off in the bedroom every morning. Now, when I get out of bed and tiptoe barefoot and shivering to the bathroom, I open the door on a wonderfully warm little room. It took me a long time to get the timer set to go off at exactly the right moment and I dread daylight saving time coming again in the spring because I'll have to reset it.

There's a radio in the bathroom and I always turn that on. I get up early and the first thing I hear, usually, is the London gold price. I don't care what the price of gold is in London but the familiar voice with the familiar information gives me some assurance that the world is still out there just the way I left it before I went to bed the night before.

The only things that go wrong these days with my morning shower are my own fault. Occasionally I get in and get wet before I realize I forgot to move my towel from the rack where I can't reach it to the little hook outside the shower door. I have to get out of the shower, wet and dripping, and get the towel.

If I ever retire and find myself looking for ways to have a good time, I think I'll just take three or four good, hot showers every day.

Neighbors

A MAN in Cambridge, Mass., took his neighbor to court because the neighbor hadn't cut his grass in fourteen years. This is the kind of story that interests me. There are something like sixty million single family homes in the United States and I'll bet ninety percent of the people living in those houses are having some kind of trouble with their neighbors.

The uncut grass in Cambridge is typical of the sort of thing that causes friction. No one likes the house next door to look worse or a lot better than his own. It's one thing to have a house of your own that needs painting but, knowing your own finances the way you do, you learn to live with it. When the house *next door* needs a coat of paint, that's a different matter. It can be a constant source of irritation. "Why doesn't that lazy bum paint it himself if he can't afford to have it done professionally?"

We have friends who are mad at their neighbors because they leave an old car in the driveway all the time instead of putting it away in the garage. I can understand that. If you have a nice-looking house and you keep the grounds in good condition, a piece of machinery like a seven-year-old automobile is not what you want to see all the time. As thoroughly well as I understand my friends' position on this matter, however, I usually leave the car in the driveway myself. As a matter of fact, I have two cars and a two-car garage but it has been fourteen years since there was room in it for both cars. One is tight.

If you basically like your neighbors, you don't make an issue of the things that bother you. If he hadn't cut his grass for fourteen years you might mention it, but smaller things you let slide in the interests of peace.

We have an almost ideal neighbor. We're friendly and would help each other in any emergency but we don't talk much and over a period of more than twenty-five years have had no confrontations.

Bill, my neighbor, works hard around his place and the only thing that ever bothered me wasn't really his fault, although I harbored a resentment toward him because of it.

For years I had watched him make a compost heap every year so I decided to compost my own leaves and grass cuttings. I built a wire mesh bin up against the fence between our properties and filled it with good stuff. I turned it over after four months and watered it regularly to hasten the rotting process.

After it had been there about two years and had diminished to a quarter of its original size, I decided to use some of it. The first few shovelfuls were rich and dark but then I struck trouble. It turned out that Bill's maple tree had discovered *my* compost heap and was eating from it. Small, fibrous tree roots had invaded the whole thing and I couldn't penetrate it with a spade. I finally gave up and today the location of my compost heap is a small hill over by the fence, dense with thriving tree roots.

It wasn't Bill's fault that his maple tree roots had gone out foraging for food but that's how neighborly feuds begin. You see *their* cat waiting to pounce on *your* birds. The outside light over *their* garage shines in *your* bedroom window. They leave *their* garbage cans out by the road all day after the garbage has been picked up in the morning.

You never know, of course, what *you've* done to annoy your neighbors. Tom, my neighbor across the street, is a nut in my opinion. He's out there mowing, seeding, raking and manicuring his place every time I look out the window. I get up at 7:30 Saturday mornings and he's already at it. I have to guess that my place bothers anyone that fussy. In the fall I don't rake the leaves much and they blow all over his property. Kids going by in cars often throw beer and soft drink cans out front where our two properties are closest and even when the cans are on my side, he picks them up.

That's the way it is with neighbors. If they're neater about their grounds than you are, they're fanatics. If they don't keep their place as well as you do, you think of them as bringing down real estate values.

My grass would never go fourteen years without being cut. Tom would sneak over when we're not home and cut it himself.

Building Satisfaction

For most of the last month I've been putting up a small building. I am not experienced in putting up buildings. My new structure is just behind the building we call the garage at our summer place. I don't know why we call that the garage, though, because it used to be an icehouse and has been full of tools for several years.

If Americans have a little bit of land near their house, they're possessed to put buildings on it. Most American farms, where there's plenty of land, are a cluster of haphazardly erected little buildings adjacent to the house and the barn. Most of the buildings were put up by someone who had an idea for their use at the time but that time has passed and they are now mostly used for what could only be called miscellaneous.

When I started my building I was going to use it for storing garden tools and a small tractor/lawn mower but now I think I may use it as a place in which to write. I'm getting to like it too much to just keep garden tools in.

My building is five-sided, eight feet tall at the sides and twelve feet tall at the crown of the roof in the middle. It's about twelve feet across although in a pentagon no side is directly opposite any other side so it's hard to measure that dimension. The base is on heavy, flat stones and the timbers are treated five-by-fives. The uprights and the roof members are two-by-fours. The sides are three-quarter-inch plywood, which I covered with tarpaper and then red cedar shingles. The floor is rough oak I bought from a farmer who has a little sawmill, and now I think if I'm going to use it as an office, I'll insulate and panel the interior.

Don't ask me why I decided on a five-sided building and don't get thinking I'm any expert. I've bungled so many things putting it up that I'd be embarrassed to have a real carpenter see it. But it's up and it's mine and I built it and I had a wonderful time doing it.

It was very hard work. Every morning I'd get up

at 6:15 and go to the garage/icehouse and write until about 8:30 and then go into the house and have breakfast. After breakfast I'd start on my building. Every evening at about 6:30 my wife would yell out the back door for me to quit. I'd work a little while longer, trying to anticipate how long I could stretch it out before she got really mad at me, then I'd go to the house, dripping wet with perspiration. I'd take a shower, have a drink, eat dinner and by 10:30 drop into bed.

It isn't often that I mix that much manual labor with writing and it got me thinking about which of the two is more satisfying. Writing is a great satisfaction to me but it's a wonderful feeling to go to bed dog-tired and twitching in every muscle after a long day's physical work in which you accomplished something. It always strikes me as surprising that it's so pleasurable to be physically tired from having used your muscles excessively. It makes me wish writing involved some kind of manual labor more strenuous than typing. If I got stiff writing, it might be even more satisfying.

Standing back and looking at my odd-shaped building, I've been impressed with how much like my writing it is. It's a little crude and not very well finished but it's direct and original.

My satisfaction in making it springs from the same well, too. For a man or a woman to take any raw material like lumber or words and shape these formless materials into a pattern that bears the stamp of his or her brain or hand, is the most satisfying thing to do in the whole world. It's what's wrong with cake mixes.

When, out of a scrambled mess of raw materials, some order starts to emerge and it is an order you have imposed on those materials, it's a good feeling. It was nothing and now it's something.

For me, writing in the early morning and working on my building the rest of the day was the ultimate vacation and I never worked harder in my life.

Now I'm back at work and I can relax a little.

III:

WORKING

Procrastination

It isn't working that's so hard, it's getting ready to work.

It isn't *being* up we all dislike in the mornning, it's *getting* up.

Once I get started at almost any job, I'm happy. I can plug away at any dull job for hours and get some satisfaction from doing it. The trouble is that sometimes I'll put off doing that job for months because it's so tough to get started.

It doesn't seem to matter what the job is. For me it can be getting at writing, getting at mowing the lawn, getting at cleaning out the trunk of the car, making a piece of furniture or putting up a shed. It's a good thing I wasn't hired to build the Golden Gate Bridge. I'd never have figured out where to put that first piece of steel to make it possible to get across all that water.

There is some complex thing going on in our brains that keeps us from getting started on a job. No matter how often we do something, we always forget how long it took us to do it last time and how hard it was. Even though we forget in our conscious mind, there is some subconscious part of the brain that remembers. This is what keeps us from getting at things. *We* may not know but our subconscious knows that the job is going to be harder than we think. It tries to keep us from rushing into it in a hurry.

There is a war going on between different elements of our brain. If I consciously remembered how difficult something was the last time I did it, I'd never do it again. The wonderful thing about memory is that it's just great at forgetting. Every Friday afternoon in summer I drive 150 miles to our summer house in the country. I always look forward to *being* there and I always forget how much I hate *getting* there. My subconscious remembers. It keeps me fiddling around the office Friday afternoons, putting off leaving. The drive can take anywhere from three to four hours, depending on the traffic, and I hate it so much that sometimes I spend two of those four hours contemplating selling the place.

The following Friday, I can't wait to leave the office for the country again but my subconscious puts it off. It keeps me from getting started. *It* remembers the drive even if I don't.

One of the jobs my subconscious is best at putting me off getting at is painting. My subconscious is absolutely right. I probably shouldn't start it even though I enjoy it once I get going. Once again, my subconscious remembers what I forget.

I look at a door or a fence or a room and I say to myself, "I ought to give that a coat of paint. It'll take two quarts of paint. I'll need some turpentine and a new brush. No sense fooling with those old brushes."

My subconscious sometimes puts me off the paint job for months but eventually, against its better judgment, I buy the paint, the turpentine and the brush. I put on my old clothes, get a screwdriver to remove the top of the paint can and then I look more carefully at the room. Now I begin to see what my subconscious saw all along.

There are many things to do before I start to paint. I have to move everything out of the room, I have to replace a piece of the baseboard that is broken and I have to scrape and sand the places where the paint is peeling. And I better go back to the hardware store to get some spackle to fill the cracks in the ceiling. While I'm there, I'll pick up some undercoater for the new piece of baseboard and the spackled cracks. I'll have to let it dry overnight so I can't start painting today.

It is quite probable that it is this wonderfully intelligent subconscious part of our brain that makes us want to stay in bed another hour every morning. *We* want to get up. *It* knows that just as soon as we get up, the trouble will start all over again.

A Microchip on My Shoulder

RECENTLY I was talked into buying a magic new machine called a Teleram Portabubble word processor. It's basically an electronic typewriter that doesn't produce anything on paper. It's all on a little screen in front of you. The good part of it is that by pressing a few buttons and putting the telephone in the cradle provided on top of it, you can send what you've written anywhere in the world in a very few minutes. Of course, you have to want to send what you've written somewhere for it to be much use to you.

The Teleram is unique in that it stores what you've written on a memory that doesn't involve any disk or moving parts. It's portable, too, weighing only eighteen pounds, and can be plugged in anywhere.

I had no natural aptitude for the word processor but after four months, I'm thoroughly familiar with it. I've written five books and hundreds of radio and television broadcasts on my Underwood No. 5 typewriter, circa 1920, and I continue to use it as my basic writing tool. It was given to me by my uncle who was a lawyer. He had used it for twenty years before me. In the past thirty-five years I spent twelve dollars on it once to have it oiled and cleaned.

Although I'm embarrassed to tell you, it's important to the story to say that I paid $5,640 for my word processor.

Several months after I bought it, I got a letter from Arline D. Walpole, Manager, Sales Administration, the Teleram Corporation. The letter informed me that my warranty was almost up and asked if I wanted to sign up for their annual flat-fee service contract.

I have written the following letter:

Dear Miss Walpole:

I have some questions regarding the letter you sent informing me that the fee for the annual service contract for my Teleram Portabubble-81 is $660.

Do I understand that $660 is the Teleram Corporation's best estimate of what it will cost to keep one of their machines in operating condition for one year?

Could you please advise me what type failure I

can expect within a year of my purchase of the word processor? I had a demonstration model belonging to your salesman for about five weeks and some kind of logjam occurred that made it necessary for me to erase and lose everything in the memory to make it operative again. Is this common? I now have the Teleram with the 260,000-character memory. What is the likelihood that I can complete the storage of that amount of material without another breakdown in your machine that would necessitate total erasure?

According to your letter, your charge for straight-time, on-site field repair is $73 an hour. Your only repair depots are in Randolph, N.J., Washington, D.C. and Dallas, Texas. None of these is in my neighborhood. Travel time for your repairmen is $53 an hour, plus costs. Weekday overtime is $90 an hour and Sunday and holiday on-site double time is $120 an hour. I estimate that if one of your repairmen works a 40-hour week plus four hours overtime and four hours double time, he could make $3,760 a week or $195,520 a year. In the event one of your repairmen worked a straight 40-hour week at your factory (at $53 per hour) with no travel and no overtime, he would only make $110,240 a year. Do you have any openings?

I have enjoyed owning my Teleram. However, if it ceases to operate, I will simply abandon it and conclude that word processors have not reached the state where they are reliable enough to be economically feasible for me to own.

I do not want the service contract you offer for $660 a year. ''Prices subject to change without notice.''

Sincerely,
Andrew A. Rooney

Hometown

MY hometown newspaper is going to start running my essays.

I view this with mixed feelings. I'm pleased that the people I know will be able to read what I write but I'm a little apprehensive about it, too. It's a small community in Connecticut and my wife and I know most of the people. We bought our house here in 1952 for $29,500 and we've brought up four children in it.

I'm apprehensive because I suspect it's better if readers don't know a writer personally. A writer ought to give readers the impression he knows what he's talking about and it's difficult for anyone to take a writer seriously if they've been watching him put the garbage out for twenty years.

A writer only has so much and it seems like less if you know where it comes from. I have what I've lived. I draw from what I see around me, from the people I know, from what I read and from the feelings I get from all these things. There's no magic. The trick in attracting people to read the kind of thing I write about is to strike a universal chord. I try to write about things almost everyone knows about. If I write about politics, it isn't from any inside knowledge I have or any special ability to interpret what's happening. I just try to put down on paper some of the thoughts that have crossed my mind because I'm average enough so they've probably crossed the reader's, too.

Knowing a writer makes you look at what he or she has written in a different way. It's like sitting way down front at a play in a theater where you can see what's going on in the wings.

If you live in one of the 350 cities or towns that carry my column but not my name in the phone book, you can read it in blissful ignorance of the fact that I'm not any smarter than you are. Friends and neighbors in my community can't do that. They know different. They've seen me bungle too many jobs to believe I have any special knowledge or ability. They saw what I did when I tried to rehang my garage doors and finally had to call a professional. They know I don't even mow my own lawn. I don't have any special standing with them except as a friend. From now on, I'm going to have to be more careful what I write and how I write it.

Up until today a lot of you strangers out there have suspected, on occasion, that I didn't know what I was talking about but you couldn't be sure. These people I've known for thirty years will know for sure.

I've always wondered how the novelist who draws heavily on his personal life—as all novelists must— handles it Saturday nights with old friends that he's used. They must recognize some of the characters in his book and they must sometimes see themselves in an unfavorable light.

I have so many friends in our community with so many problems, who often behave in such a bizarre manner that I couldn't write about them honestly and conceal their identity or maintain their friendship. I like them but they wouldn't think so if they realized I know them as well as I do. If I write about them now that they can read it, I'll have to camouflage their character. I don't want to lose the bizarrest among them.

No writer is immune to the pleasure of seeing his words in print so I'm pleased that my local paper is going to print mine. I just want all of you to understand the new note of caution and restraint you may find here. In the future I won't be able to go off half-cocked with impunity. My neighbors will be watching.

Electronic Journalism

THERE is no business so secure that the people who work in it don't worry about its future. Usually there is some technological improvement lurking in a laboratory or on a drawing board nearby that threatens the routine operation of any commercial enterprise. I suppose the manufacturers of lead pencils thought it was the end of their world when fountain pens were invented. The owners of radio stations panicked when television started moving in but I notice they're still making lead pencils and radio seems to be surviving.

More often than not, the threat is worse than anything that actually comes of it. In other cases, change comes so slowly that everyone adapts and gets in on it.

There are times, though, when an invention hits with such impact and suddenness that it threatens to destroy a business. It happens that way just often enough to keep us all worried for good reason.

The business I worry about is news. I know some of you don't really like or trust people in the news business but I like them above all others. They are my friends. When I am in a strange city and go to the newsroom of a newspaper or a television station, I am instantly on familiar ground even though I have never been in that room before. I am among friends even though I have never met any of them.

The men and women in newsrooms across the country all know the same things I know. We share common problems and we have common goals. We start our conversation further along than you normally start a conversation with someone you've never met, because of this feeling of common knowingness.

I was in Denver this year and was taken to the press club. Once inside I could have been in any of a hundred press clubs around the world. The look of the place, the look of the people and the sounds and the atmosphere of the place were as familiar to me as home. The newspapermen and women of Denver were indistinguishable from those standing at a bar or eating their lunch, in violent conversation with friends, in Hong Kong, Chicago, London or San Francisco.

Most newspaper people are as worried now about the various forms of technology creeping in on their business as carbon paper manufacturers must have been when offices started installing Xerox machines.

I'm worried about it myself even though I don't depend solely on my newspaper work for my living.

Too many newspapers are in financial trouble today and too many cities that have had healthy competition between two or more good, fighting newspapers are in danger of losing one of them. It is not clear to me why this is nor do I think all the newspaper experts know for sure. In most instances it is the afternoon paper that is in most trouble. It seems that people who once settled down with the afternoon paper after six in the evening, are now settling down to watch their news on television.

You won't find me knocking television news, nor could anything I say conceivably have any effect on a trend but television news never has been and never will be a substitute for a newspaper. Even a bad newspaper does some things better than a good television news program.

Newspapers haven't been left behind when it comes to technology. The whole process of producing a newspaper has changed more in ten years than has the process of producing a television news broadcast. Newspaper reporters have adapted to writing on a display terminal instead of a sheet of yellow copy paper but there are other innovations lurking in the shadows that worry them. If the time comes when the newspaper itself is not a paper at all but an image that can be called up on the screen of a computer in a person's home, a lot of what they love about the business will be gone. There won't be much reason for them to hold out against switching over to television, where the journalism may be worse but the pay better. Newspapermen and women wouldn't sit around the Denver

Press Club eating, drinking and arguing about a product that didn't really exist anywhere but in the memory bank of a computer.

What's News?

A YOUNG reporter I talked with last weekend said he was in trouble with his readers and with the police because of a story he'd written.

His newspaper is in a medium-sized city in the Northeast and the incident involved a holdup of a small grocery store. The two men who did it were chased into a dead-end alley and caught by three men who heard the grocer yell for help as the thieves ran out of his store.

The two men were not armed and when they were caught, they were pinned to the ground while someone called the police.

The reporter heard of the chase over his police radio and raced to the scene, arriving at about the same time as the cops.

The two suspects were released by their captors and they stood up to face the police. One of them made a smartass remark in answer to one of the cop's questions and the cop instantly pistol-whipped him to the ground and went after him again with his feet.

At this point one of the three men who had originally captured the robber pulled the cop off and told him to cool it.

When the reporter got back to the office, he realized

there were three ways to write the story. It could be the grocer's story of the robbery, it could be the story of the three citizens capturing the thieves or it could be the story of the cop beating one of the robbers.

The reporter wrote the story of the policeman beating the thief.

"You wrote the wrong story," a cop said to him after the story appeared. "Those two guys were guilty as hell."

The reporter has since been reprimanded by several cops he knows and by half a dozen letter-writing readers.

A lot of newspaper readers and almost all cops would agree that the story should have been about the holdup and the capture, not about police brutality. Not many newspaper editors would, though. They'd agree the emphasis should have been where this reporter put it: MAN BITES DOG.

It seems to me there's a news crisis in the world. The crisis has nothing to do with world events but with events in the news business itself. It has become such a big business that there is inevitable pressure for the product to make money.

This is a reasonable enough expectation for owners and stockholders but most newsmen and women like to think that news is more important than money. To increase profit on a product, you have to increase its popularity. Making news more popular is the last resort of a dying news operation.

If news is treated like any other product being sold for money, then it will be made the way people like it. Newspapers will print what people want to read, not what they ought to know. Reporters will ignore stories of police brutality because no one likes to read about it. "Those two had it coming to them."

In London during the Falkland Islands war, Margaret Thatcher complained about a BBC news broadcast that suggested that the death of a husband was just as sad for a woman in Argentina as it was for the wife of a British sailor.

Margaret didn't like that.

"The case for our country is not being put with sufficient vigor by certain journalists," she said.

Mrs. Thatcher was answered by a spokesman for the BBC.

"It is not the BBC's role to boost troops' morale or to rally British people to the flag," he said. "What we are about is not propaganda but information."

Whether a journalist is reporting a war or a grocery store holdup, it is not his business to consider whether the story will do good or harm. He has to have faith that in the long run, the truth will do good. The policeman did beat the thief. It was unusual. *It* was the news story.

The reporter was my son, Brian, too.

The Journalist's Code of Ethics

To what standards do newsmen and women adhere and how should everyone be made to adhere to them?

It is unlikely that reporters and editors are any more or less honest and ethical than doctors but I envy doctors their Hippocratic Oath, the creed they swear to when they become physicians. It's a little out of date but it has a grandeur to it that is timeless.

"I swear by Apollo, the physician," it begins.

That's not much of a beginning, but it improves even though it needs rewriting.

The Hippocratic Oath asks the young doctor to take care of the physician who taught him as he would take care of his own parents. Most young reporters don't feel all that kindly toward the editors who taught them their profession.

The Hippocratic Oath also asks the young doctor to do only what is right for his patients and to do nothing that is wrong. He promises to give no patient deadly medicine and not to induce an abortion for any pregnant woman.

The young doctor promises not to seduce any males or females and not to reveal any secrets.

If journalists had an oath of their own, it would differ from the doctor's.

The journalist certainly wouldn't start by swearing to Apollo and probably not even to Walter Lippmann or Ed Murrow. The oath should be simple and direct. I was thinking of some things that ought to be in it.

Here are some suggestions for "The Journalist's Code of Ethics":

—The word "journalist" is a little pompous and I will only use it on special occasions.

—I am a journalist because I believe that if all the world had all the facts about everything, it would be a better world.

—I understand that the facts and the truth are not always the same. It is my job to report the facts so that others can decide on the truth.

—I will try to tell people what they ought to know and avoid telling them what they want to hear, except when the two coincide, which isn't often.

—I will not do deliberate harm to any persons, except to the extent that the facts harm them and then I will not avoid the facts.

—No gift, including kind words, will be accepted when it is offered for the purpose of influencing my report.

—What I wish were the facts will not influence what investigation leads me to believe them to be.

—I will be suspicious of every self-interested source of information.

—My professional character will be superior to my private character.

—I will not use my profession to help or espouse any cause, nor alter my report for the benefit of any cause, no matter how worthy that cause may appear to be.

—I will not reveal the source of information given to me in confidence.

—I will not drink at lunch.

It needs work but it's a start on an oath for reporters and editors.

Farmers

THERE are two groups of people whose handling of money mystifies me. They are bankers and farmers.

Farmers have always been the most admired people

in our country. They were an honest, independent, hard-working bunch. More than any other single group, they have made this country what it is, great.

Little by little, though, farmers are becoming less admired than they once were. They got their good reputation in the days when they were simple, self-reliant people who raised their own food and sold what they had left over in order to buy a few things they couldn't grow or make themselves.

Everyone in town knew which were the good farmers and which were the poor farmers because the good farmers' kids were better dressed and their places were better kept. You could tell just from driving by. The farmer's standard of living depended on how hard he and his family worked.

It used to be that farmers were on their own. We let them sink or swim. If they had a drought or if the economy went bad, they sank. If there was enough rain but not too much rain and the economy was good, they could get rich. In the 1930s we decided farmers were too important to be left to the mercy of the elements and a free economy, so the government got into the business of helping them. Now it can't get out and, as a result, farmers are no more independent of government than a lot of other Americans.

The farmer who isn't very good at farming and is lazy gets just as much government money today as the good farmer does. A farmer these days is often rich or poor for reasons that have nothing to do with his ability or industry. Most farmers' families don't even eat anything they grow anymore.

Last year I visited a farmer with a reputation for being one of the best in all of Kansas. He grew wheat.

I went into his farmhouse half expecting a wood stove
and a few rocking chairs in the living room. Instead he
had two television sets, a tape recorder and a stereo
record player. I asked him how much he thought the
farm equipment in his yard was worth.

"Maybe million and a half, two million," he said,
"but the bank owns a lot of it."

I turned to his wife standing next to the electric
range in the kitchen and asked if she made bread from
the wheat her husband grew.

She broke into merry laughter.

"I've never made bread in my life," she said.
"John likes Wonder Bread."

Farmers these days aren't any less dependent on the
rest of the world than city people, either. John grows
wheat that he sells to Russia and buys Japanese television sets with the money.

There aren't any homemade pickles in *his* cellar.

Farmers seem to be victims of their own virtues.
They have worked so hard and been so smart in using
new scientific methods and better farm machinery that
they've produced themselves out of work. We not only
have a surplus of the things farmers grow, we have a
surplus of farmers.

It's both sad and strange that some of the world's
population is starving to death while we have more
food than we can eat. Why can't we work this
out?

Our farmers are growing so much that they've
created a problem we don't know how to solve. The
government has come up with all sorts of ingenious
plans. None of them really works. Last year the government paid farmers not to grow corn. The govern-

ment paid the farmers with surplus corn it had
bought from them the year before. It's a form of
welfare, even though farmers hate to have the word
applied to them.

My only real knowledge of farming comes from the
fourteen-horsepower John Deere tractor I own. I've
been wondering if I could get the government to pay
me for not mowing my lawn with it next year.

A Broken Water Hose

PEOPLE who really know how to do something and
have the ambition to do it are hard to find.

Several weeks ago I was driving the old station
wagon home on a hot summer Sunday night. I started
to smell something burning. You know how that is.
You hope it's the car next to you or something from the
outside air. Finally I couldn't deny that it emanated
from under my very own hood. I pulled off the highway into a combination gas station, grocery store and
garage. It wasn't the kind of place that gives you any
confidence that they know much about cars. I judged
my chance of getting anything done there at seven
o'clock Sunday evening to be near zero but it was the
only choice I had.

Not wishing to irritate the attendant by making him
come out to ask what I wanted, I shut off my steaming
engine, hurried out of the car and went inside. A
paunchy, balding man in his middle forties was closing

the cash register on the change he had just collected from the sale of a bag of potato chips.

"Yeah?" he said in a tone that suggested he didn't have time for me.

I told him my problem. He came out to the car and as I unlatched the hood, he lifted it and was instantly engulfed in a cloud of steam.

When the fog cleared he just shook his head.

"I dunno," he said. "You got a broken water hose here."

He went back into the store, sold two Hostess Twinkies and then went into the one-pit garage connected to the store.

I waited, uncertain about whether he'd abandoned me or not. Pretty soon he emerged with a length of hose. I was tense. He tried to fit the piece of hose on the pipe leading from the radiator but it wasn't close to the right size.

"May not have it," he said.

I was fifty miles from home. I had about twenty-seven dollars on me and didn't know anyone nearby I could call.

The man disappeared into the garage again and this time I was sure he'd lost interest in my case. When he finally emerged he had two more pieces of hose. Neither of them fitted but I knew by now that I had someone special here. This fellow had taken on my problem for his own and he was sticking at it. It was a dirty little job but he was helping me.

For the next forty-five minutes he'd wrestle with a piece of hose under my hood for a while and then go in and sell something or pump fifteen gallons of gas, but he always came back to me.

I had been there perhaps an hour when he finally found a length of hose that fit. I was happy, relieved and grateful. I could hardly believe this fellow had kept at the job until he got it done.

Next, of course, I was worried about my twenty-seven dollars. I would have been happy to pay him one hundred and twenty-seven dollars if I'd had it, but I didn't, and there was no way of knowing what he'd charge.

He went into the store area as I followed along like a faithful dog, grateful for anything my master was doing for me. Inside he took a greasy parts book down off the shelf behind him. When they go for the parts book, I'm nervous.

His finger went up and down several pages, as he uttered an occasional grunt. I don't want to suggest this fellow was a lot of fun, but by now I liked him and hoped I'd be able to pay him what he asked. Finally his finger came to rest on a serial number with a price after it.

"2749-16 JDT," he said. "I'll just charge on the cost of the hose. That'll be ten dollars and eighty-five cents."

I have no aberrant tendencies but I could have kissed this man.

"Listen," I said. "It's worth more than that to me. I've only got twenty-seven dollars. Please take the twenty dollars. I'll keep the seven dollars to get to work on in the morning."

Since that episode, I've thought of him a hundred times. Does he make as good a living as he would if he'd told me to get lost, as so many would have under similar circumstances? I hope so. I hope he gets his reward in satisfaction but I hope it turns out that it's also a good way to run a business.

Not many people are running them that way.

Getting Ahead

Do you want to get ahead in business? Are you young, just starting out and ambitious to get to the top as quickly as possible? Take some advice from someone who has seen a lot of people pass him by on the way up: Get yourself an assistant.

If you're determined to be taken seriously in business, it is absolutely essential that you have an assistant in addition to your secretary. No matter how little you actually have to do, get someone to help you do it.

Don't start thinking small. If you think you don't have enough work to do for both a secretary and an assistant, you're thinking small. Don't forget that as soon as you add one more body around the office, the time it takes to do many jobs doubles. It means getting more coffee, working out more vacation schedules and finding more office space and office equipment.

I've seen hundreds of executives and the ones who get furthest fastest are the ones who make fewest mistakes. One way to make fewer mistakes is to make fewer decisions. Get an assistant who makes mistakes for you! If you use your head, you can make it appear as though you have a very important job without ever really doing anything at all. Send your assistant to meetings. If someone wants to come to your office to talk, tell him to see your assistant. Give every visitor the impression that you have someone more important waiting to see you.

To get ahead in business you have to put yourself in a position of power and to have power you must have people working for you. The minute a person gets an assistant, his own job takes on new importance.

When you get your assistant, make sure he or she has a good job title. It won't help your stature if you're only in charge of a helper or a gofer. Your assistant should, at the very least, be called "Executive Assistant." Go to your boss once in a while and make the grand gesture. Ask for a raise or a new title, not for yourself but for your assistant. Don't forget, the more important your assistant is, the more important you are.

If you've chosen your assistant wisely, he'll come to you after a few months on the job, close the door and say he has something important to ask. He thinks *he* needs an assistant.

That could be the beginning of something big for you because if your assistant gets an assistant, the whole plan for the offices on your floor will have to be worked over to make room for your assistant's assistant. Someone else will be moved out of your area to a smaller office down the hall and you're on your way to the top. You're starting a little empire within the company.

The next step is a big one and an important one. After an assistant has made a lot of mistakes on decisions you should have made yourself, you're going to have to fire him. Firing an assistant is just one more positive way of giving yourself added stature in a company. Go to your boss, tell him how bad you feel about it but say you feel it's best for everyone if your assistant gets the axe. This instantly says to the boss that all those mistakes he's noticed in your department must be the fault of your aide. You've just been too nice a guy to say anything about it until now.

Nothing succeeds like success unless it's having people afraid of you, and if they know you can fire someone, you have acquired a new power. Having people afraid of you is absolutely the best way to acquire power and don't ever forget it. If you doubt that, just look at the former vice-president or the former general manager who has been relegated to a lesser position. Everyone knows management hoped he'd retire. His power is gone because people are no longer afraid of him. He is afraid himself.

Many of America's best companies are heavily staffed with assistants that aren't really necessary, and if you're going to be successful in business, you'd better get yourself one.

Conventions

ONE of the things businessmen love to do is get together with other people in the same business and talk business.

This great interest they have in what they're doing has created another big business, conventions. Most hotels, a lot of resorts and even some cities wouldn't make it if they didn't have conventions.

I can't figure out whether the average convention is an honest business meeting or a boondoggle wrapped as a Christmas present from the executives to themselves once a year. The money seems wasteful but if it's a corporation that's making hundreds of millions of dollars, who am I to criticize? Obviously they know more about how to do business than I do. Conventions keep a lot of nice hotels and restaurants in business, too. That isn't all bad.

Still, I can't get used to the money I see big companies spending on conventions. I went to one in San Francisco where the company hired the Goodyear blimp equipped with a big electric signboard to flash welcome messages down to the participants having a lavish outdoor party below.

Some corporations spend money on conventions as if it came from a Parker Brothers game. A company that is trying to save money back at the home office by putting a cheaper brand of paper towels in the men's and ladies' rooms, will pay first-class air fare to bring four hundred of their executives or salesmen across the country and put them up in hotel rooms that cost a hundred dollars a night.

At the reception before the banquet the final night, there are always 350 pounds of shrimp on platters around the room and piles of literature about the business on the tables. Participants eagerly grab up both. They go inside to tables with fresh flowers, have dinner with two kinds of wine and are informed, amused or entertained by an orchestra and a speaker who is being paid something like ten thousand dollars for half an hour of his time.

The business meetings are dull if you don't know

anything about the business but the participants love every dull minute of them. The speakers from various divisions of the company are terrible. They drone on with charts or other visual displays that don't make anything very clear and they tell the people in the room nothing but things they already know. If they don't know, they don't care.

A typical convention speech starts like this:

"Thanks for that introduction, Ed. I'm glad you were able to be with us today after last night's party."

This is the kind of little joke that suggests Ed is a real hell-raiser and everyone laughs. The truth is that Ed had only two weak Scotch and sodas over a four-hour period the night before and he was in bed by 10:15.

The speaker then goes on to make the following points:

—Competition will be more intense this year than ever before.

—There are difficult times ahead but he's confident the company is ready to meet the challenge of the future. (No speech would be complete at one of these meetings if it didn't mention "the challenge of the future.")

—He is confident the company will maintain its leadership position in the industry in spite of the difficult economic environment in which they operate today.

—The management team is in place. ("In place" is the most popular new phrase in business speeches.)

—Last year was one of the most difficult in the company's history but, in spite of certain setbacks with which you're all familiar, it had a record they could all be proud of.

—Nothing could be further from the truth. (This is in reference to a story in the industry that the company is in trouble.)

—Because of the ongoing efforts of this great team, they're going to take a bigger share of the market next year. He's confident it is an ever-expanding market.

—The company is fortunate in having such a forward-looking leader as its president. (This is where the speaker says nice things about his boss. Then he lists some other people who have contributed so much to the success of the company and finishes by saying "the list goes on and on." I've always wondered what the people thought whose names weren't mentioned but who were relegated to the anonymous on-and-on list.)

I have a feeling that sometime, long ago, someone wrote a convention speech and with a few name changes the same speech is still being used ten thousand times a year.

Speechmaking

IF you've ever talked in front of a group of more than ten people, you know how nervous you get. In the past few years I've spoken about twenty times to large audiences and I was as nervous before the last one as I was before the first. Being nervous before speaking just doesn't seem to go away.

There are some things I've learned about speechmaking:

—Sitting at the head table, waiting for your turn while everyone eats dinner for several hours, is the hardest part of making a speech at a banquet.

—A lot of organizations that ask you to speak don't care what you talk about as long as you show up on time and don't talk for too long.

—You have to give a longer speech when the event is held in an auditorium than you do when you're speaking at a dinner, because in an auditorium those people came for the single purpose of hearing you.

—If you make a half-hour speech, it takes about three weeks. It takes a day to get there, a day to get back, a couple of days to prepare it and several weeks to worry about it.

—It's strange to be "introduced" by someone you never met.

—The worst thing that can happen is if they give out awards, citations, trophies or plaques before you speak. Those presentations take forever and after they're over everyone's ready to go home, not listen to you speak.

—If the speech is at a dinner, you usually sit next to the wife of the president. She's almost always bright and friendly. I usually like her better than the president. It's difficult to make small talk when you're nervous, though.

—The toughest audience is at a banquet where they're all sitting at round tables. There are ten or twelve people at a table and the tables are widely separated so the waiters can get through. It's late, everyone's been drinking and eating and they can't hear what you're saying very well anyway.

—Getting dressed in a hotel room before a speech, I almost always find there's something wrong with my clothes. There's a button missing on my shirt, I brought brown socks and I'm wearing a blue suit or there's a spot on my necktie.

—Usually the podium on the speaker's platform is high enough so you don't have to worry about having your pants pressed.

—The worst introductions are when the person introducing you tries to be funny. The best introductions are invariably the shortest. I've had introductions that were as long as my speech. There really isn't that much to say about me.

—Even when I'm the main speaker, there's almost always someone on the program who speaks better than I do.

—The strange thing about speaking is that you only know for sure that you've made a point with an audience when you say something funny and they laugh. If you make what you hope is a good, serious point, there's no way for them to let you know.

—They always give you a glass of water but I never drink any.

—When there are questions afterwards, there's always one person who gets up and embarrasses everyone else by asking a really stupid question.

—No matter how bad I may have been, someone always comes up to me and tells me I was great. If most people are polite but distant when you're leaving, you know you bombed out as a speaker.

—Someone always thanks you profusely for coming even when they've paid you to do it.

—There are few pleasanter times in life than when you've finished speaking.

The Nonworking Week

A LOT of people know for sure whether they're on the side of management or labor, but I don't have a side. I vacillate. One day I'm angry at the high-handed, anything-for-a-profit corporation which is paying big dividends and small salaries, but the next I'm angry at employees who take money from the company without putting in a day's work. There's plenty to dislike on both sides.

I'm not in a position where I hire or fire people but occasionally I get so far behind on mail and paperwork that Jane Bradford, who works with me regularly, and I decide to hire a temporary secretary for a few weeks to help us get caught up.

Over the years we've had about ten. With a couple of exceptions, this is the way it goes:

Linda hears we're looking for a typist so she comes to my office to talk. She's bright, young, attractive and she knows how to type. She wants the job desperately, she says, so she can pay her part of the rent for the apartment she shares with a roommate. I don't ask about the roommate.

Linda seems like what we need so I tell her to show up Monday morning at 9 A.M.

Monday morning at 9:22, Linda waltzes in. The bus was late, she says.

First Linda puts her pocketbook down on the desk. She notices the IBM Selectric typewriter she's going to use and complains that it's an old model which she may not be able to work on.

Next she asks Jane where the ladies' room is. I know where it is too but she doesn't ask me.

Ten minutes later she reappears with a fresh makeup job. She wants to make a good impression on me, I guess.

"Is it okay if I go down to the cafeteria and get a cup of coffee?" she asks.

I had assumed that by quarter of ten she'd already had breakfast but I want to be Mr. Nice Guy with Linda, so I, of course, say sure.

Linda is in the cafeteria long enough to have fresh-squeezed orange juice, pancakes and sausage and a third cup of coffee, but when she comes back she's carrying a bag with coffee and a Danish in it. She spreads her little breakfast out on the desk and proceeds to have it while she reads the newspaper. This is not the kind of help Jane and I had in mind.

I finally put some things on her desk that I want typed. She asks me a few questions about the material and then says is it okay if she makes a phone call first.

Mr. Nice Guy says sure.

I hear her talking to her mother. She's been on the payroll for an hour and a half now and she hasn't done anything at all for me yet but she's telling her mother how good I am to work for.

It turns out Linda is a telephone junkie. She spends more time making personal phone calls than she does drinking coffee or going to the ladies' room, and by the end of the third day she's getting more incoming calls than Jane, Bob Forte, the editor, and I put together.

Several days later Linda confides in Bob, who tells

me, that she really hates this kind of work. She wants to be an actress and only took the job in hopes she'd see Walter Cronkite or Dan Rather in the halls. She'd like to meet Dan because if she can't make it on Broadway, she wants to be the first anchorwoman on the network evening news show.

On Friday of the first week, Linda calls in at 11 A.M. and says she's going to be a little late because she has a dental appointment she forgot to tell me about. All the temporary secretaries I've ever had have an awful lot of dental work done and their buses are later than anyone else's.

I thought of all this because I've read where, when unemployment is high, the absenteeism rate in industry goes way down. Workers don't goof off as much. I hope it's true even though I know it could mean less business for dentists during a recession.

Unemployment

LOOKING for work is one of the worst things to have to do. There's nothing good about it. You don't really know how to get started, you feel like a jerk and it's demeaning every step of the way.

There aren't many of us who haven't looked for work at some time in our lives. There are ten million Americans doing it at almost any time and I feel terrible for them. I feel almost as bad for them because they have to *look* for work as I do because they're *out* of work. Being out of work is bad enough but having to look for it is even worse.

If you aren't working, it's almost impossible not to feel a little ashamed of yourself. If you're a man, you feel a little less of a man; if you're a woman, I don't know how you feel.

Considering that just about everyone has looked for work, it's amazing how mean the people *with* the jobs are to the people without them. You'd think they'd never looked for jobs themselves. You'd think they were born with jobs.

Once a person gets to be in the position of hiring or firing someone, he or she seems to forget what it's like to be unemployed. Why is that?

When you fill out the form for the personnel department, the man or woman who takes it from you always makes you feel like dirt. It's as if they don't like associating with someone who doesn't have a job.

The person who interviews you always acts as if he or she was president of the company. You know darn well it's just a flunky's job but you don't dare let on you know that because your application could end up in the wasketbasket. When he turns away from you and walks to a desk or file cabinet, you feel like giving him a swift kick in his smug tail.

I remember the first time I looked for work. There were hundreds of classified ads in the paper under the Help Wanted heading and I figured it was going to be easy.

Well, it didn't take me long to find out that the number of Help Wanted pages in the classified section of the newspaper has very little to do with getting a job.

First you count out all the ads looking for nuclear physicists, registered nurses, animal trainers and, if you don't know anything about computers, you count out the ads looking for computer programmers. I mention that because there seem to be a lot of ads for them these days. I don't know what they do but I assume it's a terrible job that doesn't pay much. If it wasn't, there wouldn't be so many ads for them under Help Wanted.

As soon as you get some experience looking in the classified section, you get discouraged. You begin to read the classifieds the way you read the phone book when you're looking for one number. You know all those hundreds of listings don't mean anything. You get to spot the ones looking for door-to-door salesmen to work on commission only. There's usually only one or two categories that mean anything to you and if anything is listed there, you're probably too late for it.

Unemployment is as much of a mystery as cancer and almost as bad. I've never understood why there should be any real unemployment. Do we mean there isn't any work to be done anywhere in the country? Do we mean people have everything they want to eat? Everything they need by way of housing? All the clothes, cars and creature comforts they want? Of course not. Then why isn't there work for everyone?

What we need is a President who can figure out a way to match up those ten million unemployed with the ten million Help Wanted ads. And when that's done, I hope everyone fires those miserable people in the personnel offices so they have to go out and look for work themselves.

Economic Indicators

Yesterday, for the first time, I noticed I've been using two tissues or paper handkerchiefs instead of one. I think I've been using two more often than one for some time now but I never thought about it until yesterday. It's a sign of the times. They're making smaller, cheaper paper handkerchiefs.

Will we ever reverse the present trend in which everything gets smaller, of less quality and more expensive? Is there a company in America that has improved its product and given us more for our money this year than it did last year? There are some, of course, but they're far outnumbered by the ones giving us less for more.

Each of us has his or her own scale on which the past economy is measured against the present. We have our own personal equivalents of the government's Gross National Product and economic indicators. It may be the price of a cup of coffee, a bus ride or a pair of stockings. (I hate to tell you but thirty-five cents for a movie is one of my standards. That's what we used to pay when we went to a cowboys and Indians double feature at the Madison when I was a kid.)

I can understand having to raise the price of a product when the cost of labor and materials goes up but how do they explain the deterioration in the quality of the product? That shouldn't have anything to do with inflation. And why is it that when the economy is good and everyone's working, prices go up but when the economy's bad and people are out of work, prices still go up?

When a well-known watch company first started making something other than the old-fashioned spring watch, I bought one. They had obviously put a lot of research and technique into it. It was the first watch I ever had that operated on a tiny battery and it was just great. It kept near-perfect time and the quality of the workmanship was first-rate. I retired my trusty old Hamilton railroad watch with a few tears and gave way to progress. The new watch gave me ten years of good service before I finally left it in a locker at the place where I play tennis and lost it.

From loyalty to the company and because I wanted another good watch, I went back to the jeweler. Well, they don't make that model anymore. The jeweler conceded their new equivalent isn't as good.

You can't tell me razor blades last as long as they did ten or twenty years ago, either. How in the world does a company make razor blades that aren't as good? That must take real technical know-how.

The gasoline we buy for our cars isn't as powerful as it used to be. Forget about the increase in price. Maybe they had to raise the price from the thirty-three cents a gallon we were paying not so long ago but did they also have to lower the octane rating so that one gallon of gas won't push a car as far? A lot of gas sold now is only eighty-seven octane and the highest octane you can buy is ninety-three. An octane rating in the nineties used to be regular gas and high test could be ninety-nine octane.

For the past ten years I've had a popular brand-name suitcase. It's been the best suitcase I ever owned even though, for a while, it looked like everyone else's suitcase. It's been all over the world and back and it's a little shabby so last month I decided to retire it. I was going to stay at an expensive hotel and I didn't want to embarrass the bellboy who would have had to carry my battered bag to the room so I went to a luggage store to buy another like it. Three guesses? They don't make it any longer. The one they do make to replace it is shoddy by comparison.

Every time a big company takes over a smaller one in this country in order to promise its stockholders a bigger return on their investment, the product suffers. They raise the price and make it cheaper. I'm not a Communist, and I own some stocks but I'd gladly settle for a little more quality as a consumer and a smaller dividend as an investor.

IV:

MONEY

A Cash Standard

THERE'S something about having a thick stack of money in your pocket that gives you a feeling of well-being. I smile more when I have money in my pocket. Even too much change will do it for me if the change is mostly in quarters and quite heavy.

It occurs to me to mention this today because I've noticed that the more money I make, the less I use. I'm talking about actual cash, green paper money. Earlier in the week I took an overnight trip from New York to Washington. Before I left, I cashed a check for a hundred and fifty dollars. When I got back to New York late the next afternoon, I still had more than a hundred dollars. The surprising thing was that I had that little left because I hadn't really paid for anything. The fifty dollars went out in petty cash for tips, taxis and newspapers. I charged my air fare, my hotel room and my meals.

Like most people, when I sign for something on my credit card I consider it to be free. Paying for the item is postponed to some indefinite time in the future. The bill will come in a lump sum and will bear no relationship in my mind to any service or goods that I actually got for that amount.

The trouble with doing all these things with numbers

instead of with real money is that it takes the fun and the satisfaction out of the exchange process. What's rewarding is to work hard to make money and then to take that money and buy something with it that makes life pleasant or easier.

There used to be a joke about a wealthy recluse who went to his bank once a week and made them show him his money. He wanted to make sure it was still there.

We all know our money isn't really in the bank, it's in the bookkeeping machinery, but I feel the way that old guy did. I'd like to see my money in real life once in a while. Those numbers they send me aren't any fun at all.

I can't get over how little I see of my money these days. One summer when I was in college I worked at a paper mill for forty dollars a week. Every Friday afternoon they gave me my pay in an envelope and I've never made money that was as satisfying to me as that. I don't care how big my check is, it can't match that forty dollars I got in cold cash.

Today the company mails my check directly to the bank. After a while, the bank mails me a slip of paper saying the check has been deposited. When I owe someone something, I write out a check and my bank deducts that from my account. It's all terribly unsatisfactory. Collecting money or paying it out can be a rewarding experience but bookkeeping is no fun at all. If I had my way, I'd have every penny I earned turned over to me in cash and I'd pay most of the people I owe with the money in my pocket.

I understand perfectly well that it wouldn't be practical sometimes but it would be more satisfactory and, furthermore, if the federal government handled its accounts in cash, there'd be a lot less waste. It's one thing for a government official to sign his name to a piece of paper transferring a billion dollars from one place to another, but it would be quite different if he had to show up with the actual money in dollar bills and hand it over. Just counting it would make everyone think twice and there'd surely be cameras around to record the event.

Money ought to be more tangible than it is today, not less. We're treating it too lightly because we can't see it. I don't understand the ramifications of a return to the gold standard but I have a feeling pennies ought to be copper, dimes ought to be silver and it wouldn't do any harm if we had some little fifty or hundred-dollar gold coins in circulation. We need money that's really worth something.

The money game is being played with numbers that are too big for most of us to comprehend. Only lawyers, bankers, computer experts and government officials understand money as a statistic. Most of us get no kick at all from a computer printout of a bank's idea of our net worth. What we want is that lump in our pocket.

Broke

Has everyone been desperately broke?

Maybe not. I always assume that there are very few experiences or emotions that aren't universal. I've been seriously broke twice in my life.

It's a feeling you never forget and although it's been twenty-six years since I didn't know which way to turn for money, I never see anyone out of a job and without a dollar in his pocket without knowing how he feels.

There are still times when I think about being broke. At night when I empty the change out of my pocket and put it on top of my dresser, I often recall, in those terrible old days, adding up my change to see if I had two dollars.

There are chronically poor people who would laugh at what I went through because it wouldn't seem very bad to them. My wife and I were never hungry. My father was retired but he had made a comfortable living even during the Depression, and my wife's father was a doctor. They wouldn't have let us get to the point where we were out on the street and without food, but you know how that is. There's an unwritten code. There are people you don't ask for money and my father and my wife's father were two of them.

I don't know who makes those rules but we all know them. Certainly if I'd asked, either would have given me money. Maybe that was it. They'd have given it to me, not loaned it to me. They would have been disappointed that I had to ask.

My father's brother was a salt-of-the-earth lawyer in a small town in New York State, fighting petty political corruption and providing free legal services to people who couldn't afford to pay him. He and my aunt never had children and I was the closest thing to a son he had. When he came to visit us when I was a child he would often slip me a five-dollar bill as he was leaving. You don't forget an uncle like that.

In desperation one year, I went to him and asked for

five hundred dollars. One of the terrible memories of my life is that I never repaid him. He died three years later without ever having been able to take pleasure from thinking that his favorite nephew was a responsible person. He didn't need the money but he must have looked for some token payment from me and I never made it. I always meant to but I never did.

About fifteen years ago we were doing better but we needed $2,500 to help pay for one of the kids' college tuition and my wife went to the bank for a loan. Banks are a better place to go for a loan than an uncle is. They aren't disappointed if you don't pay them back. They get you.

By this time I was making enough money so we weren't in desperate need of the loan, so as the joke goes, we didn't have any trouble getting it. The interest was probably seven percent.

A year or so later I asked my wife if we were going to pay off the loan in a lump sum, or just continue paying the seven percent interest each year. Being in no way a business tycoon, I had the feeling we should pay it off. She does all our bookkeeping and banking, and she didn't think we should. She was right. I'm not sure to this day if we ever paid off the loan.

Now, of course, I appreciate that it's the only good joke we ever played on a bank. We won because interest rates rose. If we have the $2,500, and it's invested, maybe in the same bank's money-market fund, and we get nine percent interest, we are beating the bank for two percent on $2,500. It is not at all like failing to pay back my uncle.

This all occurred to me today because yesterday an old friend asked me to loan him money. Of course I'll loan it to him but I wish he hadn't asked. It breaks the unwritten law. It changes our relationship. I don't want to think about it every time I see him and I don't want him feeling uneasy about it when he sees me but that's what will happen.

Being broke is a terrible feeling but it's probably an experience everyone ought to have once in a lifetime. If you've never been really broke, you can't possibly understand how nice it is to have a little money in the bank.

Money in Stress

I WAS listening to one of those financial experts being interviewed on the radio the other day and he used the term "money in stress." I never heard the phrase before and I don't know what it means but I think it's where my money is. It's in stress because I don't know where else to put it.

Now that the kids are out of college and the mortgage is paid off, I'm making more money and don't need as much.

Wasn't money easier to deal with ten years ago than it is now? I don't remember hearing about a "money-market fund" until five years ago. It used to be that the solid citizens kept most of their paycheck to pay bills with and put what they had left in the savings bank. Their savings account paid four percent interest and they just let it accumulate year after year, secure in the knowledge that they had a little nest egg. It was the American way.

There was less wheeling and dealing going on and it must have been better for the average person, because when there's a lot of wheeling and dealing, the only ones who get rich are the wheeler-dealers.

Handling money has become complicated, even for someone with a modest income. If a person makes $35,000 a year, he or she could easily spend full time figuring out what to do with it. The trouble is, if you spend full time figuring out what to do with the money you're making, you couldn't keep the job that pays you the $35,000. It's so complicated for most of us that we just give up.

This year I've saved some money and because it doesn't interest me that much, I never got around to doing anything with it. At lunch with a friend last week we were talking about money and I said I had quite a bit in my checking account. He went to work on a paper napkin and figured out how much I was losing every week by having it in the checking account instead of invested in something else.

When I got back from lunch I called a woman at the bank who's been helpful to me over the years—she calls and says I'm overdrawn instead of bouncing checks when I write one for more than I have—and she suggested Treasury notes. Or, at least I think she said Treasury notes. I next called someone at the bank who deals in that kind of thing.

"Were you interested in Treasury bonds, Treasury bills or Treasury notes?" he asked. "If you put your money in ninety-day Treasury notes at five point six percent with a real earning of six point five percent . . ."

"Listen," I said, interrupting what he was telling me, "I've got another call I have to make but I'll get back to you on this."

The money is still in the checking account.

Most of us aren't that interested in getting rich—we just don't want to get poor. We want to stay even. It's very difficult for anyone whose chief interest in life isn't money to do that. If we're surrounded by people who have a serious interest in acquiring money, they usually get it. I've always thought it was unfair for anyone to try to get rich.

On the train I take to work, I often see people going to their offices in the financial district. For them, money is both business and hobby. It's all they want to read about. The only newspaper they buy is *The Wall Street Journal*. If the world ever comes to an end, I'm sure that paper will carry news of the event in a brief, well-written story summarizing the effect Doomsday will likely have on the Dow Jones average, long-term bond rates and pork belly futures. The people who follow money will have had advance inside information about it so they'd have done a lot of late profit taking the day before.

My life's savings, on the other hand, will be "money in stress."

Paying Bills

PAYING a bill isn't just a matter of having the money. Like writing a letter, there's more to paying a bill than just thinking you ought to do it. Paying a bill is easy to put off even if your bank account is in reasonably good shape. I pay my bills now slower than I did when I was broke.

If you've ever talked to a small businessman, or if you are one, you know how slow people are to pay. Most slow payers aren't dishonest or broke. They just don't get at it. That doesn't make it any easier for the small businessman, of course.

Doctors always have a lot of unpaid bills. They often have so many deadbeats that they overcharge the patients that do pay what they owe, to make up for those who don't. I, personally, don't like a lot of talk about money when it involves a doctor. I think of doctors as being above the idea of money. I'm crazy, of course.

A lot of people pay the doctor last and this strikes me as strange because you have a first-person relationship with a doctor that you don't have with the power company. It would be difficult to rush into the doctor's office in an emergency if you still owed him for the last two visits you made a year ago.

You and I may live with a vague kind of guilt over bills we haven't paid that are more than thirty days old but not paying bills quickly is a way of life for some

businesses. The longer a business puts off paying what
it owes, the longer it can keep its money in the bank
making big interest.

Recently there was a story about what Yale University and a lot of other educational institutions are doing
with their government grants. Yale, for example, was
getting $82 million from the federal government for research grants, contracts and loans. The money came to
Yale on the twentieth of each month. By holding on to
half of it and investing it for only ten days, until the
end of each month, the university made $535,000 on it
over a year's time. Obviously it pays not to pay.

Some businesses have turned the tables on slow payers. They charge high interest rates on any unpaid
amount and they make so much money on the interest
that they don't care whether you pay on time or not.
They like it better when you don't pay quickly. For example, I have a VISA card but I've learned not to use it
any more often than I have to, because when my bill
comes from them it's so confusing I can't figure out
how much I owe. I think they do it intentionally. If I
don't pay what I owe on time, they charge me high interest on that amount and on any new items I charge.
They seem to do everything possible to keep me from
paying my bill on time because they make more money
by charging me eighteen percent interest for every
twenty minutes I'm overdue.

We have a good system for paying bills in our home.
My wife and I divide up the responsibilities. I open the
mail and give her the bills to pay. If we get a second
bill the next month, it's my responsibility to say to her,
"Haven't you paid that yet?"

Yesterday I got a postcard from our town water department saying they hadn't been paid because they had not been able to get in to read our water meter for more than ninety days. When I get home tonight, I'm going to take care of that bill so I don't have to feel guilty taking a shower tomorrow morning.

I'm going to say to my wife, "How come you haven't let them in to read the water meter so they can bill us and you can pay the water bill?"

I know her. She'll say, "The water bill will be for about twelve dollars and ninety-five cents. I'm in no hurry to pay because I have it in a high interest-bearing money-market account."

Banks and Jesse James

BANKS have discovered that people are a waste of time. They've discovered that money is a waste of time, too, so they're phasing out both people and money. They don't want to have anything to do with either. All they want is their computers computing away.

Banks are already trying to discourage people from coming in to get fifty or a hundred dollars in cash by keeping customers waiting a long time. They also don't keep as much cash around as they used to. If Jesse James were reincarnated in 1990, he might have to go on welfare because the tellers wouldn't have enough money on hand to make it worth his while holding them up. If he stood in line often to rob banks, he could end up making less than the minimum hourly wage.

Our daughter, Ellen, lives and works in New York. She's been saving some money for a down payment on a cooperative apartment. A while ago things started coming together for the deal and she had to give the owners a certified check for ten thousand dollars. It's hard for me to get used to the idea that a daughter of mine would *have* ten thousand dollars, but that's another story.

On the day she had to pay the money, she went to the bank where she had it stored and asked the teller to give her a bank check for ten thousand dollars. It was normal banking procedure except the bank told her their check "wouldn't clear" for three days. In other words, it couldn't be collected immediately by the people she was giving it to.

You know real estate people. They wanted it that day. My daughter, having been brought up right, said to the bank teller, "Okay then. I'll take my ten thousand in cash."

It was forty-five minutes and three vice-presidents later that she walked out with her money, much of it in one-dollar bills. They were either short of cash or trying to teach her a lesson.

A retail trade in any business is irritating because people can be so difficult. Big deals are where the money is. Obviously banks are tired of the retail trade. They can make more money loaning ten billion dollars to a bankrupt nation that can't pay them back than they can from solid citizens with modest bank accounts.

The handwriting is on the wall. All of us are going to be handling fewer dollars in the future. When we buy something the cashier will punch up our code on a machine and that will transfer money electronically from our account to the store's. The cashier won't deal in cash.

There's a lot we could all learn from banks. I've been awfully slow learning. I could kick myself for all the bills I've paid on time. Banks are teaching us it isn't the way to do business. The way to do business is to put off paying a bill until the very last minute.

Today, in many large city banks, if you deposit money in your checking account with a check written by someone else on a bank next door to yours, you cannot withdraw any of that money for ten days. That banking practice ought to be illegal.

In the past, banks have said it takes two or three days for a check "to clear." Exactly when they actually get the money no longer has anything to do with when you can have it. They hold your money, sometimes for more than a week, and won't let you use it. Of course, they make interest on your money while they withhold it from you.

It's almost impossible to find out when a bank actually collects on a check. When I deposit a check written to me by a major company on a bank within two blocks of my own bank, I can't believe it takes more than two days for them to get the money.

Why can't I use it for a week?

Companies have already learned from banks. The accounting departments of many corporations routinely stall on paying bills because every day they hold onto the money, they're making interest on it.

I recall, from some of those old movies, that Jesse James wasn't all bad. He did have a code of honor. If

Jesse James were around today, it wouldn't surprise me to hear that he was refusing to do business with some banks by holding them up because their shoddy business ethics didn't meet his standards.

The Ultimate Cigarette

THE other night I turned in my ticket at a parking garage in midtown New York and waited for them to extricate my car from the pile upstairs.

A man in his mid-thirties came over and stood beside me. He had a briefcase with him and before he spoke to me I could tell he was going to speak to me.

"You're Andy Rooney, aren't you?" he said.

I don't deny that, except under extreme circumstances, so I admitted it although I was sure I didn't want to hear what he was going to say next.

"Would you like to see an idea I just presented to one of the biggest ad agencies in town?" he asked.

I shrugged. I didn't have any interest at all in seeing it but before I answered he opened his briefcase and unfolded a glossy page of paper.

"The ultimate cigarette," it said, "for people to whom money is no object."

He had a name for the cigarette but I forget it.

"My idea," he said, "is to make this cigarette a status symbol. The package will be black and the cigarette itself will be black. That way everyone will know when you pull out this pack of cigarettes that you smoke the most expensive cigarette in the world. It'll give you instant class."

"Did they like the idea?" I asked.

"Have to like it," he said. "How they not gonna like an idea this surefire. Listen. We got Cadillacs and Rolls-Royces for people who want to spend a lot on a car. We got swimming pools for status symbols for a house. We got Countess Mara neckties. We got status symbols for everything except cigarettes."

"How will you make them so expensive?" I asked. "Will the tobacco be better? Could they make a really great cigarette if they wanted to?"

"They won't be any different," he said. "That isn't my business though. I don't know how they'd make them. The big thing is, they'd be really expensive. That's what'll get people to buy them. Expensive."

My car came and it was a good thing because about then I felt like wrestling this guy to the ground and kicking him in a sensitive place.

I think you'll believe that story because it's not the kind of story I could invent. Not only that, I wouldn't be surprised if we all see his expensive black cigarette on the market in another year or so. They could probably make the cigarette a lot quicker than that. It's laying out the advertising campaign that will take the time.

The cigarette industry is representative of a lot of businesses that depend more on their advertising than on their product for sales. Cigarette brands are not very different, one from another. It's their advertising, not their tobacco, that counts. If they take on this guy in the garage with the expensive black cigarette, and get the right advertising campaign going, he won't be get-

ting his own car out of the garage next time I see him.
He'll have a chauffeur waiting.

This fellow in the garage said he was suggesting
they sell his new cigarettes for two dollars a pack. I admit it could be a very effective sales gimmick. There
are idiots who'll buy anything as long as it costs
enough.

Made in Japan

I LOVE America. I salute the flag and I go around saying "We're the greatest!" but I'd be lying if I said I
wasn't worried.

The funny thing is, unlike my government and some
of my friends, I'm not worried about the Russians. I'm
a little worried about the Chinese, I'll never get over
worrying about the Germans, and the Japanese make
me nervous but the people I'm most worried about are
ourselves. We aren't doing it.

In 1950 we were making seventy-five percent of all
the cars driven anywhere in the world. Now thirty percent of all the cars sold just in this country alone are
made somewhere else. They're not only made somewhere else, they're made very well in Japan, Germany, France, Sweden. I've driven Russian cars and
they're no threat.

Only 25 years ago airlines throughout the world
were all flying America-made Boeings, Douglasses
and Lockheeds. Now, the more you travel on the
smaller airlines both in the United States and abroad,

the more you see commercial planes made in other countries.

Our computers, our television sets, our electronic games and much of our office equipment is made in Japan. It may have the name of some fine old American company on it but don't let them kid you, the chances are the component parts come from Japan.

Our steel mills are running less than half capacity and that's partly because of the economy but even more because other countries have better technology for making steel than we do. Did you ever think it would happen? It's cheaper, even for American companies, to buy foreign steel and have it shipped here.

The same auto companies in Detroit that have workers demanding that the rest of us buy cars made in America, are producing cars they call "American" in foreign countries. Even the cars that are actually assembled in Detroit are often put together with some parts made in Japan. They're about as American as chopsticks.

Statistics show that for the first time in our history, more people are employed in service industries than in production. Today seventy-three percent of the work force deals in services. Only twenty-seven percent work in the production of goods. In other words, more people are selling it than making it.

"Service" may sound like a good word but a lot of what goes under that heading is duplicating order forms on Xerox machines, selling insurance and figuring out interest rates on bank loans.

I recognize the need for bankers, financial experts and figure jugglers but there's just so long the money-manipulators can keep their numbers in the air while they make money off each exchange. Eventually someone has to come up with a product, without which all the statistics in the world mean nothing.

If it's hard to do, we aren't doing it anymore. We buy it from someone else, double the price and sell it back to ourselves at a profit. No wonder we're in trouble. In the last three months we spent 13.1 billion dollars more in foreign countries buying their goods than they spent here buying ours. Oil is something we can't help but machinery and manufactured goods are things we ought to be able to produce better than anyone else in the world.

The basis for everything is not money but hard work. You don't have to be a Communist to believe that Wall Street doesn't deal in that kind of work and the Dow Jones average doesn't reflect it from day to day. The engineers, the chemists, the architects, the scientists, the designers ought to be predominant in our society. If anyone's going to get rich, it ought to be them. The mechanics, the carpenters, the electricians, the construction experts, the plumbers and the repair people and all the other craftsmen who really know how to do something ought to be making it, too.

The only subject you read about or hear about is money. It's as if the products on which all money is based don't make any difference at all. Why are so many foreign goods selling so well here? Usually it's because those products are being made cheaper and better than comparable products made in America.

Why shouldn't I be worried?

Automobile Costs

I⊤ costs us almost a quarter for every mile we drive a car. That's what the government says in a study it issued called "Cost of Owning and Operating Automobiles."

The actual figure is 23.8 cents a mile and the government includes everything in that. It inclúdes how much you paid for the car, your insurance, your gas, oil and even your parking fees. The only thing it hasn't included is parking tickets.

The study says the average car in the United States is now six years and six months old, but they base their overall statistic on a car that is twelve years old and has been driven 120,000 miles. I'd like to see the government keèp all its cars for twelve years and drive them 120,000 miles.

If I thought about the fact that it was costing me a dollar for every four miles I drove, I'd probably walk more. I've always enjoyed trying to save money on a car but I've never been very successful. Last month, just after I decided to keep my old one for another year, the muffler went. I went to a Midas shop and paid $247 for a new one. Do you think I got taken? The muffler itself was only about $45 but they hit me for $125, for something called a crossover pipe. I don't think I've ever heard Midas mention a crossover pipe in their advertising.

It's difficult for most of us to know when we're getting taken by a garage mechanic. You just have to find a good one and trust him. The chances are that even an honest one will add a little on for something he didn't do to make up for something else that took him longer than he expected for reasons he couldn't possibly explain to you unless you were a mechanic.

The people who give advice say to get a written estimate from a garage but if I were a mechanic and you asked me to tell you exactly how much a job was going to cost, I'd tell you to get lost. It's like asking a doctor to tell you exactly how much it's going to cost to make you well again. When I get a bill for work done on my car, it's always twice what I thought it would be but I don't notice a lot of rich mechanics.

Driving bores me but I get a kick out of saving money in little ways on my car. It's dumb that I waste so much money on so many things and get such petty pleasure from saving thirty-five cents on a quart of oil by buying it at a department store and adding it myself, instead of having them do it at the gas station.

The most expensive thing I ever paid for was a car wash. Two weeks ago I took the car to one of those automatic car wash places. They didn't have a sign out front and I should have been suspicious but when I got to the cashier he asked for six dollars. It was too late to turn back but that's the last professional car wash I'll be getting. It's satisfying to wash a car anyway and now that I know it costs six dollars to have it done, it's going to be twice as satisfying for me.

I spend less time in gas stations than most people because I don't go in as often. I don't make many pit stops. Some people get nervous when the gas indicator shows the tank is down below half full. They always fill it before it reaches the quarter mark. I, on the other hand, seldom buy gas before it gets exciting to consider whether I'm going to make it to the next gas station or not. It keeps me awake on the road. I've only run out of gas once with my present car and after you've done it once, you know exactly how far you can go with the tank registering "Empty."

If the government knows of a good mechanic who can keep my car going until it's twelve years old, I'd like to hear from them.

Money and Sports

You can't watch the World Series on television without thinking about money. The same thing happens watching pro football Sunday afternoon.

Money is dominating sports. People are tired of it and I don't know what's going to happen. Nothing, probably. People are tired of a lot of things that don't change.

The commercials in the World Series aren't as annoying as those during the football games because it's easier to make room for a commercial during a baseball game. It isn't the real commercials that most people object to, anyway. They aren't bad. Some of them are even good, and we accept a certain number of commercials as fair exchange for what we're getting free.

The trouble comes when the broadcasters start stealing a little time here and a little time there. It's all those minor promotional intrusions that are making games on television seem like one long interruption. I don't want to be told during the World Series how different Peter Jennings is or how wonderful Dan Rather and Tom Brokaw are during football games. Leave me alone.

The networks snip away at program content on the theory that viewers won't notice the loss of a mere ten seconds or thirty seconds here and there. After a while, though, we do notice.

In an attempt to build a rating for a show of its own later in the day's schedule, the network will often interrupt the flow of the game with a promotional tease for a situation comedy "coming up at nine." They'll cover the time it takes for the batter to walk to the plate with their little in-house ad. On the football field, the promo is superimposed while the team huddles and they don't take it down until the ball is ready to be snapped.

It ought to be mandatory for a broadcaster to superimpose a dollar sign over any picture or announcement which is not a commercial but which is specifically designed to produce income for the network.

Broadcasters don't seem to understand that watching the batter walk to the plate is part of what people enjoy about baseball. Neither do fans want to watch only the part of a football game that takes place while the ball is being run or thrown. Everything that happens down there is part of the game and we want to see it. We are not interested in knowing what mediocre situation comedy is coming up later. We don't want to be lectured to about how bad drugs are for us while our quarterback is flat on his back after being blind-sided by a 270-pound tackle.

Broadcasters are lucky that team owners are as greedy as they are. The owners and associated businessmen in the sports world make the games so unpleasant to attend in person that people would rather be irritated by television in the comfort of their own homes. I speak with authority because I go to all the New York Giants home games.

The parking lot is so badly organized that it can take an hour to get into it and an hour to get out.

My ticket for a seat in the end zone costs $14 a game. If I want to know the names and numbers of the players on the other team, I have to buy a fat magazine with a lot of dull stories, which they erroneously call a program, for $1.50.

If I get thirsty, beer in a paper cup costs $1.90. If I'm very thirsty, a large beer costs $2.75.

A box of Cracker Jacks is $1.00 and a hot dog costs $1.35. They don't sell peanuts in the ball park anymore because they don't like paying to have someone sweep up the shells. They'll have to rewrite the words to "Take Me Out to the Ball Game" and eliminate the peanuts.

Ballpark owners have even found a way to annoy fans electronically, too. They now have electronic scoreboards with commercials interspersed with phony exhortations for the home team.

It'll be interesting to see how far they can go with money before they kill sports.

Charity Is Never Easy

IF you have your health, some happiness, a job, a place to live and some money in the bank, you don't need help. The chances are you ought to be helping someone who does need help. I have those things but whom do I help and how?

At least twice a week I feel guilty as I drop some letter asking for a contribution into the little wicker wastebasket next to my chair. Do I not care about the blind? Don't I want to help wipe out cancer? Am I in favor of muscular dystrophy? What about the school and college I attended? Am I ungrateful to them because I don't always give them as much as they want?

There are so many people and organizations that need and deserve help that it's more than I can stand to think about sometimes. I'm eating too much and there are people starving. It would be better for all of us if I split what's on my plate with them but how do I do that? It is not easy to be charitable.

One of the difficult things about charity is deciding whom to give to. You can't give to everyone who asks and sometimes those who don't ask need help worse than those who do. I don't give to the blind beggar with the dog on the sidewalk outside Saks Fifth Avenue because he demeans every blind man who does not beg. Where *do* I make my contribution?

The United Way has been a partial answer to the problem of how to give but most of us aren't satisfied with such an impersonal charitable contribution. We'd like to do something in a more direct way for a person or for some specific organization. At the time of year when I begin to get my tax stuff together, I'm often embarrassed to see how little I've given compared to how much I have.

We all want to know for sure that any charitable contribution we make is not stolen or wasted and it's impossible not to look for some kind of appreciation from others who know we've given.

"Take heed," it says somewhere in the Bible, "that ye do not give alms before men, to be seen of them."

I always look with suspicion on the people who give to that blind man outside Saks. I can't read the looks on their faces but I think they're taking some smug satisfaction from giving where so many people can see them give. They may drop a quarter in his tin cup in a crowd but I wonder how much they give to the United Way in private?

A lot of rich people make wills and keep everything they have for themselves until they die. This comes mostly from the fear of not ending up with enough, I suppose. I've always thought—and I suppose everyone has thought this—that if I ever became really rich, I'd give away everything except what I needed to live on. Not being really rich, that's easy for me to think. And, of course, each of us gets to define what's really rich. If I had what I have now twenty years ago, I'd have considered myself "really rich."

Very few of us "give 'til it hurts." We wait until we have enough so it doesn't hurt much, then we give. We find ways to let ourselves off. We say to ourselves that we're suspicious of how this charity spends its money or we don't like the new policy of this school or that organization. It's easy to find an excuse for not giving and, of course, it's necessary that we have excuses. It is true that we can't give to everyone.

The mayor of New York once complained that too many New York neighborhoods are selfish. They only want good things for themselves, he said. The Mayor, a Jew, said it in a synagogue and made a wonderfully strong, honest, almost familial complaint. He said no synagogue in New York was providing a single bed for the homeless.

It isn't easy, the Mayor said, to care for the sort of people who need a bed for overnight.

Charity is never easy. So many of the people who need it don't seem to deserve it and that provides a wonderful excuse for all of us not to give much.

Place Your Bets

THE gambling casinos in Atlantic City took 193 million dollars from people visiting that city in one month last year.

That is one of the most disgraceful and sad figures I've ever seen. For gambling casinos to be legal is disgraceful; for people to be dumb enough to go to them and lose 193 million dollars in a month is sad.

If it's mandatory for people to wear seat belts in an automobile for their own protection, how come the government doesn't protect its citizens from losing their money by strapping it into their wallets when they go to Atlantic City?

The thing that bothers me most about it is that when people gamble away their money, they don't spend it on an honest product that someone has worked to make. There's only so much money and if it is lost at a gambling table, it is taken out of the productive part of our economy. Whom would you rather see employed, a blackjack dealer in a casino in Las Vegas or a machinist at an automobile assembly plant in Detroit? Who contributes most to what's good about American life?

It's estimated that the casinos in Atlantic City will take two billion dollars in profit this year. The State of New Jersey takes eight percent of the casinos' profit. This amount is what government exacts in exchange for issuing a license to steal.

I was surprised to read that Atlantic City is now grossing more than Las Vegas. I didn't think anything could be as gross as Las Vegas. Las Vegas estimates it will only take one billion seven hundred and fifty million from customers this year. (I've spelled that out so there won't be any mistake with zeros.)

That means that between the two cities they'll haul in three billion seven hundred and fifty million dollars from customers. Make it an even four billion.

I've been doing some arithmetic, figuring out what could be bought for four billion dollars.

Here are some suggestions:

—It would buy 500,000 Chrysler Le Barons at $8,000 each.

—Four years in an average college costs roughly

$30,000 for tuition, room and board now. It would buy a college education for 133,000 young Americans.

—People could buy one billion copies of this book to give each other for Christmas. This would make one writer very happy.

—One hundred sixty million Americans could each buy a new pair of shoes for $25.

—You could rent an apartment at $350 a month for 952,380 years.

—It would build 66,666 new homes for $60,000 each or 26,666 expensive homes at $150,000 each.

—Two million couples could spend an all-expense-paid week in Hawaii, including air fare.

—It would feed a lot of hungry Americans. That amount would provide food stamps for 1,326,259 families of four, for an entire year.

The slot machines account for about half of a casino's take. The dumbest money goes into those and into something called the Big Six Wheel. It's referred to as the Idiot Wheel because it takes about forty-five cents of every dollar bet on it.

The blackjack tables take fifteen to eighteen percent from a player and the craps tables, twelve percent. The roulette tables take close to twenty-five percent.

The players with the most money play baccarat. They're the smart ones. They only lose twelve percent of their money on an average evening.

The casinos refer to the money that they don't take from the customers as "the drop." The money they take is called "the hold."

Some day I'd like to rent a huge billboard on the outskirts of Atlantic City with a simple Dante-like announcement:

"Abandon hope all ye who enter here!"

Over all, the gambling casinos take eighteen percent of everything bet so there's no chance whatsoever of anyone winning over a period of time. It isn't a gamble, it's a sure thing. You lose.

V:

YOUR
WASHINGTON
REPORTER

Your Washington Reporter

I WENT to the Capitol in Washington the other day to check on things for you.

With press credentials I was able to eat in the congressional restaurant, where I had a bowl of warm milk with six oysters in it for $2.50. It had been advertised as "oyster stew" on the menu but was so unsatisfying that I also ordered a hamburg. That cost $2.75 and was barely fair. I'm telling you about lunch because you may have thought your congressman has a better place to eat lunch than you do.

It was 2:10 when I walked into the gallery of the Senate chamber. The Senate was in session but I didn't think so at first because there were exactly four senators down there on the floor. Three of them, Howard Baker, John Stennis and Russell Long, were debating whether they ought to allow television cameras into the Senate and the fourth, Orrin Hatch of Utah, was Acting Speaker.

The three senators were no more than fifteen feet apart. Senator Stennis was speaking and the stenotypist, with his machine on his chest, hanging from a broad strap around his neck, stood too close to him. The stenotypist looked like the accordionist in a bad restaurant . . . the one you hope doesn't come to your table.

Senator Stennis has never been a favorite of mine but as I sat there, I was impressed with how good he was making his case against televising Senate debate.

"All these empty seats . . ." he was saying. "All these empty seats . . . someone's gonna have to explain 'em . . . make an explanation of where these senators are. This is a dishonest picture. It doesn't tell the story of what's going on . . . all these senators doin' their work in committee meetings somewhere else."

He had a point, I thought. I'd walked in there a few minutes earlier and my first impression was that four senators were working and the other ninety-six were goofing off. It wasn't true, of course. Probably only twenty-five were goofing off and the rest were working elsewhere.

Senator Stennis went on to say how distracting television would be. He said he was easily distracted although he didn't look as if he would be.

He gave an example:

"It takes a lot of wind out of me," he said, "if I'm talkin' and I look up and see the Speaker chattin' with someone else. I think maybe I've said something good that caught his attention and he's talkin' to that other person about it . . . but probably not."

What a wonderfully funny and human thing for this tough old warhorse to say. I liked him better.

Senator Baker got up when Senator Stennis had finished. The stenotypist, with his machine on his chest, moved toward Baker to catch his every word.

Baker spoke as if he was excerpting little phrases out of old speeches he remembered but he said some good things in favor of televising Senate proceedings.

"The Senate is a microcosm of America," Baker said. "We are what we are and America's entitled to watch. The business of the Senate is to do the public's business in a public place!"

"Hear, hear!" I would have shouted but I didn't want to get thrown out.

Senator Long, the third man in the debate, had already betrayed his opinion of the public's IQ by saying that if television was allowed in, Senate debates would have to be tailored "to appeal to the most common denominator, let us say those with a fourth-grade education."

During the debate, Senator Robert Byrd walked in. He paid no attention to anyone, walking between Baker and Stennis and taking his seat near the Speaker's platform. Senator Dole and one or two others had drifted in and were standing in back at the fringe of the chamber. When the debate about television coverage had come to an end, Baker stood up, walked over to Long's desk and as they laughed about something, Long offered Baker a cough drop. Baker took it, put it in his mouth and wandered up the aisle toward the back. They'd been through it all before.

At this point, Senator Byrd stood up, asked for the floor and addressed almost no one with a perfunctory message about protecting the American eagle as our national symbol.

I didn't understand whether he was for it or against it but if I know Senator Byrd, he was for it.

I left.

This concludes my report from the nation's Capitol.

Is Politics Child's Play?

I'm a Democrat," an eleven-year-old girl wrote me in a letter the other day.

An eleven-year-old probably doesn't know whether she's a Democrat or a Republican but that doesn't make her much different from the rest of us. We may think we know and we may announce what we think we are at regular intervals but don't ask us for a list of the differences between the two parties.

When I was a kid, my father always voted Republican but I don't think he had a lot of well-thought-out reasons for it. Like most people, he picked a couple of little things he thought the Republicans stood for and that he agreed with and concluded from those that he was one of them. People fall in love with the idea that they're either Republicans or Democrats.

When I asked my father the difference between the two, he told me the Democrats wanted to lower the import taxes on the things foreign countries shipped here to sell, and the Republicans wanted to raise the taxes to keep foreign goods out. Even way back in the 1930s, he worked for a company that was in competition with the Japanese. A person's bread and butter usually has more to do with his political affiliation than his ideals do.

You can't trust anyone's definition of what a Republican or a Democrat is. Each party likes to pretend it has hard-and-fast economic, social and philosophic principles that are cast in stone but they don't.

Generally speaking, the Democrats have always been thought of as being on the side of labor and the Republicans are thought of as being on the side of business. Obviously that isn't the way things really are or we'd never have had a Republican president. There are always going to be more working people than businessmen and women but we've elected sixteen Republican presidents and only thirteen Democratic ones.

The funny thing that happened in recent elections in both England and the United States is that a lot of blue-collar working people teamed up with a lot of white-collar business people and elected Republicans. (In England, the Republicans are called the Conservatives.) These two groups at opposite ends of the social and economic scale—low-income workers, high-income executives—agreed on politics.

The people who voted for the Democratic or Liberal party candidate in each country were all the rest and it wasn't enough. It seems as strange to have a young, college-educated businessman making $35,000 a year supporting a Democrat as it is to have a truck driver with less than a high school education making $35,000, supporting Reagan. I'm not knocking it in either case but it does seem funny. Why would the bricklayer and the owner of the construction company agree on such issues as abortion, prayer in schools, busing and the ERA Amendment?

It's all very confusing and I have an idea it's better that way. As soon as a nation's political parties begin to get too orderly and predictable, there's trouble. I'm pleased that there are no deep, sharply defined party principles the Democrats and Republicans swear by. During an election year we listen to a lot of campaign oratory that gives the impression the world will come to an end if the candidate speaking isn't elected. Someone is always beaten, though, and the world never ends because of it. When our candidate is defeated we swallow the defeat and go about our business again, confident that things won't really change much.

I don't know what to tell that eleven-year-old girl who wrote me. I don't want to discourage her interest in politics but I would like to point out to her that she probably hasn't thought out why she thinks she's a Democrat with any more clarity than why she thinks she's a Methodist, a Catholic, a Buddhist or none of the above. People fall in love with their religious affiliation for reasons that are about as well thought out as their political ones.

Imputing Motives

In the past year something like twenty congressmen or high-ranking public officials in Washington have quit politics. They have quit either because they aren't satisfied with the money they can make in government as compared to private business or because they don't like having every decision or statement they make inspected under a microscope by the public and the press.

Senator Howard Baker of Tennessee said, when he

announced he was retiring, that a lot of the pleasure he used to get out of public service was gone.

"I think that news is so current," Senator Baker said, "and so often analytical and so frequently wrong, imputing motives that really don't exist in many cases, that a lot of people are just getting tired of it."

Senator Baker's decision not to run for office again was a loss for all of us. Most of us are either not capable, too selfish or not ambitious enough to help in the process of governing ourselves. We'd rather sit back and criticize the people who do involve themselves in politics. Senator Baker was one of the best. We were lucky to have had him. He's nice, honest and competent. He has simply decided he doesn't want to take all the heat he's been taking any longer. He's going to look into what he calls "a delicious range of things to do."

Print and broadcast journalists have had a lot to do with the decision many government officials have made to get out of politics, Senator Baker says.

"I can't think of a single case where someone decided to run for public office because of investigative reporting. But I can sure think of people who decided not to run because, day in and day out, they don't like having to explain the reasons for their votes."

The public, the courts and government officials have almost always been in favor of freedom of the press in the abstract and against it in the particular. The public complains about politicians who get rich from dishonest deals while they're in office and the public complains about the press reporting such incidents because news of dishonesty is so depressing. I'm disappointed that Senator Baker, one of the good guys in my opinion, has joined the popular complaint that the press is too negative. It is exactly the same as the know-nothing attitude you hear from so many uneducated people talking about politicians as being "all a bunch of crooks."

Politicians are not all a bunch of crooks but there are some crooks among them and the public has a right to know who they are. Politicians have no more right to expect perfection from journalists than the public has any business expecting perfection from politicians. They're all people and there are going to be roughly the same number of good guys and bad guys in both professions. They both have to be watched.

The best journalists assume that if all the facts are revealed, it will be a better world. Politicians often honestly believe that the public is best served if it *doesn't* know everything. This is where the battle lines are drawn between politicians and the press. For some reason that always puzzles journalists, the public agrees with the politicians. If it's bad news, they don't want to hear it even if it's true.

By retiring, Senator Baker made a politically expedient move if he wants to be President someday and by suggesting that a tough press is part of the reason for his retirement, he's getting himself a little bonus. Maybe the press will take it easier if it thinks it's driving good men like him out of politics.

Senator Baker would, I'm sure, say that I am being "analytical and frequently wrong, imputing motives that really don't exist."

Andy Rooney for President

THE candidates for office seem to have so much fun trying to kill each other with television commercials that I've decided to run for office myself. In light of this decision, I'm asking each and every one of you to make a small sacrifice in the interests of better government and mail me $10,000 so that I can start a campaign fund.

It's illegal to contribute more than $1,000 to any one person's campaign so you'll have to find some way to work this out. Check around and learn how it's being done by others. You might consult one of your local Political Action Committees, known familiarly as "PACS."

If only 2,500 of you respond to this appeal for campaign funds, it will provide me with $25 million with which I'll buy my first two thirty-second commercials on network television. Through these commercials, I hope to make my position as well-known to America as Preparation H.

Because you have a right to know where I stand on the issues before you commit $10,000 to my campaign, I'll give you a preview of the two commercials. Here are the scripts.

(CANDIDATE, DRESSED IN BUSINESS SUIT WITH VEST, IS SEEN STANDING BEHIND IMPORTANT-LOOKING DESK. BEHIND HIM ARE SHELVES FULL

OF IMPORTANT-LOOKING BOOKS, BOUND IN RED
LEATHER.)

"Good evening. I'm Andy Rooney, the Middle-of-
the-Road Party's candidate in this important election.

"Are you familiar with the voting record of my opponent? Do you know where he stands on crime, for
instance?

"My opponent is in favor of crime. He has sup-
ported crime in the past and will continue to do so if
reelected. For more than forty years now, ever since I
was twenty, I have been against crime.

"Taxes. My opponent seems to feel that the solution to every problem is higher taxes. If you want
higher taxes, vote for my opponent.

"My opponent thinks the rich are an underprivi-
leged class. He's against the working man. He hates
farmers. He's never been seen in church and he locks
his dog out at night even when it's cold.

"This is where I stand and I hope I can look forward
to your support on election day."

That's the first commercial. If it runs a little longer
than thirty seconds, I may take out the part about the
dog. Here's the second script prepared for me by the
same advertising agency that writes them for my opponent.

(CANDIDATE IS FOUND SITTING ON THE COUCH IN
A MODEST LIVING ROOM INTERVIEWING AN AC-
TOR, AN ACTRESS AND TWO CHILD ACTORS. THEY
ARE POSING AS THE TYPICAL AMERICAN FAMILY OF
GEORGE AND BETTY MORGAN.)

ANDY: I'm here today with George Morgan and his wife, Betty. How are things going, George?

GEORGE: Terrible, Andy. I've been out of work for an hour and twenty minutes. I can't make the payments on any of our cars and the man won't come and clean our swimming pool because I still owe him for last time.

ANDY: How are you going to vote this year, George?

GEORGE: You're the kind of leadership we need in America, Andy. You're honest, forthright, fair, hardworking, easygoing, patriotic and you go to church Easter. You're going to lower taxes, raise Social Security benefits, cut inflation and reduce unemployment.

CHILD AT TABLE: I'm hungry, Mommy.

BETTY MORGAN: Hush, Linda. We can't have dinner until Mr. Rooney is elected and gets the economy going again so Daddy can get a job.

ANDY: Thanks for inviting me into your home, George and Betty. You're good Americans. Good Americans will be voting for me this election day.

The preceding political announcements have been paid for by the Committee to Elect Andy Rooney.

The Elected Official Speaks

GOOD evening. This is your Elected Official speaking. I've bought this one last television commercial because now that you've elected me, I'm going to tell you the truth.

"It will come as no surprise to many of you to hear

that most of what I said when I was trying to get elected was pure baloney. Those commercials, for instance, were someone else's idea. I just came into the studio and read them. They wanted me to sound folksy and honest and I had to do them over about ten times before I sounded folksy and honest enough. How'd you like the one where I was in shirtsleeves and suspenders? The media consultant who did the commercials brought the suspenders to the studio for me. They were his uncle's.

"He produced the commercials for my opponent, too. They used the same suspenders on him but I think I sounded folksier and more honest. That's why I won.

"But I've given you so much doubletalk during the campaign that tonight I thought I'd level with you. Here's where I really stand on the issues.

"Taxes. You didn't really believe me when I said I wasn't going to raise your taxes, did you? If you did, you deserve what you're going to get. I'm going to raise taxes and I'm going to do it as soon as possible. That way, you may have forgotten it by the next time I run for office.

"Crime. Let's face it, voters. We got a lot of weirdos out there who'll do anything to anyone to get themselves some cash for a drug fix. I told you I'm against crime and I am but I'm not a magician. My advice to you is lock your doors at night and watch where you walk after dark.

"Social Security. I'm sorry to have to tell you this but if you're very social, you don't have much security. If you're retired, I hope you got rich while you were working because if you didn't, there's no way in hell you're going to be able to live on what you get from Social Security. You can't get blood from a stone, you know.

"Abortion. To tell you the truth, I was so scared of this issue I forget what I told you I was for or against. I figured there was no sense making a lot of enemies by coming out on either side. The truth is, I haven't thought much about abortion.

"Gun control. I hedged on this, too, but actually I'm in favor of gun control. If I had my way, no one in the United States would own a handgun except me.

"Unemployment. We have a lot of unemployment in this country and I feel sorry for some of those people but let's face it, you know and I know some of those bums wouldn't work if you drove them to the job in a Rolls-Royce. Unemployment's only bad for the people who aren't working and more than ninety percent of you are working. You're the ones who voted for me.

"In the next few weeks I'll be making a lot of appointments to important, high-paying jobs in my Administration. Those jobs are going to the people who contributed the most money to my campaign. Why should I lie to you now?"

The Queen and the President

EVERY few years an American president and the king or queen of some country meet on a formal occasion.

It's always been a mystery to me what a Queen and a President talk about when they have dinner together. Everything about it must be awkward, even the way they're seated. They're almost always seated side by side instead of across the table from each other and right there you have a problem. They can't look each other in the eye easily and it's difficult to bring anyone else into the conversation. The person on the President's other side can't talk to the Queen without leaning over and talking across the President's dinner, and the person on the other side of the Queen can't talk to the President for the same reason. If the person on the other side of the Queen wanted to talk to the person way on the other side of the President, he'd have to yell or get up and walk around behind him. This would probably bring the Secret Service and the Queen's Guards to their feet. It must limit the conversation.

It would be bad form, I should think, for the President to stop talking to the Queen and turn to someone else but they really don't have that much they can talk about except horses, if it's the Queen of England. There are things they *could* talk about but wouldn't. I've been thinking about some examples of things they wouldn't talk about. This is a conversation that would never take place between Queen Elizabeth and our President:

PRESIDENT: How are all the kids these days?

QUEEN: Fine thanks. You know, they can be a pain in the royal tail sometimes but they're good kids.

PRESIDENT: Let's see, you have two . . . or is it three?

QUEEN: Four. Charles, Anne, Andrew and Edward. Everyone forgets Edward.

PRESIDENT: It must be tough on Edward, the youngest boy. How does he feel about having so little chance of ever being King?

QUEEN: We've never talked about it.

PRESIDENT: That seems to be a nice girl Charles has. Is Andrew seeing anyone?

QUEEN: Yes, and I could just kill him.

PRESIDENT: That would give Edward a better chance of getting to be King.

QUEEN: Not funny, Mr. President. He's been chasing after this road company Playboy bunny. It's awfully hard to explain to Mother, I'll tell you that. He must have gotten it from Philip's side of the family.

PRESIDENT: Maybe. At least Wallis Warfield Simpson was always well dressed.

QUEEN: You really know how to hurt a Queen, Mr. President.

PRESIDENT: It certainly wasn't intended that way. Can I get you more champagne?

QUEEN: If it's French, yes. If it's more of that California, no.

PRESIDENT: Hey, if you want to play rough I'll ask you what you do with your old hats . . . the ones your mother gave you?

QUEEN: I *wear* them, sir! At least Philip doesn't put on a pair of those macho cowboy boots you wear every time you get within four miles of a horse. And how often do you get the grease changed in your hair?

PRESIDENT: Boy, you got a sharp tongue, lady.

QUEEN: Let me ask you this. If you could be King or President, which would you be?

PRESIDENT: Hmmm . . . of the United States or Great Britain?

QUEEN: The United States.

PRESIDENT: The way things are going I'd like to be Queen for a Day and then quit the whole mess!

We'll never know what the Queen and the President talk about when they meet, but you can bet it must set some kind of world's record for dull.

Presidential Friendship

By the time you've done all the things the President's been doing all his life, you get to know a lot of people. You've even gotten to like a lot of people and consider them to be friends. Do you send them all Christmas cards? Do you sit down with your wife in the private quarters of the White House and make a list?

There are some things a President can delegate but making a list of friends is a strictly personal matter. How do you handle old friends?

Say you're President and your best friend from high school calls. Somehow he gets through the outer layer of secretarial protection a President has and gets to one of your personal secretaries. This is a kid whose house you used to go to after school. He even stayed at your house one week when his parents were away.

What instructions does your secretary have for handling this kind of a call? If she pokes her head in the Oval Office door and asks if you want to speak to Billy Reidy, do you pick up the phone or do you tell her to brush him off politely?

Handling any kind of personal relationship would be one of the most difficult things about being President.

Do you have a telephone in the private quarters of the White House with a number you've given only a few close friends? I don't mean important congressmen or Cabinet officials. I mean do you have a number you've only given real friends, not just important people?

What about money? If you're President do you keep track of what you have in the bank? What about domestic problems? Aren't there some problems with the house at the ranch that ought to be taken care of personally? Something out there must be falling apart that no one knows about but you.

If you're the President in Washington and you notice there's a crack in the tiles around the shower in your house in Santa Barbara, do you call someone to have it fixed? Whom do you call? Even calling someone takes more time than a President has.

In 1965, Walter Cronkite was interviewing President Lyndon Johnson. There were, as always, a lot of serious problems facing the President. There was also a minor problem with the White House staff. They'd been asking for a raise for some time and just that morning it had finally been approved and signed by President Johnson.

At one point in Cronkite's talk with Johnson, a senior aide to the President came in and interrupted.

"That raise for the staff," the aide asked, "will it be retroactive to the first of the year?"

Lyndon Johnson flushed with anger, pointed his finger at the aide and started to sputter.

"I'm the President of The United States, I've got a war in Vietnam, I've got the weight of the world on my shoulders, I'm talking to this important man here and you come in with a chicken s—— question like that."

Presidents must often feel that way.

Some U.S. presidents have been accused of working only four or five hours a day, but even if it's true, I wouldn't complain. There's no way in the world one person could sit in the Oval Office all day worrying about the life and death of the universe. A President would almost have to find a way to shut out some of the problems pressing in on him or he'd go crazy.

I often have a guilty feeling going past a hospital. I know how many sick and dying people there are in those rooms and yet how long can any one of us feel sad about everyone in trouble in the world? We have to shut out the thought of some of what we know is going on and proceed with our lives.

The President must do that. Once in a while when an old bit-part player in a movie they made together called the White House, Ron must have answered the phone and said, "Hey, I'm not doing anything. Why don't you come over and we'll shoot the breeze . . ."

The National Academy of History

I'M not at all satisfied with history the way it's being written. We've all taken history courses in school and most of us were skeptical of some of the information given us as historical fact.

There's a lot more history piling up on us every day but we ought to be gaining on it, because with pictures and sound recording it's easier to preserve original documents than it was a hundred or a thousand years ago. Everyone five hundred years from now ought to know everything about us. They won't though because too many of the things being saved as history won't present an accurate picture of what was going on this year.

I propose we establish a National Academy of History. It would be this group's job to pass on to the future exactly what happened and what we were like in our years here on earth. I even have some specific suggestions for how the National Academy of History (NAH) would go about the job.

For example, it would insist that Presidents Reagan, Carter, Ford and Nixon get together for a long weekend at Camp David, with no one else around, and let their hair down. (In Gerald Ford's case, I'm speaking figuratively.) They'd be promised that nothing they said would be released for fifty years.

The four of them would be given anything they wanted to eat or drink but they'd also be given an occasional shot of sodium pentothal, the drug that makes people blab the truth.

There are, as I write, six living wives of Presidents, Jackie, Lady Bird, Pat, Betty, Rosalynn and Nancy. These women have a view of history that is different and more accurate in many specific details than any historian will ever get. The girls ought to get together while the boys are at Camp David. If they'd relax, they'd probably like each other. If they'd talk, we'd have some real history.

This newly established NAH of mine would organize all kinds of groups to get at and preserve the details of history that are being lost now. It wouldn't be simply the history of power. It would be the history of Us.

We study the day before yesterday looking for clues about how to behave so we'll be happier tomorrow. That's what history is for and we haven't been keeping it accurately enough. There are dozens of reasons why history doesn't ring true to us.

Too many historians aren't reporters looking for facts, they're theoreticians. They have some idea about the grand sweep of history and they write their books, choosing only the facts that support their theories.

Historians like to promote the idea that there's a rhythm to history and that events follow a pattern. They're often more interested in the pattern they think they see than the facts. They can't stand the thought that there might not be a pattern and that a lot of important things happened in history, not by the design of a king, a president or a dictator, but because of some insignificant unrecorded incident or accident that started things going one way instead of another.

It's difficult to make people from one century intelligible to the people of another and if reporters can't find out what's going on right now in our own country, how can we expect the historians of ten, fifty or a hundred years from now to know anything at all that's true about us?

Russian Bombs/Russian Hotels

You can go into a strange restaurant and make a good guess about how the food is going to taste long before they've actually served you any of it. There are telltale signs that give you advanced warning. When the rolls or the bread comes, you know for sure how the whole meal is going to be.

This idea can be extended to everything and everybody. You can tell a lot about the whole from a small part. You can tell a lot about how a person does everything from watching him or her do just one thing. We are all victims of our own character and we find it impossible to do something that isn't characteristic of us.

This idea applies to whole countries just as certainly as it applies to individuals. We keep doing things like Americans, the Germans keep doing things like Germans, the French like the French.

The President said the other night that the Soviet Union has "a definite margin of superiority" over the United States in nuclear arms. Using my theory about being able to tell a lot from a sample, I doubt it. I've spent a good deal of time in Russia and hold some opinions about the people and the nation that no one can talk me out of.

One of my firmly held beliefs is that the Russians are not naturally mechanical people. They may acquire the ability and they may be better at it than they used to be but working with machinery does not come naturally to the average Russian. They have a great heritage in music and literature and the arts in general but they build terrible automobiles and don't know how to fix them when they break down.

One of the most incredible travel experiences I've ever had is a week in a Russian hotel in Moscow. The second time I stayed there they had installed telephones in every room but the telephones were not connected through any hotel switchboard. There was no way for anyone to call the hotel and be connected with me by phone in my room. It had a number just like any other telephone in a home in Moscow.

Does this sound like a country that is apt to be ahead of us in nuclear weapons?

The Russians, in their desperate attempt to get hard, Western currency away from tourists, opened what they call "Dollar Stores." They put their best merchandise in these small shops located in their best hotels and offer it for sale in exchange for dollars, not rubles. Russian citizens can't buy there.

I've bought nail clippers, razors, razor blades and ballpoint pens in those dollar stores and I've carefully inspected such items as cameras, camera lenses, binoculars, cigarette lighters, scissors and watches there. The best Russian goods are poor by our standards. The workmanship is inferior and the design is either imitative or just bad.

This isn't being written by some blindly anti-Russian nut. I don't hate the Russians. I hate their oppressive government. As a matter of fact, I kind of like the Russians. They're often wonderfully free-spirited and fun to be with but, for whatever facet of their national character it is, they do a lot of things badly. From what

I've seen of their binoculars and their ballpoint pens, I'd guess nuclear weapons would be one of the things they make poorly. There are things Americans don't do well, either, but these are different things.

Obviously the Russians have learned how to do some things. Their space program is not as sophisticated as ours but it works. I have no doubt that their nuclear bombs go off with a big bang and I'm also sure they've built rockets that will take their missiles to New York. What I can't believe, from what I know firsthand about the Russians, is that they have more and better nuclear weapons than we do.

I can't help myself from thinking that the President is just trying to scare us into approving a huge defense budget. If the Russians could build great nuclear bombs, their hotels wouldn't be as poorly constructed as they are. I go into a place for a week and judge a whole country by one hotel. The Russians would be accurate in saying that's the kind of person I am.

Spies

THIS has been a bad year for spies. Every couple of days you read in the paper where they've caught some of ours or we've caught some of theirs. The French, for instance, recently expelled forty-seven Soviet Embassy people because they said they were spying. Forty-seven is a lot of spies.

It would be interesting to know what secrets all those Russian agents got from the French. They'd have to get an awful lot of secrets to make it worth-while because keeping forty-seven agents in Paris, at those prices, isn't cheap. Even spies have to eat. I've eaten in Paris and I've eaten in Moscow and if all forty-seven of those Russians were really spies, and were smart, they'd have been trying to steal the secret of French cooking.

Being a spy in Paris must be one of the most desir-able jobs any spy could have. The living is good and the French don't take spies that seriously. You could probably go to a cocktail party in Paris and discuss what you did without surprising anyone.

"What is your business, Mr. Standoffsky, if I may ask?"

"I'm in espionage. I spy for the Russian Govern-ment."

"How interesting. You must meet so many fascinat-ing people when you're a spy."

"True, and most of them are other spies."

Recently, a Soviet citizen was apprehended (spies are "apprehended" not "caught") while he was in the process of picking up some rolls of film from the trunk of a hollow tree in Maryland. It shows that Russian spies know little about this country. Everyone knows you pick up your film at the drugstore.

We never get any information about what it is spies find out. It's always suggested that the information they take back to their country will have grave conse-quences on ours but I'd like more specific information. I suspect that in the past twenty-five years the most se-rious information one country has gotten about another is a list of its spies.

There must be a lot of wasted effort in the spy business, too. Scientists working on new developments don't have any contact with the CIA or the KGB. I can imagine a spy working for years to get hold of the plans for a new aircraft and by the time he gets them, he finds they've already been printed in *Popular Mechanics*. Or a spy might come running home with what he thinks is a secret formula for a new chemical weapon only to discover that U.S. and Soviet scientists had exchanged that information at a meeting in Sweden three years ago.

Spies are having a tough time of it everywhere and I wouldn't be surprised to see them organize and form a union. Soviet and U.S. spies would all belong to the same labor organization but in different locals. Soviet spies would have to honor the picket lines of U.S. spies and vice versa.

Any espionage union would probably make several demands on behalf of its members. It would certainly demand the right for them to be double agents. Spies, like professional athletes, ought to have the right to become free agents after a certain length of time, too. If the Russians have a really good spy, he should have the right to bargain and switch his allegiance if another country offers him more money.

An espionage union would certainly take up the matter of women's rights. Women seem to have been almost completely frozen out of the spy business ever since the unfortunate demise of Mata Hari. That could have happened to anyone. Mata Hari just happened to be a woman.

I don't have a very high regard for spies. I think we should keep track of what's going on in other countries in a general way but I don't think we need the blueprints for their nuclear energy plants or even the formula for their chemical warfare weapons. Their World Almanac is all we need.

Americans have never been very good spies. It's something we can all be proud of.

VI:

FAMILIAR THINGS

A Place to Stare

THERE'S a major renovation going on in the building I work in and it looks as if I may have to move out of my office.

The people in any company who assign offices are always thinkings of reasons why people should move. Everyone should resist them. Their reasons are usually not good enough and they don't understand what a serious effect moving an office can have on a person's life.

I've known some people who don't seem to mind moving. They're usually executives with better-organized minds than mine. They know where everything is in their office and they can move it to another and still find things. That would not be the case with me. I know that if I have to move, there are things I'll never find again in my whole life. They'll be lost at the bottom of a packing box and some survivor of mine down the road will have to go through the box and throw the stuff out. He won't dare throw anything out without looking through it because I often hide a ten-dollar bill in a book or envelope around my office so I'll have emergency money the day I come to work without a nickel.

I don't know what's wrong with me but I take inanimate objects in my life too seriously. I get to have quite an affection for a car that's given me good service and I've always hated to turn one like that over to the secondhand dealers. I feel terrible thinking of someone who doesn't care, buying it and then abusing it. How can I be so disloyal?

That's the way I feel about my office. To the building planners it's nothing more than some marks on a blueprint. It's four walls that need painting, a worn carpet and a radiator that spits water from a bad valve when the heat is up. As far as the planner goes, my office is just another secondhand car. He'll get what he can out of it without a thought for what it has meant to me.

I can remember every office I've ever had. In 1962 I had one I wrote a book in. Everyone called the office ''the submarine'' because it didn't have any windows and was buried in a basement area of the building but I liked it. The temperature was easy to control and it wasn't on anyone's way to their own office so people didn't drop in and chat a lot. If you're trying to write a book, it's better if you don't chat much.

The office in which I sit at this moment is one I've occupied for ten years. That's my personal world record for office occupancy and I've not only been in it longer than any other but I like it better. I've had more professional success in the years between 1972 and 1982 than I ever had before and naturally I give a lot of the credit for it to this office. If anyone gives me an award of any kind and asks me to make a speech, I'm going to mention this office when I modestly start passing credit around. ''Without this office,'' I'll say, ''I never would have been able to do what I've done.''

That's what I'll say and all the people at the awards dinner will applaud me for passing the credit around and congratulate my office for its contribution to my success.

No one will ever know this office as well as I do this moment. I can't tell you how many times I've leaned back in my chair, propped my feet against the angle where my desk meets the attached typing table, and simply stared at some part of my wall or ceiling. If anyone goes past my door when I'm staring, they get the impression I'm thinking about something but I'm not. I'm just staring. A writer has to get quite a bit of staring out of his system before he goes to work.

I hate the thought of moving. This office has been a great old friend to me. Losing it is going to be like a death in the family. Building planners don't understand that. They don't understand why I'm not pleased.

"The one you're going to get is bigger than this," they tell me. "Got two windows and we'll put down new carpet. It's a better office."

What do they know about staring?

Elevators

IF you've ever worked or lived in a building where you had to use an elevator, you know that it becomes part of your life. It's often as much a barrier between you and the ground, or the ground and your office or apartment, as an open drawbridge.

No one is ever completely comfortable in an elevator. There's something about them we don't trust. Lurking in the back of our memory is the story we once read about the twelve people who were stuck between the seventh and eighth floors for nine hours. We look around, imagining what it would be like to be stuck with the people now on our elevator.

There's an uncertainty in our minds about the engineering principles of an elevator. We've all had little glimpses into the dirty, dark elevator shaft and seen the greasy cables passing each other. They never look totally safe. The idea of being trapped in a small box going up and down on strings induces a kind of phobia in all of us. There we are, standing on a platform, enclosed on all six sides, that could drop to the bottom of the building in an instant if any of the strings and the emergency brakes failed.

There's a predictable sequence to the little drama of an elevator ride. If you arrive at the elevator door first and the elevator is on another floor, you press the button and stand there with absolutely nothing to do. Usually someone else arrives before the elevator does. Depending on your relationship with that person, you say nothing, nod or say hello.

Invariably the second person, and subsequent persons who arrive, stand there for ten seconds and then step forward and press the button themselves.

I've never been sure what motivates a person to press the button when I'm already standing there. Does he think I'm so dumb I was standing there without pressing it myself?

More often I think it's just a little action that relieves the embarrassment of standing there close to another person without saying anything. It's something to do. Often it's done with an impatient gesture, designed to produce a rapport among the standees, by suggesting a mutual disapproval of the machinery.

I work on the sixth floor of a building. I know some of the elevator riders well. Others I have only that nodding acquaintance with and some are total strangers.

I prefer riding with the strangers. Those elevator friends whose names I'm not always sure of aren't comfortable with the silence, but we don't know each other well enough to talk about anything of substance. The conversation often turns to the elevator itself.

If it stops at more than one floor, they'll say, "We've got a local here."

I suppose that remark has been made in my presence in that elevator a thousand times.

Any other conversation is limited to three topics and they begin with a question. Those are:

1—"They keepin' you busy?"
2—"What's new with you?"
3—"Is it hot (cold) enough for you?"

My inclination is to just nod and smile when these are directed at me. I don't want to be unfriendly but I'm not going to make a fool of myself by answering a question that wasn't really meant to be one.

Escalators have always been more fun than elevators, although most women approach them gingerly. Years ago I talked to a hotel architect named William Tabler who had just designed a new Hilton in New York. He'd put in lots of elevators but he'd connected three meeting-room floors with escalators.

"They're really slower even if you have to wait for

the elevator," he said, "but people like to be moving."

This week I've decided to get in shape by walking up and down the six flights in my building. It's something I've decided to do three or four times a year for the last ten years. My resolve disappears in a few days in a fit of heavy breathing and I go back to the elevator.

Hotels and Motels

A HOTEL or motel can be a pleasure to stay in for a night or two. You don't have to do the dishes, there isn't a mess in the garage you ought to be cleaning out, and whatever needs fixing isn't your problem.

For more than a night or two, though, hotels and motels are less satisfactory. They begin to get on your nerves and you yearn for the familiar disarray of home. I've been staying in a lot of hotels and motels recently. They've ranged from seedy motels that I stayed in for convenience because they were near the airport, to a very expensive, high-class hotel in Houston.

What follows are some random notes I've made on hotels and motels:

—If you're traveling and only want a night's sleep, a motel is better than a hotel. I call it a motel if there's no elevator and you carry your own bags to your room.

—The coffee shop doesn't open until too late in most places. Seven A.M. is too late if you want to return to your room after you eat and still get going early.

—I'm always surprised that hotels don't make more of

a point of having you turn in the key when you pay the bill. I often walk off with the key by accident.

—It isn't easy to read in a motel room. The light over the bed is never where you want it and all the bulbs are low-powered. Charles Kuralt carries a hundred-watt bulb in his suitcase when he's "On the Road."

—If you're only staying one day, it's hard to wash socks and underwear at night and have them dry in time to pack them in the morning. When my socks don't dry, I drape them over the lampshade while I go have breakfast. If they still aren't dry when I come back, I put them in a plastic bag and put that in my suitcase.

—I can never bring myself to use two bars of soap. I open one for the sink but then in the morning, when I take a shower, I use that one again instead of opening the bigger one they gave me for the shower. It doesn't save me any money but it seems wasteful to use two.

—I never eat where I sleep. Motel restaurants aren't usually very good. The best restaurants are owned and run by individuals. I prefer to take a chance on one of them when I'm in a strange city. On the other hand, I usually stay in a motel that's part of a big chain instead of taking a chance on a privately owned, local motel.

—The pile rug in the bathroom of the hotel I stayed in last night was so thick the bathroom door didn't clear it and that made it difficult every time I opened or closed the door. You'd think a hotel with 250 rooms would have worked that out. They must have 250 bathroom doors that are hard to open because of the carpet.

—It's gotten so you can hardly pay cash for a motel room anymore. They insist on a credit card when you check in.

—There ought to be a law standardizing the controls for hot and cold in hotel and motel showers. It's easy to burn yourself or freeze before you catch on to how they work.

—Most places have those hangers you can't steal now. They don't have a hook on the end. The hook is attached to a bar and a little knob on the hanger fits into the hook. I hate them.

—Hotels and motels cover every flat space in the room with literature and picture folders telling you how wonderful their place is and how good their services are. I always dump these in a drawer. I need the space myself. I figure while I'm paying for the room, I shouldn't have to read their advertisements.

Some Sound Ideas

A FEW minutes ago, walking back from lunch, I started to cross the street when I heard the sound of a coin dropping. It wasn't much but, as I turned, my eyes caught the heads of several other people turning too. A woman had dropped what appeared to be a dime.

The tinkling sound of a coin dropping on pavement is an attention-getter. It can be nothing more than a penny. Whatever the coin is, no one ignores the sound of it. It got me thinking about sounds again.

We are beseiged by so many sounds from every side these days that it isn't the loudest sounds that attract the most attention. People in New York City seldom turn to look when a fire engine, a police car or an ambulance comes screaming along the street.

When I'm in New York, I'm a New Yorker. I don't turn either. Like the natives, I hardly hear a siren there.

At home in my little town in Connecticut, it's different. The distant wail of a police car, an emergency vehicle or a fire siren brings me to my feet if I'm seated and brings me to the window if I'm in bed.

The people who drive cars or trucks equipped with sirens ought to be more careful about when they use them. I'm often suspicious of ambulances that careen down the street with sirens wailing. It can't always be a matter of life and death and if they're used when it isn't, they're less effective when it is. I suspect quite a few broken legs have gone through a lot of red lights rushing too fast and too loud to an emergency room where they waited two hours for a docotor to set them.

It's the quietest sounds that have most effect on us, not the loudest. In the middle of the night, I can hear a dripping faucet a hundred yards away through three closed doors. I've been hearing little creaking noises and sounds which my imagination turns into footsteps in the middle of the night for twenty-five years in our house. How come I never hear those sounds in the daytime?

Some people, of course, never hear anything in the middle of the night. There are light sleepers and heavy sleepers and they always seem to sleep together. One gets up in the middle of the night to check the noises; the other hears nothing. The sleeper awakens four hours later to ask, ''What happened?''

''Nothing happened, dear. There was a burglar

downstairs walking around in hobnailed boots, the oil burner exploded and two cars hit head-on in front of the house. The cops came, the fire engines were here and the ambulance picked up the injured. Everything's all right now. Go back to sleep.''

In a book by W. S. Gilbert I had when I was a kid, there was a character named King Borria Bungalee Boo, ''an African swell . . . whose whisper was a horrible, horrible yell.''

There are people who find it impossible to whisper or even talk softly. For some reason, they're the ones who try to do most of it. There's nothing more embarrassing than to have someone whisper to you about someone else in the room, in a voice everyone in the room can hear.

Car horns are an irritating noise. There are very few times when it's important to blow the horn of a car. When someone on our street parks out in front of someone else's house and blows the horn, I feel like throwing rocks.

I'm quite clear in my mind what the good sounds are and what the bad sounds are.

I've turned against whistling, for instance. I used to think of it as the mark of a happy worker but lately I've been associating the whistler with a nervous person making compulsive noises.

Walking through the woods in the fall of the year, with the leaves up around your ankles, is a great sound.

Someone else in the room sniffling and without a handkerchief is an annoying sound.

The tapping, tapping, tapping of my typewriter as the keys hit the paper is a lovely sound to me. I often like the sound of what I write better than the looks of it.

Let It Rain

IT is raining as I write. I'm snug and comfortable here in this room. I'm surrounded by familiar things and tools like this typewriter that I know how to use. The rain can't get at me. I'm dry. Being warm and dry inside when it's cold and wet outside is one of the few victories man scores over Nature. We ought to enjoy it. This isn't a wet cave I've crept into in order to avoid the worst of the storm. This is a comfortable home where I can forget all about the rain if I choose to.

I've never understood why Longfellow wrote that famous line of his or why it's famous. You remember:

> Into each life some rain must fall,
> Some days must be dark and dreary.

It's clear that Longfellow associated rain with all the bad things that happen to us. I don't associate rain with that at all. Maybe it was raining when I was born. Rain is as important to people as it is to plants. I've lived in climates where they don't have much rain and hated it. I'm not the cactus type. The human brain needs a good, hard rain at least once every two weeks . . . snow if it's cold. You can't keep going out in the bright sun every day without having it get on your nerves and dry you up. Maybe smog is nature's way of protecting Los Angelenos from all that sun they used to get.

One of the few lines I remember from what little Chaucer I read is better than Longfellow's. I never really understood Chaucer's olde English spelling but even that adds flavor to the lines he wrote about rain:

> Lord, this is an huge rayn!
> This were a weder for to slepen inne.

That has a wonderful feel to it and it evokes memories of all the good Saturday mornings I've decided to turn over and sleep for another hour under the lulling rhythm of the rayn on the roof.

People are always knocking rain but I don't think they mean it. It's just pass-the-time-of-day weather talk. We're all expected to make negative comments about a rainy day. "It's raining cats and dogs," someone will say. I've never understood what that means or where the phrase came from. No rain ever reminds me of cats and dogs coming down from the clouds and I don't know why we keep saying it.

I went to a football game in the rain earlier this year and had the time of my life. I had rubber shoes, a sailor's rubber, foul-weather suit and a wide-brimmed rain hat that kept the water from going down my neck. In addition, I had a four-foot-square rubber sheet that I brought along to keep on my lap. Under that I kept my program, my lunch and a thermos bottle filled with hot chicken broth. There I sat in a dry little island, surrounded by a sea of rain trying unsuccessfully to get at me. I was happily isolated from every outside distraction except the good game on the lighted playing field below me.

The players on the field were as happy as I was although it would be hard to explain that to anyone who has never played football. Football players don't mind rain at all unless they're quarterbacks or pass catchers. Once a player gets sloppy and wet all over, it's fun slopping around in the mud. It's John Madden's kind of football weather.

Nothing is perfect, of course, and there are one or two little things that keep me from being totally enthusiastic about rain. First there's that persistent leak in the back corner of the basement by my woodworking shop. It isn't much but a small puddle always forms on the cellar floor after a hard rain and I can't seem to find a way to stop it.

The only other thing I don't like about rain is that eight or ten inches of pants between the tops of my shoes and the bottom of my raincoat that always get soaked when I go out in a downpour.

Other than those two minor inconveniences, I say, let it rain!

The Greenhouse Effect

THE Earth is going to get a lot warmer in the near future, according to an announcement from a government agency in Washington. Our temperatures will be rising an average of nine degrees by the year 2100.

This comes as a surprise to me, because I've always

assumed that the Earth would get colder, not warmer. The fire up there has to go out sooner or later, but apparently it's going to be later. First the Earth's going to get hot because of a gas barrier of carbon dioxide that's drifted up into the atmosphere from all the stuff we burn. If you always thought smoke just went up, up and away, you were only half right. It goes up but it doesn't go away. The barrier it forms lets the sun in but prevents heat from leaving the Earth.

The Environmental Protection Agency, which made the announcement, says that New York City could end up with Daytona Beach's temperatures.

If that's true, it proves beyond a doubt that there is a God and that everything works out okay in the end. For the past fifty years, residents of the Northeast have worried because so many people and so much industry have left for the Sun Belt. All kinds of industries with aging factories have been abandoning their old red brick plants in New England and moving to cinder block buildings in the South.

During the oil shortage, the exodus reached epidemic proportions. Factory operators and ordinary people who didn't like the cold wanted to go where heat didn't cost so much.

Now, apparently, the cycle has come around and it will be the Northeast's turn to prosper. If it gets warm in New England, all those factories that moved south will be moving back. They'll want to move out of the Sun Belt because they're spending too much on the electricity they need for all the air conditioning the unions require in their contracts.

The State of Maine, which has always handled its poverty with more grace than other poor states, may prosper. Maine could become the new Sun Belt. If New York has the temperature of Daytona, Maine ought to get what North Carolina has. That would be a big improvement over what Maine has now and would certainly bring industry and prosperity to it.

The thing that worries me about this warming trend is that people don't work as hard when it's warm. Most of the good work of the world has been accomplished in temperate, not tropical, climates. People work better when it's cold than when it's hot. Bad weather brings out the good in people so I hope this warming trend doesn't mean we're in for a lot of nice weather. We can't lie around in the sun if we're going to stay ahead of the Japanese.

The Environmental Protection Agency only predicted what results this warming or "greenhouse effect," as they call it, will have on the United States. It never mentioned the potential effect on world affairs.

What temperatures will the Soviet Union get?

Will Moscow be like Miami Beach or more like San Francisco?

If the Russians have San Francisco weather, will they become nicer people, like San Franciscans?

If Paris ends up with temperatures like Zambia, will Yves Saint Laurent be presenting a new collection of designer loincloths in his fall collection?

They say the polar ice cap will melt as the Earth warms. Is this the end of the igloo as we know it today?

Will Eskimos be living in thatched-roof cottages?

The environmental experts predict that the ocean could rise four feet. This is bad news for the people living in the expensive houses right on the shoreline but it's good news for me. Our house is one hundred yards from the water now and if the ocean rises, we could end up with valuable property right on the beach.

Insects

WHY are there flies? I suppose they have as much right in the universe as we do but if they have their place in the grand plan of things, I don't know what it is and I'd be just as pleased if no one told me.

Yesterday I went for a walk in the woods and what might otherwise have been a very pleasant time of admiring nature and thinking good thoughts, was ruined by a couple of horseflies that took the walk with me. They're so infernally clever, those flies. They know I don't have eyes on the top of my head so they stay low over my hair, making passes at my ears in order to get the maximum effect out of their irritating little buzz. I swipe at them but I seldom hit one and if, by some lucky accident, I make contact with a waving arm and knock one to the ground, he just gets up again and buzzes off.

I not only fail to understand what flies are for but I'm not sure why they're as annoying as they are. That noise they make isn't really loud and they don't bite much. Even if they do bite, it isn't like a broken arm. There's a better reason to hate mosquitoes than flies.

Because I couldn't think of anything else on my walk, with the flies around me, I got thinking of some of the other creatures we live with that bring out some latent desire to kill in the mildest-mannered of us. We have a house in the country with both chipmunks and mice around. They are, after all, about the same size and if you were describing them to someone who'd never seen either a mouse or a chipmunk, they'd sound the same. They're awfully close to being the same thing for such a difference in my opinion of them. I'd hate to hurt a chipmunk but I've caught quite a few mice by the neck in that cruel little trap.

Ants don't bother me much. At certain times of year we have some ants in the kitchen but I don't have any primal urge to kill them. I wish they'd go away but they don't bug me the way flies do. Maybe I'm more irritated with the fly because he's superior to me in the way that an ant isn't. The ant can't hover over my head, buzzing in my ears and tantalizing me with his ability to evade every swipe I take at him.

Keep in mind I am reconstructing this from the memory of the thoughts that came to me yesterday on my walk. I got thinking about an experience I had with a couple of ants just the day before. I saw a black ant on my workshop floor trying to run off with a smaller, red ant. They were all tangled up together and I suspected all sorts of things might have been going on there but as I watched, I decided that it was the red ant who was attacking the black ant and the black ant was trying to get away. The red ant had attached himself (or, according to my darkest thoughts *herself*) to him. I got the two of them on a piece of paper and dropped them into an empty coffee can. The two came apart and seemed to ignore each other and I left them trying to scramble up the shiny walls of the can while I went to do something else, at which I probably had about the same chance of success as they had of getting out of the can.

I came back an hour later and learned a lesson about black and red ants. I had been wrong. The red ant was in six or eight little pieces and the black ant was still trying to get out. I felt terrible about having left that little red ant in there with that black killer but how was I to know? Imagine the terror the red ant felt when I left him or her alone in the can with the black ant!

I don't suppose you could teach one of those black ants not to kill a red one. You can't teach a cat not to kill birds. Why do cats do it? Maybe it's a matter of territory. The black ants want to preserve their home-land and the red ants think they ought to have one for themselves. It seems to me there's room enough for all the ants on my workshop floor but what do I know?

I don't understand what's going on in nature any more than I understand what's going on among people in the world and I certainly can't say why I was deter-mined to kill those harmless flies buzzing around my head in the woods yesterday.

Matches

KEEP this page out of the reach of young children be-cause it's about matches.

With the possible exception of pennies, nothing piles up in places where you don't need them and dis-appears from places where you could use them faster than packs of paper matches. I have a little drawer in my dresser, next to the one I keep my clean socks in, and there must be a hundred packs of matches in it. They'd be handy except that I never light a match looking for socks.

I've never smoked cigarettes and we have a range with pilot lights so I don't really use many matches. I want to be honest with you though. I played with matches as a kid and I've never gotten over the fascination they had for me then. I still play with matches. For instance, if I light one for anything, I always try to burn it all the way to the end. After it has burned halfway, I wet the tip of my thumb and forefinger and grab hold of the hot, bulbous end to see if I can burn the whole match.

We have a grill in the backyard and I use matches most often starting the fire for cooking there in the summer. That's where I do most of my thinking about matches.

I wish the people who make matches wouldn't be so protective of us. They keep thinking up new safety features that make matches more inconvenient and no safer. I don't think many fires are set accidentally by people using matches for a good purpose and I don't appreciate some of the ways match makers try to protect us from ourselves.

For instance, I have a strong aversion to book matches that have the striking pads on the opposite side from where the cover lifts open. They aren't handy at all and I doubt if they've ever prevented one fire. I'm careful to throw them all away without looking at the advertising displayed on them.

Last weekend I cooked out for the first time this season. I use a combination of those commercial charcoal briquettes and a few pieces of wood from the dead limbs of several hickory and maple trees we have. The charcoal briquettes are not really what I call charcoal at all, of course. They're made mostly of coal dust and a binding material like clay or starch, but they're handy.

While I was buying the bag of briquettes that morning, I also bought a box of wooden matches. It is my habit to keep matchboxes on the mantelpiece over the fireplace when I'm starting a fire in the backyard. That's what I did last weekend but after setting the fire with newspapers underneath, I couldn't get the match to light.

I went back inside to look at the box the matches came in and, of course, they were called "safety" matches. They couldn't be struck just anywhere. They had to be scratched on the strip on the side of the matchbox.

Well, when I go out to the backyard, I don't want to take the whole box of matches with me and I'd be pleased if the wooden match makers wouldn't try to make life so safe for me. There are even laws in many states making it illegal to sell matches that will strike anywhere. There are states in which you can buy a rifle at the hardware store but not a box of matches that will strike on the seat of your pants.

Most of us are fascinated with fire and it isn't hard to understand why. We're suspicious that the world will eventually grow cold and fire is a great comfort to us because of the heat it produces. The fact that it's dangerous only makes it fascinating. Civilization's ability to use fire may be the most important thing it has learned how to do.

In the movie version of Mark Twain's *A Connecti-*

cut Yankee in King Arthur's Court, Will Rogers saved his life by amazing the king with his cigarette lighter. A dream or fantasy that often recurs in my mind is one in which I'm the only person in the world with matches. If I had lived a thousand years ago and had no other possession than those book matches in my dresser drawer, I wouldn't have needed anything else.

Of course, with my luck, I'd have gone before King Arthur with my life on the line and discovered, when I reached into my pocket to amaze him by lighting a wooden match, that they were safety matches and I'd left the box home.

Dislikes

LIFE is pleasant most of the time but there are some things it would be better without. I've made a partial list of things I dislike:

—Special or clever license plates with the owner's nickname on them.

—Magazines that hide their index where you can't find it. The index to a magazine belongs inside the first page after the cover.

—Television commercials for hemorrhoid cures, toilet paper, sanitary pads or dental adhesives. Newspaper ads for these same products don't bother me.

—Flip-top beer and soft drink cans.

—People who take up two parking spaces with one car.

—Anything stapled together.

—Announcements in the mail that I'm the potential winner of a million-dollar sweepstakes.

—A space that's too small on a form where I'm supposed to put my signature. I scrawl when I write and if I have to put it in a little space, it isn't really my signature.

—Having to open a new can of coffee when I only need two tablespoons more.

—Telephone answering machines with messages at the beginning that are too long or too cute.

—Newspapers with sections that have different numbering systems from the main news sections. There may be no good way to handle this problem but that doesn't stop me from disliking it.

—The middle seat in a crowded airplane.

—Trunks of cars that have to be opened with a key. Why can't I leave the trunk of my car unlocked if I want to?

—Religious quacks on radio and television thinking up new ways to take money from ignorant listeners and incidentally from legitimate churches.

—Dirty magazines prominently displayed at a newsstand.

—A cart in the supermarket with a wobbly wheel.

—Waiting in line to pay for anything.

—Secretaries who say, "May I ask what this is in reference to?" when you call their boss.

—Admonitions from weathermen to "drive safely." All I want to know from them is whether it's going to rain or not. I'll decide how to drive.

—Recipes in a bag of flour that you can't remove without spilling flour all over.

—Hot-air hand dryers in public washrooms. I'd rather use my shirttail.

—People who play radios in public places.

—Baseball or basketball scores on the radio for teams I don't care anything about.

—People who stand too close to my face when they're talking to me. I think they're cousins of the people who move you gradually over toward the buildings when you walk down the street with them.

—Screws with slots that aren't deep enough so that they tear when you twist with the screwdriver.

—Having to check a shopping bag when I go into a store. I know shoplifting is a problem but I don't like the idea of being a suspect.

—Cars with too many red taillights.

The Flu

THIS isn't going to be easy. As I write, I'm having the flu. The brain seems to be thinking all right but I can't keep it thinking about one subject for long. My body is quaking just enough so that when I go for the *h* on my typewriter, I'm often hitting the *g* or *j* on either side of it.

This is my fourth day. That's the longest I've ever had what they used to call the forty-eight-hour virus. I think I may be pulling out of it because this morning I was interested enough in life again to read the newspaper for a little while. My daily paper is one of the great pleasures of my life and when I'm not interested in it, I know I'm sick.

Strange things happen to time when you're sick. The minutes and the hours seem interminably long when you're lying in bed tossing and turning . . . 2:35 A.M. . . . 2:50 A.M. . . . my gosh, is it only 3:15? But then in the morning it all seems so condensed. You have no point of interest to which the memory can attach itself so the night is all one brief unpleasant blur.

In regard to time, I'm furthermore convinced that there is definitely some state in between sleep and wakefulness that we don't identify very often. There have been times over the past four days when I would have sworn in court that I never fell asleep between midnight and five A.M., but looking back at it rationally, I suspect that if I was not really asleep I was for part of the time, at least, in a state of suspended animation. This can happen to anyone who simply isn't sleeping very well even if they don't have the flu. When a husband or wife claims not to have slept all night, the partner is often tempted to ask what all the snoring was about then.

Considering the flu is not usually a serious disease, it sure is uncomfortable. I lie in bed wondering how I'd feel if this were a disease I'd never get over. At noon of the second day Margie said I ought to eat a little chicken broth. I said I didn't want any. I didn't feel like it and I was afraid it would make me sick to my stomach. She brought some upstairs to the bedroom anyway and in deference to her concern and effort, I drank some of it. I was soon sick to my stomach. It's a tough way to prove a point.

All day Margie kept bringing me things I didn't

want. I don't suppose there was a single thing in the world I could name that I wanted except my health back. I didn't even want to turn over in bed when I ached from lying on one side for too long. When I had to go to the bathroom, I kept putting it off, thinking I might be in better shape to get up in another half hour.

You get very aware of the parts of your body lying in bed with it for four days. You get very aware of its shortcomings and dissatisfied with it. In the bathroom, I look in the mirror, unshaved, hair uncombed, face drooping and I think, "My God, this is what I really look like when I'm not fixed up."

One of the things I notice that's wrong with my body is that there's too much of it. I've been thinking about all the food I would have eaten that I haven't eaten in the past four days. I'm still alive. I have no desire for food. Why can't I have this attitude toward food when I'm well?

It's the old story, I know. It's easy to decide not to eat so much when you feel the way I do. As a matter of fact, it's difficult to remember how you felt when you were well while you're sick; and difficult to recall how you felt when you were sick when you're well.

Yesterday the inevitable happened. Margie got it. She had been so good to me that I dragged myself out of bed and started bringing her hot tea, which she likes. I noticed she didn't drink her tea. The next morning she came in to see how I was. She brought me tea and said she felt stronger.

It made me feel terrible to have her waiting on me again. She said she felt much better today but I couldn't help wondering if some people aren't just better at being sick than others.

I hope you don't get anything from reading this.

Coughing

MY life has been dominated for the past four days by coughing. I must have coughed almost as often as I've exhaled.

Coughing is one of the least attractive things we do in public and I hate to do it but I can't stop myself. I have a cold or a virus or some flu bug and it seems to have settled in the spot just below my throat where that indentation is between the collarbones.

When I was young and people coughed as much as I have the last few days, they were said to have "consumption." I don't know where the word came from. The more knowledgeable word was "tuberculosis."

I don't have either of those. I have a cough. I don't smoke cigarettes and I know my body well enough to be sure I don't have any dread disease.

I was in Florida over the weekend. The temperature hit ninety degrees one day and Florida when it's ninety degrees is the worst place to be with a coughing cold. It's humid and when you're inside you need air conditioning. Air conditioning, as we all know, is a cold's best friend. A cold loves air conditioning.

Friends have been sympathetic enough about my cold. They've been properly worried and they keep saying things like "You ought to take care of your-

self,'' but it hasn't helped. Not only that, even though
I can tell they genuinely feel sorry for me, I've noticed
a certain edge in their voices a couple of times. They
wouldn't say it but I know what they want to say. They
want to burst out loud and yell, "Will you *for goodness sake* stop that infernal coughing!"

It's irritating to have someone around you coughing
all the time. No matter how much you try to keep yourself from thinking it, you always have the sneaking
suspicion they could stop if they wanted to.

When I was a kid I coughed a lot when I had a cold
and even now I have an annoying way of clearing my
throat when I'm not sick. I'm more aware of this than I
used to be because two of my four grown children do
it. Drives me crazy. "Stop clearing your throat," I
want to yell at them, as I clear my throat.

I've never found a legal cough syrup or cough drop
that did anything at all for a cough. There was one ten
or fifteen years ago that helped but it had more codeine
in it than the law allows now so you can't buy it today
without a prescription. I don't go to a doctor when I
have a cold, no matter how bad it is. I've probably had
more colds than he has and I know just as much,
maybe more, about them. All the doctor can do in a
case like that is give you medicine that's stronger than
is good for you. I don't take much medicine, not because of any religious conviction or anything like that
but because anything you can buy without a prescription probably doesn't work.

As kids we used to argue about whether the black
licorice Smith Brothers Cough Drops were best or
whether the menthol ones in the yellow package were.

In desperation the other day I bought a package of

Luden's Menthol Cough Drops. That's a familiar old package I remember with affection, too, and I thought perhaps over the years they'd learned how to sneak something into their cough drops that would really help a cough.

I paid thirty-five cents for fifteen cough drops. That's only a little more than two cents each and you can't expect a miracle drug for that. The front of the package says they're "MEDICATED." I don't know what that word could be broadened to include but when you look further on the package for all the active ingredients, there are just two. Luden's Menthol Cough Drops are made of sugar and menthol. Menthol is the principal ingredient of peppermint. It's obtained from oil of peppermint. It sounds like candy to me.

Considering how good our bodies are at curing themselves of the worst things that happen to them all but once, it's interesting that none of us is ever totally free of every single malady or irritation. If we check closely, there's always something that isn't quite right. It may be nothing more than a hangnail but there it is, stopping our bodies just short of perfection.

I'm not going to eat any more of these cough drops. (I think "eat" is a better word than "take.") I'll put them in a dresser drawer. Next time I get a hangnail, I'll see if sugar and peppermint helps that.

Pacemakers

EVERY three or four years it occurs to me that my heart has been beating away about seventy times a minute night and day, day after day but most of the time I don't pay any attention to my heart. It's the same with breathing. If you start getting conscious of the fact that you're taking air in and pushing it out again 28,000 times a day, it can be disconcerting.

I got thinking about my heart and all our hearts the other day when I read a story about pacemakers. A Senate study found that doctors and pacemaker makers may have overcharged patients a billion dollars a year for putting the device in their hearts. About 150,000 people are having them put in every year and they are charged as much as $10,000 each. Medicare pays most of that cost and the average American's attitude is that if Medicare pays for it, it's free. If it's free to the patient, he or she doesn't care much what it costs Medicare.

Most of us are so naïve it wouldn't occur to us that there was any hanky-panky going on between the manufacturers of this really wonderful little device and the doctors who put it in. It's really disheartening to hear that while we're thinking about our hearts, some doctors and pacemaker businessmen are thinking about money. There's no reason they shouldn't think about money. It's just that the rest of us like to think the world is nicer than that.

Now that I know how aggressive these pacemaker salesmen are in selling their product to doctors, I've thought of a couple of new ways for them to get rich. They can have this idea free.

There ought to be a huge market for pacemakers that control the speed at which other parts our bodies operate. My heart is pumping away in perfectly satisfactory condition and it doesn't give me any trouble but I could sure use a pacemaker for my brain. If these pacemaker people could come up with a little device they could implant in some inconspicuous place to control the speed at which I think, I'd be mighty pleased. Maybe they could get one in my earlobe, in which case I might take two. One brain pacemaker would control the right side of my brain, the other the left.

I'd want a dial on my brain pacemaker so I'd be in control of it. Sometimes I want to think faster than other times. When I sit down to write, I'd turn it up to full speed so my brain would be thinking its very fastest. In the evening, when I'm home watching television, I'd turn it down to idle. Thre's no sense having your brain thinking fast when you're watching "Dallas" or "The A Team."

As I understand the heart pacemaker, it provides a small, regular electrical impulse that controls the speed of the heartbeat. Is there anyone alive who wouldn't like one of these for his or her brain? If I went to a party where there were a lot of people I should know, I'd set my brain pacemaker for medium speed. If I saw someone whose name I should know but couldn't remember, I'd simply pinch my earlobe and turn my variable speed brain control up a few notches.

"Hey! If it isn't my old friend George Forbisher!

How you been, fella! How's Grace? And the kids George Junior, Marybeth, Sarah and Walter?''

I don't want to get too clinical but there are a lot of parts of my body I'd like to have a pacemaker for. Some parts work too fast and some don't work fast enough. I'd like to be in control of all of them. If they could work something out to speed up my fingers when I'm typing, I'd be mighty appreciative. I'm a slow reader and I wouldn't mind picking up the pace of the movement of my eyes. Often my feet don't move as fast as I want them to. A couple of little pacemakers inserted somewhere near the anklebones might help. I know for certain I'd like to be able to speed up the digestive process going on down there in my stomach. I'm always eating dinner too late and then having indigestion in the middle of the night.

If the pacemaker makers get at some of these auxiliary aids, maybe they could stop overselling the heart pacemakers.

My New Lifestyle

You may have seen something about a report issued by the National Academy of Sciences saying that half of us die when we do, not because of old age but because of our lifestyle. The people from the Institute of Medicine who issued the report recommend that if we want to live longer, we ought to change our lifestyle. The NAS and IOM give official advice to the federal government.

I want to live a good long while so I've been thinking about following these recommendations. What's the sense of paying someone like your government to help you if you won't take their advice?

The problem I have with trying to change my lifestyle is that I don't think of my life as having any particular style. The word "style" to me is something that appears in certain sections of the newspaper and in magazines like *Vogue*. I just plod along, living day after day and having a pretty good time doing it, too, but it isn't what anyone would call stylish. Whatever it is though, I'm thinking of changing the way I do it to conform to government recommendations.

The report says a lot of us die from things that are unnecessary. We die from driving cars, eating too much of the wrong food, drinking too much of the wrong liquids, smoking and generally living at too fast a pace.

I don't know where to start breaking up this style the government thinks my life has. I guess I'll start with breakfast. I know the government wouldn't want me to eat bacon and eggs although it would be afraid to say so because of all the farmers who make their living selling them. I'll have a simple breakfast of two slices of plain toast without butter. I won't toast the bread much because that nice brown color comes from carbon and carbon has been found to be a potential cause of cancer. My grandmother gave me milk toast once for breakfast when I was sick. It was terrible but it must be good for you or my grandmother never would have given it to me, so maybe I'll start the day with milk toast. Of course, it won't give me much incentive to get up.

I better not drive to work anymore. The report says too many of us die before our time in automobile accidents. I don't know how I'll get to work. It's too far to walk and anyway, the government also says too many of us are killed as pedestrians. I was thinking maybe I won't go to work at all because I won't be needing as much money because everything I spend money for is bad for me according to this report.

The only thing I'll need really big money for is fresh fruit and vegetables. I know I'll have to be eating more of those. They cost plenty. I saw California oranges for sale in a fruit store last month and they were two for eighty-nine cents. The most remarkable thing about asking that much for two California oranges was, the store was in California. I'd like to know how the government proposes we pay for all this healthy fruit it wants us to eat.

The report says too many of us die before our time because of heart attacks brought on by stress. I guess I'll stop working so hard. I sure wouldn't mind taking a month off from writing some summer. I like to play tennis too but I suppose I'd better be safe and give that up. The government wouldn't want me dropping dead on the court unnaturally.

Life is going to be pretty quiet for me for the next fifty years. I should live that long with my new lifestyle. Long and dull, my life's going to be. When I wake up in the morning, I'll get up, go to the bathroom, brush my teeth and go back to bed to get some rest. I'll cancel the newspaper because that only creates stress by getting me all worked up. I can't eat, I can't get to work safely, I can't play and from what I gather, my government would just as soon I didn't have a drink before dinner. About all my new lifestyle calls for is devoting full time to living forever.

I don't really know whether I'm going to change my lifestyle or not. I'd feel like an awful fool if I gave up all these things I like and then choked to death lying down trying to take a vitamin pill with a glass of water.

You'll Never Have to Diet Again!!!

Do you want to lose weight without pain? Do you want to drop ten pounds in ten days?

If I were writing this for one of the ladies' magazines, I'd title it YOU'LL NEVER HAVE TO DIET AGAIN!!! (I'd have those three exclamation points in the headline.)

This morning I made the final decision to lose some weight and being a basically unselfish person, I'm going to share my foolproof weight loss plan with you. It's so simple I can't believe I never thought of it before.

I'm going to give up food as a hobby.

A hobby is defined as being an interest or pursuit outside one's regular occupation that is engaged in for relaxation. That's what food is for me. I'm interested in it far beyond the need I have for it to sustain me. I spend idle hours looking at it, shopping for it, reading about it and cooking it. I use food as a diversion from the problems of life and I'm going to stop that.

No longer will you find me in the interesting food stores along the area known as Hell's Kitchen in New York. On Saturdays I'm not going to spend all morning shopping for food, all afternoon preparing it and all evening eating it. I'm going to suppress my interest in food and in so doing, cut down on my consumption of it.

I'm a gourmand and a gourmet. They are not the same thing and I am both. A gourmand is a person who has an unusual interest in eating. A gourmet is someone who knows a lot about food. Being both is tough on the weight.

Over the years I've made a study of the best places to buy good food. I know where the best crusty loaf of Italian bread in America is made, for instance, in a real brick oven in the Bronx. In San Francisco, I know where the best sourdough is.

I've traveled all over this country and there are very few towns or cities you could mention in which I couldn't name the best restaurant. I might not remember the name of the hotel or why I ever went there in the first place, but as a collector of restaurants, I'd remember that.

That's all in the past, though. As of today, or tomorrow at the very latest, I'm dropping food as one of my hobbies. I'll eat supermarket cheese, the kind that comes with paper between the slices, on two pieces of Wonder Bread with margarine.

As things stand now I divide my free time between woodworking and food, but beginning soon I'm going to spend all of my hobby hours with my tools and my wood. I'll come up out of my workshop only when called for dinner.

I'm so devoted to food as a hobby that it isn't going to be an easy break, but once I make it, I'm sure the fat will melt away. At present I eat things long after I've finished being hungry, just because the food tastes good. No more of that. Once I've had as much food as I need, I'll quit eating. No more eating for the fun of it or to pass the time away.

One side effect this plan will have for me is that in addition to losing weight, I'll save time and money. When food is your hobby, you spend a lot of money on things you can't even eat. I have more good knives than we have drawers to keep them in and I'm always buying a new pan or a gadget.

I could write a novel with the time I'll save eliminating food as a hobby. Last weekend I didn't have any of that good Italian bread. I was determined to duplicate the brick-oven conditions in which it's baked, so I bought two of those red clay drainage pipes six inches in diameter. I cut them off so they'd fit into my oven and baked my own bread in them. That's the kind of fun I've got to stop having if I'm going to eliminate food as a pastime.

After I cut out food as a hobby, I'll probably lose so much weight that you won't recognize my picture on the cover of a book.

Corn

I⊤ would be difficult to describe to a stranger what you talk about at the dinner table. One of the subjects that always comes up in our house, at certain times of the year, is the question of which ear of corn is best. I have the nervous feeling that they're fooling around too much with vegetables in agricultural laboratories and one of the vegetables they aren't helping is corn.

If you like corn as I do, you don't like the way they've been growing it the past few years. The kernels are getting smaller and smaller and whiter and whiter. I used to like a variety called Golden Bantam but I haven't seen any in years. Next came something called Country Gentlemen. Country Gentlemen had huge ears and small kernels. In recent years corn has been called Sugar and Spice, Salt and Pepper and Silver Queen. I yearn for the days of Golden Bantam but I'm in the minority at our dinner table.

We're still getting pretty good corn in our part of the country although the pumpkins are in the markets now, and when the pumpkins come, we know we're getting near the end of the fresh fruit and vegetable season.

It's been a fairly good season for vegetables in the Northeast quadrant of the United States. It hasn't been any *better* than fairly good, though. We had torrents of rain in the late spring and then almost nothing during July and August. At least that gets the roots headed down. That's what the farmers say anyway and all I know is what the farmers tell me.

Farming is desperately hard work and often it's so heartbreaking you wonder why anyone sticks at it. There is *always* a reason why the crop isn't as good as it should be. If there isn't too much rain, there's too little. If the amount of rain is just right, there's an early freeze. I stopped for apples last weekend and the farmer was complaining as usual.

"Too warm for this time of year," he said. "It takes all the color out of the apples. They're dropping off the trees before we can pick them. I got a couple hundred bushels of apples out there on the ground."

Last year he couldn't get anyone to pick them off the trees and the year before there was a freeze in September. For most of us the weather is just a topic of conversation but for a farmer, it's his life.

In most parts of the country, we've had bumper crops of everything. There was never a better year for apples in the East. Wheat is abundant in the Midwest. I read where there are so many avocados in California that they're going to make dog food out of them.

Avocados suffer from an image problem that corn on the cob doesn't have. Most Americans think of avocados as a very elitist food and not something you'd have more than a few times a year on special occasions. The day after I read about how many extra avocados there were, I went to the store with every intention of buying several. They were $1.29 each. Some dog food! The farmers have trouble with the weather; the rest of us have trouble with prices.

Yesterday I had a sign as clear as a falling leaf that

the season is changing. For the past few months we've been having corn several times a week at dinner and melons or berries for breakfast. Yesterday my wife said she couldn't get corn and for breakfast we had the first Florida grapefruit of the new year. They were small and sour but it was still good to have them back. Now I can't wait until the price of juice oranges comes back down to where I can afford to squeeze a few for breakfast Saturday and Sunday mornings. There's a time for melons and a time to forget melons. There's a time for corn on the cob and a time to forget corn on the cob.

Confessions of a Tea-Totaler

I HATE tea.

Tea is so universally respected that I've hardly dared say it before. To tell you the truth, I never even realized I disliked it until about four o'clock yesterday afternoon. There I was sitting at my desk drinking tea out of a Styrofoam cup and it hit me like a ton of bricks.

"I hate this stuff," I said to myself. "And I don't care much for this cup, either."

After that, I tried to remember how I got started drinking tea in the first place. I think I know how it happened. Several years ago some of us were sitting around the office thinking of ways not to do any work when one of us—I think it was me—said, "Let's have a nice cup of tea!"

We had a cup of tea and ever since then, that's what someone says almost every day around four.

"Let's have a cup of tea."

My grandmother never called it just a cup of tea. She always referred to it as "a *nice* cup of tea." It was practically all one word to her.

My grandmother would be very disappointed to hear me say I don't like tea. I also have a good friend I've been keeping the secret from for years and he may never speak to me civilly again. He's spent most of his adult life tasting tea for one of the big tea companies and he drinks the stuff all the time, even when he isn't working. Many of you will, no doubt, want to say you liked me up until now but if I don't like tea, you will never read anything I've written again. I'm sorry but there are things a man has to do, and I had to tell you I don't like tea. Please don't write.

Tea is a nervous habit. It's like chewing gum or your fingernails. A drink of tea is so close to nothing that it hardly even dirties the cup it's served in. If it had become fashionable to drink a cup of steaming hot water, tea never would have gained a foothold in America.

It's only a matter of time, too, before someone discovers that tea is bad for laboratory mice and should therefore be labeled as potentially dangerous for human consumption. Tea is one of the few things I can think of that hasn't been called a health hazard and you can bet its day is coming.

Drinking tea seems like a simple thing to do but it isn't simple at all. For an example of how confused tea drinkers are about it, consider how many different ways they think tea should be drunk. Tea drinkers are

divided into three categories of roughly equal numbers. Each category further subdivides into those who like it with or without sugar.
—The first group likes tea with nothing in it.
—The second drinks tea with milk.
—The third wants tea with lemon.

There are no three tastes more different than milk, lemon and nothing . . . with and without sugar.

Keep in mind none of this has anything to do with iced tea. Iced tea is as different a drink from tea as lemonade is from hot cocoa with whipped cream. I like iced tea but iced tea is not considered socially acceptable in the same way a cup of tea is.

You may think of tea as an innocuous beverage but historically tea has been a troublemaker. In the 1760s and 1770s, the amount of tea smuggled illegally into this country dwarfs anything ever smuggled in since. The marijuana trade is petty cash in comparison.

If anyone wishes to argue that the idea of afternoon tea is a civilized social convention. I'll accept that. In England everyone breaks for afternoon tea. That's fine. It's the beverage itself I can't stand.

It's almost four o'clock now. I've had a tough day and I could use a break. I guess I'll have a cup of tea. A *nice* cup of tea.

Milk

WHAT is the fourth most popular drink in the United States?

The answer to today's news quiz is one four-letter word: milk.

The three fluids other than water that Americans drink more of than milk are soft drinks, coffee and beer, in that order.

I haven't been so surprised by a statistic since I read that women buy more razor blades than men.

For years milk was associated with wholesomeness and goodness. The all-American kid came home after school, dropped his homework books on the kitchen table and had a glass of milk and a cookie. After that he went out and played for several hours until supper was ready. The kid had milk at supper, too.

According to the statistics, that has changed. Now when school is over a child buys a bottle or a can of sweet-flavored carbonated water and throws the can or bottle on someone else's lawn on the way home from school.

Nothing seems to hurt the booming sale of soft drinks. I had noticed the increasing popularity of something called Sunkist, so I bought a can of it to have with a sandwich at lunch the other day. The can, because of its name and color, gives the clear impression that the drink inside is made of orange juice. Sunkist is *not* made of orange juice. A carbonated beverage can be called "orange soda" without having any orange juice at all in it. For lawyers worried for me because of the legal implications of that statement, be advised that I have talked to the administrators of the regulation at the Food and Drug Administration in Washington, D.C., within the last four minutes. *They* told me that.

The makers of carbonated orange soda often put in

orange pulp to help it masquerade as being made of orange juice and they may include an additive that gives the drink the cloudy appearance that real orange juice has but unless it says "orange juice" on its list of ingredients, it has none.

The dairy industry blames the decline in our consumption of milk on the medical profession. Doctors have suggested that too much milk produces cholesterol, the substance that clogs the pipes that carry our blood through our bodies.

There's no doubt that the American wish to cut down on fattening foods and foods that produce cholesterol has had an adverse effect on milk consumption, but I'm not convinced this is the principal reason for the decline. The medical profession has just as often attacked soft drinks for a variety of medical reasons and it hasn't hurt their sales.

The dairy industry can think what it likes but I think people aren't drinking as much milk and cream as they used to because it doesn't taste as good. They've made factories out of cows and the milk tastes more as if it were manufactured than given.

Jersey cows living in a pasture give wonderfully rich, good-tasting milk. It's dessert all by itself. The Jersey cows are a minority in America, though, because they only produce three-quarters as much milk as Holstein cows do. The Holstein's milk is about half as good.

Dairy farmers no longer chase their cows into the barn to milk them twice a day. A lot of cows live like broiler-bound chickens, in a narrow stall for most of their lives. They're fed from a trough in front of them that is resupplied from a conveyor belt and they're artificially inseminated once a year so they have calves and keep producing milk. A cow doesn't have any fun at all anymore and her milk tastes that way. Dairy farmers work hard. It's a tough way to make a living but many of them have become part-time scientists and their dairies are laboratories.

Milk processors take the milk apart, do unnatural things to it and then put it back together so it's more like orange soda than what the cow intended for her calf when she produced it.

That's why so few people are drinking milk.

Milk Again

IT occurs to me that I'm not finished talking about milk. There was a recent exhibition by an organization called Dairymen, Inc., that I saw and they were showing how they're producing milk they process at such high temperature that it can be stored for months anywhere without refrigeration. You could keep a bottle in the trunk of your car all summer.

If the world of the future is going to serve me milk that can be kept for a long time out of the icebox, I won't have a glass, thank you. Is this really what people want from science? I personally like ice cream that melts and milk that turns sour after a reasonable period of time.

The words "natural" and "organic" have been overused in advertising. That's because advertisers recognize that almost anything that comes to us direct from nature is better than something we've concocted with the help of man-made chemicals. They know we know it, too, so they pretend their product is "natural."

We were all propagandized to believe from infancy that milk was the perfect food and one reason for its perfection was, it was natural. Well, those days are gone forever. The average quart of milk today is about as natural as Gatorade or a thick shake at McDonald's.

Almost all the good, natural foods we have ruined, have been ruined because some giant corporation in the food business wanted a product that was easier to handle and had a longer shelf life in the stores. The farmers don't ruin it.

Tomatoes were ruined by the companies that didn't care much what a tomato tastes like as long as it could be picked by a machine or packed and shipped in a crate without being crushed.

Bread isn't any good in this country because the big bakers undercook it to keep the moisture content high. Water is heavy and by law a loaf of bread can be thirty-eight percent water. Water is cheaper than anything else they can put in bread and that mushy, wet feeling gives people the idea the bread is fresh. The average commercial loaf of bread will stay soft and mushy in its wrapper for months. That's as long as the super-pasteurized milk stays "fresh." The soft feeling bakers build into their bread has nothing to do with freshness.

There are surprisingly good commercial ice creams on the market. The bad ones have too much air and too many stabilizers in them. These ingredients, along with preservatives, allow ice cream to be mistreated by truckers and kept longer by store managers. If the ice cream is good, they have to treat it carefully and sell it quickly. They don't like that.

I am infuriated every time I fly on an airplane and the flight attendant pours me coffee and asks if I want cream or sugar. I always say, "Yes, I'll have cream."

The flight attendant then hands me a little container of liquid white plastic called For Your Coffee or Coffee Lightener.

This new process that will enable the big dairies to produce milk that will keep for months without refrigeration is a giant step in the wrong direction. It serves nothing but the convenience of the distributors. It will be one more technological improvement that further hurts the hurting dairy farmer by making milk less attractive to drink.

VII:

OPINIONS

Driving

JUNE is the beginning of the time of year when Americans do the most driving. I often spend 20 hours a week in my car during the summer months. It seems like an awful lot of time now that I've written it down. If I sleep for 42 hours a week and drive for 20, that means I'm not doing much of anything for 62 of the 168 hours in a week. Maybe we better get a weekend place nearer home.

The trouble with driving is that you often do it in a state of agitation. I'm not usually very relaxed when I drive because I'm mad at the guy behind me or the woman in front of me or the truck that just cut me off. As soon as I do relax, I get sleepy. I'd rather be angry than sleepy when I'm driving. I'm not a very safe driver when I'm driving slowly to be safe. When I'm mad, I drive faster but at least I'm alert to everything that's going on. I'm trying to get that dirty so-and-so who cut in front of me.

It is my opinion that the slow drivers are a greater menace on the road than the ones driving at, or slightly above, the speed limit. The slow drivers sit there, slumped way down behind the wheel, smug in the knowledge that they are safe drivers but they're wrong. They're the ones who don't know how to move. They're the ones who can't get out of their own way. They cause the rest of us to pile into something to avoid them.

You can tell I'm just off the road because I'm writing in an agitated state. I just drove 150 miles from upstate New York to New York City and it was the kind of drive that makes you wonder whether the weekend was worth it.

I confess to being a competitive driver. I'm vaguely irritated when someone passes me, even when the other driver has a perfect right to do it. The chances are, though, that he doesn't have a legal right because I'm probably driving as fast as the law allows, or faster. What irritates me on a major highway is that there are some nuts who won't let you maintain a reasonable distance between your car and the car in front of you. If you do leave a sensible opening, someone comes along and cuts into it and then you have to drop four or five car lengths behind him. You're losing ground and it makes you mad. I think this is the cause of a lot of accidents. People tailgate because they don't want anyone getting in between them and the car ahead. When there's a sudden stop or slowdown, it can be too late to brake to a stop before hitting the car you're following.

The single most annoying driving habit Americans have on and off the major highways is their practice of hitting the right turn signal just after they've started to turn right. By then, you *know* they're turning right. What you would have liked is some indication of their intentions a few hundred yards back. It would have helped you make plans. Why do so many drivers think it does any good to hit the turn signal after they've started their turn?

In city driving, the principal menace for the average driver is the panel truck. I don't know where they get the people who drive panel trucks. Every year there are a lot of race drivers who fail to qualify for the Indianapolis 500. Maybe they all take jobs driving panel trucks in cities. They're trying to make enough money to enter the Indy 500 again next year.

The average driver puts 10,000 miles on his car every year, according to Federal Highway Administration statistics. One statistic I'd like to see that no one has kept is, how much I've paid out in automobile insurance in the past twenty-five years and how much I've collected. We've owned two cars for most of that time and I guess we've paid out a total of more than $20,000. The insurance company didn't get the perfect driver when they got me but they haven't done badly. During that time I doubt if they've paid out $2,000, mostly in dents.

I had all my accidents when I was driving carefully.

Dear American Airlines

DEAR American Airlines:

Please accept what I am going to tell you as friendly criticism. I could probably say it just as well about United, TWA, Pan Am, Delta or any of the others but I just flew into New York on the overnight from Los Angeles and you're fresh on my groggy mind.

When we landed your flight attendant, formerly stewardess, thanked us all for "flying American." I felt guilty accepting her thanks because I choose an airline, not for its name or from my past experience with it, but because it has a plane going where I have to get to at a time I want to go there. I'm as loyal to American over TWA as I am loyal to Hertz over Avis if the line is shorter at Avis. So don't go to a lot of trouble thanking me for "flying American." I don't do it as a favor to you.

I'm probably grumpier than usual because I've only been off your plane for three hours and I haven't had either a shower or any sleep. I got about half an hour's sleep on the four-hour flight. I would have gotten more but ten minutes after I dozed off, one of the flight attendants tapped me on the shoulder to ask if there was anything I wanted. All I wanted was sleep.

It was an hour later before I fell asleep again and this time I had fifteen minutes before the captain woke us all to say we were over the Grand Canyon. I've been down in the Grand Canyon on a mule but I'm not interested in being awakened from a sound sleep to be told I'm flying over it at three A.M. New York time. Does American Airlines own a piece of the canyon or something? Why are you always promoting it? Sure it's a nice canyon.

I've read where eleven major airlines lost a total of $330 million in the first nine months of this year. *You* think you're losing money because business is bad. *I* think business is bad because people are getting so they hate to fly. A flight used to be an experience we looked forward to. Now we're being treated like cattle and a lot of us dread traveling. There used to be a difference between a flight and a trip on a Greyhound bus.

You tell us to get to the airport an hour before flight time. Is this so you won't have to hire enough ticket agents to handle the crowd comfortably?

I'm always impressed with how hard your flight attendants work. You've trained them well and they're invariably courteous under trying conditions. They're often as mad at you as we are. We hear them grumble—not at us but at you. They know better than anyone that you're cutting down on space and service and they're the ones who face an irritated public and have to smile.

They don't seem to be making that announcement much anymore . . . the one where they say, "If there's anything we can do to make your flight more enjoyable, please don't hesitate to call on us." That's good judgment on their part because the attendants are so overprogrammed with jobs they absolutely have to get done now that they have no time for any personal service whatsoever, even in first class. First class is not as good as economy was ten years ago.

To tell you the truth, you got off to a bad start with me last week in New York before I ever got to the airport. I bought my ticket on a Tuesday for a Saturday flight. Round-trip economy class cost $377 each way, a total of $754. On Friday of that week you announced the new economy ticket one way was going to cost $99, beginning in about ten days. That's a difference of $556. What does it cost to fly me to Los Angeles and back? Doesn't what you charge bear any relationship to what it costs?

I hope you can accept this in the spirit in which it

was intended, the spirit of a dissatisfied customer who just had a lousy trip from L.A.

We all like you, airlines. We just don't want to see you go the way of the railroads.

Sincerely,
Andrew A. Rooney

Pilots

PILOTS are the good guys. No one hates a pilot.

Pilots are the ones who know how to do it. They're successful. They're smart, skillful and daring but careful. There's a little of Charles Lindbergh and Eddie Rickenbacker in each of them.

Commercial airline pilots are getting it in the neck now and it's too bad. You hate to see it happen to the good guys even if they were asking for it. The airlines are in such trouble and the unions, including the pilots' union, the Air Line Pilots Association, pushed salaries and benefits so high and work hours so low that the hurting airlines can't afford them.

Do the pilots deserve it? A good friend of mine flew for a major airline for thirty years. He made good money, went everywhere and on top of it, it seemed to the rest of us that he was home all the time. For four or five days a month it was work, work, work but then he'd get two or three weeks off for good behavior. He's smart enough to run the airline. When he wasn't flying, how come he wasn't pitching in at the office instead of raking leaves?

With airline deregulation, it's become easy for someone with a relatively small amount of money to start an airline. Unfortunately for the great old-timers flying for the traditional airlines, there are a lot of young-timers who also know how to fly. The new airlines, with no union contracts, are hiring them to do twice the work for half the price.

I hope the new pilots fit my pilot image. One thing I never worry about when I get on an airplane is the pilot. I may complain about standing in line at the ticket counter and I may not like the food or the cramped seating but I have absolute faith that the pilot sitting up front, whom I've never seen, is faultless. He's tall, square-shouldered and he has a faint smile on his face but a glint of steel in his eyes.

Bill Casey was the first pilot who took my life in his hands and I've felt safe with pilots ever since. Casey lives somewhere in Florida now. I hope dark glasses haven't dimmed that glint of steel in his eyes.

He was the pilot of the B-17 Banshee that took off one February day in 1943 for the first U.S. bombing raid on Germany. I was a nervous reporter who went along, up front with the navigator and bombardier, and with far too good a view of everything that was coming at us, from the flak on the ground to the Luftwaffe Messerschmitts and Focke-Wulfs in the air.

When they shot off the plastic nose of the Banshee, the bombardier froze his hands trying to stuff his jacket in the gaping hole. The navigator, his oxygen hose pierced, collapsed unconscious on his little table. I was healthy but helpless until Casey called me on the intercom.

"Take your parachute off so you can get through

here," he said. "Then take twenty deep breaths, take your mask off and get back here and pick up the emergency oxygen tank for those guys."

I did what he said. I got oxygen to the navigator, he regained consciousness, we got back from the battle and all lived happily ever after.

You can see why I defer to pilots.

Even the pilots with their own small planes at the little airfields all across the country are special people. They have some unique ability to do things right.

An airline pilot's life is a strange combination of exciting and dull. Pilots seem to have a great appetite for excitement and a high tolerance for dullness. These are characteristics you wouldn't think you'd find in one person.

Commercial airline pilots constantly experience the excitement of new places. They're charged with the life or death of a lot of people but there's very little interesting in what they do most of the time. The best and biggest of the new commercial liners practically fly themselves. The pilot sits there in the sun, knowing he can't go back to the bathroom in the main cabin or people will know he's mortal.

I like to think of pilots as better than that. Pilots may be mortal but they're the kind of people I trust my life to.

Culture Shock

IT's easy for a writer in America to make people laugh by poking fun at anything cultural, artistic or intellectual. It's easy because people think they ought to understand or appreciate those things but they often don't. When someone suggests it's all nonsense anyway, they laugh with relief. The other reason it's easy to have fun with art, culture and intellectuality is that there's so much fake art, pretentious culture and so many imitation intellectuals around.

Last evening, I sat in a box at the season's first performance by the New York Philharmonic Orchestra at Lincoln Center. Because I do not appreciate or understand the great bulk of the music they play, I am tempted to appeal to readers I know are out there for jokes about it.

I'm not going to do it though because I wish I liked good music better. I am respectful of people who do and consider them superior to myself because of it. I don't know what's wrong with me.

Rudolf Serkin was the soloist last night and he's one of the greatest pianists in the world. I appreciate his technical expertise. He hits those little keys, all so close together, without ever hitting the one next to the one he's after, by mistake. I don't understand what the composer is trying to do though. How did the composer know when he was finished? What does he mean by these sounds or doesn't he mean anything? Should they make me think? If so, of what?

A box at the Philharmonic sounds better than it is. Avery Fisher Hall is rectangular and the box seats are not angled toward the stage. They face directly across the hall so you're looking, not at the stage, but at the people in the boxes across the way. There was an attractive woman over there but that wasn't what I had been invited to see, so I craned my neck to look at the orchestra.

My neck was further craned by the fact that the steel railing was directly in my line of sight with the conductor.

Inevitably I started drawing comparisons to my box seat at the New York Giants football games. My seat there is on the ten-yard line but the action moves up and down the field so sometimes it's directly in front of me and the seat is so high that I never miss any of the action anyway. Last night, the box was way back where the side meets the balcony. It was the equivalent of a seat low in the end zone at Giants Stadium and the ball never moves downfield at the Philharmonic.

At Giants games, the reaction of the audience is spontaneous. We cheer when our team is good, boo when it's bad. There is no reason to think that the members of the Philharmonic are any better musicians than the Giants are athletes but there is a strict form to the protocol of applause at the Philharmonic. You don't just applaud when you feel like it. You applaud during gaps in the music which are approved for applause. You follow the people who know where those places are. If you applaud when you feel like it, you make a fool of yourself at the Philharmonic. You never boo, no matter how badly the musicians play.

Because I did not understand the phonic subtleties of a piece by Gustav Mahler, I sat there, staring at the attractive woman across the way, thinking nonmusical little thoughts.

—Could Louis Armstrong have played in the Philharmonic? Could that Philharmonic trumpet player stay with Benny Goodman?

—If the Philharmonic were broadcast like a sports event and Leonard Bernstein were in the announcing booth, would he point out errors the conductor was making?

—Is the worst piece of Beethoven's music better than the best popular song ever written?

All symphonies end with a musical cliché. There is a lot of loud noise that makes them all sound like the *1812 Overture*.

At the end, I stood when the others stood. They shouted "bravo" and I clapped but I didn't really make much noise doing it. I wanted them to think I was one of them but I wasn't.

Movies

It's beginning to look as though I'm going to miss seeing the Academy Award-winning movie again this year. In the last few years I've missed *The Deer Hunter, Kramer vs. Kramer, Gandhi* and *Terms of Endearment*.

When I was young, there was nothing I liked better than going to the movies on a Saturday afternoon when I should have been outdoors playing. It was always a double feature and we'd come out of the Madison Theater feeling all funny from having been cooped up in the dark for so long. All the kids I played with liked the movies even if they were bad. In those days I don't ever recall having any critical opinion. It was just "the movies."

I still like the movies but I don't see more than one or two a year now. It isn't television that keeps me in. It's that I like what I do around the house when I'm not doing anything more than I like going out to the movies. Going to a movie is a small event and I don't need another event in my life. I find life itself eventful enough. (You could say the same thing about reading this book.)

A second reason I don't go to many movies is that I'm never very impressed with movies that set out to be arty. They're filled with meaning that doesn't mean anything to me. I sense their depth but cannot fathom it.

Motion-picture makers, more than most artists, have consciously set out to make their product arty and that never produces much art. Art is a by-product of an honest and successful attempt to do something well.

I hope motion pictures prosper as an art form because the best of them are wonderfully good art. There's no reason not to rank motion pictures along with opera, literature, the stage, music or sculpture and painting as legitimate art. The fact that most movies are junk doesn't enter into it. Most art in any form is junk.

Nudity in the movies is a good example of fake art. Most producers have found it good box office in the past ten years to include some sexy nakedness but they almost always pretend it's art. I don't mind the nudity but I object to the pretense that it's art. As a matter of fact, sometimes it just doesn't last long enough. I've seen some very beautiful women take all or most of their clothes off in movies. They looked just fine and I didn't turn my head away but the movie lasted for two hours and they only had their clothes off for maybe thirty seconds and the rest of the movie was terrible.

I'm not interested in wasting an hour and fifty-nine minutes and five dollars just to see thirty seconds of nudity.

Movies are better than they were when I was growing up. I wish I liked them as much as I did then. The shortcoming is more mine than theirs. They're doing their part. Movies have an important, well-done, big-time air about them. Even the worst ones don't look as though they were done by amateur film makers.

They aren't making movies I want to see, though. When I go to the movies, I want to be entertained, not educated. I don't go to the movies to learn how terribly sad life can be for a married couple who hate each other and have two children. I've seen dozens of examples of that in real life and it doesn't amuse, divert or educate me.

Setting the Rules

THE relationship between government officials and reporters has sure deteriorated since the last time I covered a war. They no longer trust each other.

The press was all over President Reagan because no reporters or cameramen were allowed to go with the invasion troops to Grenada and tell Americans back home what was happening. Information about the invasion was controlled by our government and, as we all know, governments aren't famous for handing out information that makes them look bad.

Secretly is how governments we don't like always invade a country. The issue of whether it was right to invade Grenada is completely separate from whether or not reporters should have been included in the action.

Secretary of Defense Caspar Weinberger said they were only thinking of the safety of the news people. Baloney, Caspar, if I may call you by your first name. Reporters have risked their lives and died in every war we've ever fought and there are hundreds who would have jumped at the chance to do it again. Thanks for your concern but sacrificing truth for safety is a bad swap.

Dwight Eisenhower was setting the rules when I was first a war reporter. He's my idea of a great American, a great general, an okay President and a fine human being. I was thinking about how differently reporters were treated under his direction. I was covering the Eighth Air Force bombing raids over Germany then. The story of how reporters got word that there would be a raid the following morning so that they could get from London to one of the bomber bases to cover it would seem incredible now to any admiral, general or White House press secretary:

The other people living in the various buildings in London where the correspondents lived must have thought the newsmen were very strange people. We were always getting mysterious phone calls at three or four A.M. The voice of Colonel Jack Redding or Major Hal Leyshon at the other end of the phone at Eighth Air Force Headquarters would say, ''We're having a little party tomorrow and hope you can come.''

The metaphor might have varied but we all got the message. At least eight trusted news people knew hours in advance that there would be an air raid on Germany. This was heavy intelligence. It would have been of crucial importance to the Luftwaffe. Reporters were no less critical of government and the military than they ar?M now but no one questioned their loyalty to their country.

In many official statements about the censorship of information, there is the faint, faraway suggestion that government officials are doing what's best for the country while newspaper and television reporters are only interested in getting the story for commercial reasons. It's strange how difficult it is to convince some people that the whole story is what's best for the country. If President Reagan thinks he's more of an American than the columnists who question his judgment because he talks about patriotism a lot, he's wrong.

One of the most disappointing facts of life is how effective press censorship can be. It was shocking to see those pictures from Havana showing thousands of young Cubans marching in the streets supporting Castro's statements on Grenada. It had never been so clear before how effectively Cuban citizens have been propagandized into believing that Castro's form of communism is best for them. The same is true in the Soviet Union. Any American who thinks the average Soviet citizen doesn't support his government is kidding himself. Why wouldn't the average Russian think it's great? Through the government-controlled press and television he's never heard anything but good about it. Government censorship of the news works for the government in power. No wonder every government is tempted to use it.

Income Tax

BY April fifteenth, we have all paid—or avoided paying—our federal income tax and it feels so good to have it over with that it doesn't hurt as much as it ought to. I made more money last year than I've ever made before but my taxes were the most I ever paid, too. To tell you the truth, I have a feeling I paid more than my share. I suppose a lot of people feel that. There must be others, though, who know darn well they didn't pay enough. They beat the system.

I have an idea how the IRS could get more money out of the tax cheaters and it wouldn't cost the government a nickel. They would make income tax records open to everyone. Once a year the amount we each paid in tax would be posted in the Town Hall or printed in the newspaper. At the very least, the figures would be readily available to anyone who wanted to look them up. This would be the way to get better compliance with the tax laws.

People who wouldn't cheat or steal anywhere else have no hestiation about cheating on their tax returns. If they think they can get away with it. Most of those same people wouldn't cheat at all if they knew their neighbors were going to see what they'd done. They don't mind cheating the big, anonymous bureaucracy but they wouldn't steal from their friends. The fact that cheating on their tax is the same as stealing from their friends doesn't occur to them.

The government goes about trying to get us to pay our taxes the wrong way. They need the review system and I suppose they have to scare some people with the threat of a jail sentence, but the IRS has never appealed much to our sense of national pride. Americans would be proud to pay their income tax if they thought their money was not being wasted in Washington. If everyone knew what everyone else was paying, it would make it easier to be proud, too. No one gets much of a kick out of being proud in front of a computer checking a return for errors in arithmetic.

I don't know why income tax returns are secret. They're considered nobody else's business even though what we earn isn't usually much of a secret to anyone who knows us or to anyone who wants to find out. We all have a pretty good idea how much our friends and our enemies are making. We may not be able to pin it down to the dollar but unless they've found some way to steal and are hiding the money under the mattress, our friends' salary ranges are apparent to us. If they're driving a Mercedes, they're making more than we are.

If we know how much our neighbors make, what's wrong with knowing how much tax they pay? It would be a way of applying a kind of strong peer pressure that the government could never apply. We'd all be embarrassed into paying our fair share. Very likely there would be people who'd pay *more* than they had to just to keep up with the Joneses.

More than half the income of the federal government comes from taxing the salaries of individuals. Most of that comes from money that is withheld from their paycheck. No one gets rich on a salary that is withheld from their paycheck. No one gets rich on a salary no matter how high it is, and no one can cheat much on his tax if it's withheld, either. I'd like to see the federal government concentrate their investigative efforts toward the people whose income is derived from sources other than salary. I'd like to be able to look at the tax books and find out how much the guy with the house with the four-car garage and the chauffeur-driver Cadillac is paying because if he's getting off easier than I am, I'm damn sore about it.

A Dumb Idea, Made in Ohio

You want to hear something really dumb?

The State of Ohio has put into effect a "Buy Ohio" law, saying that any state agency has to buy things made in Ohio, even if they cost more and aren't as good as the same things made someplace else.

By implication, the law suggests that the ordinary citizens of Ohio, as well as government agencies, ought to buy products made in their own state.

The governor of Ohio explained what he thought was the necessity for the law by saying, "We have a lot of unemployment."

This makes Ohio different? Every state has a lot of unemployment.

Minnesota has a comparable law. A lot of states do. What would happen if all forty-eight states enacted similar laws of their own? What if they simply decided to strike back? What effect, for example, would a nationwide "Don't Buy Ohio!" campaign have?

What if neighbors of Ohio like Michigan, West Virginia and Pennsylvania started driving around with "DON'T BUY OHIO" bumper stickers?

If this law works for Ohio, and the others, perhaps the idea will spread. If states put up trade barriers between themselves, why shouldn't towns, counties and cities? Why should Cleveland buy products made in Akron when Cleveland has so many unemployed itself?

If that works, Berea, a relatively poor section of the Cleveland area, might start refusing to do business with Shaker Heights, a wealthy section.

Carried to its logical conclusion, this kind of economic isolation that Ohio is practicing could even spread into the home. This could be the salvation of America. If each one of us refused to do business with neighbors or anyone else, we'd all have to learn how to do things for ourselves to stay alive. We could become self-sufficient individuals again, building our own homes, growing our own food and making by hand the things we need in order to keep from doing business with anyone else. It could save the nation.

Short of that, there's nothing good about Ohio's plan to make it on its own. By asking the people of Ohio to be loyal to their state, legislators are asking them to be disloyal to the rest of the country. It's easier to be loyal to something small than something big. It's easier to be loyal to your family, your school or your town than it is to be loyal to the whole world or to the whole country. Loyalty, in the form of patriotism, has produced some good things, but it is basically an unthinking human reaction.

Under the patriotic stimulus of loyalty to the United States during World War II, this country produced better than at any time in its whole history. The only trouble with taking any pleasure from that is, Nazi loyalty to Adolf Hitler was the identical attribute. It produced the same extraordinary results, though. The fact that the effort was on behalf of evil doesn't bear on the quality of loyalty.

Loyalty to a country, a team, a family, a city, a school, without any question, isn't always good. Is it sadder that there are people in Ohio who don't have enough to eat because they aren't working than it is that there are hungry and unemployed people in New Jersey?

If our economy is going to be managed by our government, as it appears it has to be, it ought to be managed as a whole. It has to be done by the federal government, unpopular as that so often is. The economy can't be managed in little pieces, even pieces as big as Ohio.

There are good ways a government can use the enthusiasm of its citizens for their country, their state or their city, but "Buy Ohio" isn't one of them.

Revolutions

IT always amazed me that my mother lived from before the time we had automobiles until long after we had sent a spaceship to the moon. That's some lifespan.

From day to day, though, progress seems slow and often we don't notice what's happening around us. I realize now that I've lived through half a dozen major social or mechanical revolutions that I didn't see occurring at the time.

When I was very young and unable to understand what it was all about, Franklin Roosevelt was changing the whole way we took care of ourselves in this country. It was one of the most important things that ever happened here and I was oblivious to it. All I knew was that the few rich friends my parents had, hated Roosevelt. All their poor friends loved him. I didn't understand why.

At about the same time my father bought his first Atwater Kent radio. He used to sit in front of it nights and get stations like KDKA, Pittsburgh. A few years later the whole family sat in the living room listening to Ed Wynn, Eddie Cantor or "Myrt and Marge," the "Dallas" of its day.

I was about ten and I accepted the radio the same way I accepted running water in the house. I didn't realize it was new magic. I didn't realize I'd been in on a revolution, the beginning of radio.

Radio broke the ground for television and because we already had sound coming to us out of nowhere through the air, I was too dumb in 1949 to be amazed when they started sending us pictures, too. All I wanted to know was who was fighting.

In retrospect it makes me mad to think of all the big changes I watched happen and didn't notice. I went through World War II with a front-seat view of it and I knew how exciting it was but I was oblivious to the fact that I was watching history being made.

I'm trying to be more alert to events now. I'm trying to notice what's happening right before me and maintain some awareness of what the event will look like in a history book. There are about five things I have my eye on. Not necessarily in order of their importance, they are:

1—The Reagan Administration's dismantling of the system of government Roosevelt started. The bureaucracy grew for almost fifty years before Reagan started taking it apart. For better or for worse, it was a turning point in history.

2—The tendency of bright young men and women to marry later, if at all, and to have fewer children, if any, is the most important hidden revolution of our time. It could have a profound effect on the makeup of the human race.

3—The dramatic rise in quality of products made in Japan. The Japanese first took the camera business away from the Germans and then ended the worldwide dominance of the United States as the maker of automobiles. When Roosevelt was President, the phrase "Made in Japan" printed on anything, meant "cheap and poorly made." America's reputation for hard work and excellence has declined in proportion to Japan's progress.

4—The gradual intrusion into broadcast television of the cable networks and smaller, local broadcasters. We may find, in ten or twenty years, that we're looking back at the good old days when ABC, CBS and NBC had a virtual monopoly on the mass market and were therefore able to attract advertisers who could pay for expensive news coverage and elaborate dramatic productions. If it happens, it will be the reverse of what happened in the 1930s and 1940s when big supermarket chains took over small, independent grocery stores.

5—Money seems to be disappearing and I suspect the time isn't far off when cash won't be used except for small purchases. The computers will take the place of our pocketbooks and money will be transferred directly from my account to yours without anything material ever having changed hands between us. If someone wants to steal from us, he won't hit us over the head, he'll simply hit a few keys on the computer.

Twenty years from now I don't want to look back and say I didn't realize these things were happening.

The Generation War

IT seems likely that young people will be at war with old people in another fifteen or twenty years. You can see it coming in the numbers. In 1900 only one percent of the population was older than seventy-five years old and in a few years it's going to be five percent . . . 13 million people.

The trouble with being seventy-five years old, if you aren't rich, is that with inflation, everyone working keeps getting more and more dollars for what they do but the dollars you've saved stay the same and are worth less. You have less money and, sooner or later, you'll need more medical care.

We try to be nice to old people in this country but very often self-interest wins out over compassion. If the Social Security system breaks down—and it appears as though it might—the old will have to depend on the young to support them. I'm not talking about a son or daughter taking care of a mother or father. The young are not only going to have to do something for their own parents and grandparents but for everyone else's, too. Do you think young working people in twenty years will stand for a tax on their income that goes to support the elderly? Will they be willing to go without something for themselves in order to provide for a whole generation of the old? I think they'll rebel against it and it'll be war.

There's always plenty of evidence of friction between ages. For example, when there is a vote in any community on an issue involving schools, the lines are drawn along age boundaries. The old people who already have their education and whose children also have theirs, don't want to raise taxes to pay for better wages for teachers or a new wing for the school. The young people with children are in favor of better schools.

If war comes between youth and age, I'm not sure who'll win. You'd think it would be youth but age has a lot of power. Because of age's growing numbers and the degree to which it is united because it shares this one problem, it will elect a lot of people to government office. It will have a lot of influence in Congress.

On the other hand, older people don't have much influence on day-to-day affairs unless they have a lot of money. As soon as someone leaves a job at a company, he becomes powerless because no one's afraid of him any longer. To be powerful, you have to scare people. No one fears the elderly because they don't control jobs or anyone's destiny.

When the young see the old no longer doing what they did best in their lives, it's difficult for the young to believe they ever did anything very well. We always tend to think that even the best brains of the centuries past are inferior to our own. You can't believe the doddering old man of ninety ever ran a race or that the wrinkled, gray and bent woman of ninety was ever a beauty. The young sometimes honor the old but in their hearts they feel superior to them. The old hate the young for it and that's why the war will begin.

Prejudice toward age, any age, changes with birthdays. The ten-year-old feels vastly superior to the four-year-old but at about age thirty it becomes apparent that the eighteen- and twenty-year-olds can do things you can't. Having lost the feeling of superiority you used to have over the young, you look elsewhere for it.

By the time people are forty, they no longer feel at all physically superior to anyone twenty so they satisfy themselves feeling superior to those fifty. This continues for life. When my mother was eighty, she spoke in disparaging terms of several women who were still playing bridge at ninety. When my mother turned ninety she was convinced her bridge was as good as ever.

I hope I'm wrong about the war between generations that could be fought over money. I like both the young and the old and I wouldn't want anything like a war to come between them.

Executions

THERE'S an arugment going on all across the country about the best way to kill a person. Even states that have decided on capital punishment can't decide how a prisoner should be put to death.

There are thirty-seven states that have the death penalty now. Eighteen have approved the electric chair as the nicest way to kill a murderer, nine gas them to death, four give them lethal injections, four hang them by the neck from a rope and Idaho shoots them. The Governor of New Jersey says he's leaning toward the intravenous death method because it's the most humane.

I have such a vindictive streak in me that I am surprised to find myself in opposition to the death penalty. Some days getting back at someone is the most fun I have and yet I do not approve of society putting anyone to death. Most of the people in the United States who do approve think of themselves as Christians. I wonder whether Jesus Christ would have voted for or against the death penalty. I should think the people who worship Christ would suspect that he'd be against it.

Those of you who approve of the death penalty might be able to give New Jersey some advice on what you think the best way is to execute someone. It's one of the states that can't decide. Everyone is always looking for the most humane method but if you are among the people who think the death penalty is a deterrent to crime, putting someone to death in the most humane manner isn't the best way to get what you're after. If you want to scare criminals off murder, maybe you'd want to consider a law that would call for torturing them to death.

How about burying them in sand up to their chins and leaving them out in the hot sun? I've read where they do it that way in some Middle Eastern countries. That would sure deter any would-be murderer who can't take the heat, I should think.

Another thing you should consider as a deterrent is the firing squad. It's dramatic, it's long drawn out and if you also made it mandatory for the television networks to show it on the evening news, everyone would watch and think twice or perhaps even three or four times before murdering anyone.

I wouldn't want to be in the state legislature if I had to decide which was the best way of executing someone. When I was eight I was playing marbles with Buddy Duffey and he asked me if I had to kill either my mother or my father, which would I? I remember I refused to try and decide that and I feel the same way now about the death penalty. Being against the whole thing, I don't have to decide which method of execution is best.

My objection to the death penalty doesn't come out of any sympathy I have for the murderers. What I object to is making a murderer of anyone else. My objection could be eliminated, of course, by a simple addition to the capital punishment laws. Have the executions carried out by other people on death row who are already murderers. Make them strap the victims in the electric chair and throw the switch. If death is to come by hanging, make them slip the noose over the victim's head and drop him through the trapdoor.

To make capital punishment a real deterrent, there are a lot of things that should be done differently. Why give a murderer the "last meal"? Traditionally the person about to die can have what he wants as his last meal. Suddenly we're being nice to this guy? And should a doctor be present? Why the minister or priest? A doctor is a saver of life. Does the clergyman ask God's forgiveness for the murderer? Does God give it? If God forgives him, who are people to take his life?

The Dead Land

It is difficult to understand how people who talk as much about being religious and about loving their country as Americans do, can so consistently spoil what they've been blessed with. Too many of us throw the debris from a McDonald's Quarter Pounder out the car window. Too many young people throw their Coke or beer bottles on someone else's lawn as they drive by Saturday night and too many major American industries dig up the good things out of the earth, spit out what they can't use and produce poisonous waste by-products that are eventually going to kill the land and then us.

> "This is the way the world ends
> Not with a bang but a whimper."

T.S. Eliot wrote that in a poem called "The Hollow Men" fifty years ago and it was sadly prophetic. While the leaders of government everywhere are worrying about the Big Bomb, mankind everywhere is poisoning the ground and the waters we depend on for life.

I drive alongside the East River down the edge of the island of Manhattan on my way to work most mornings. The garbage barges are loaded high with all the sophisticated debris the twentieth century produces in such abundance. The barges will shortly be towed out into the Atlantic Ocean and dumped. And again tomorrow and tomorrow and tomorrow. It's a big ocean but we will certainly someday have ruined its clear, briny beauty with garbage.

How can anyone who professes to love this country or even the earth and life itself, *not* be an environmentalist? Maybe we need a better word than that. How can a businessman or a government official think and say that there is such a thing as environmental "extremism"? We are going to die or the inhabitants of the earth in future generations are going to die because the land and the water are all poisoned. Is anything more certain than that? Do we ignore it because for us today it is only a few people living near the Love Canal or in the dioxin-contaminated town of Times Beach, Missouri?

I don't think you blame Big Business for having dumped toxic wastes. Big Business wasn't malicious. It didn't set out with the intention of killing anyone. Big Business was just selfish and stupid, that's all. Big Business is just like the kid who throws the beer can out the car window. "What difference does one more make?" "This place is a mess anyway." He's not a bad kid.

Americans have taken most of their money out of the savings banks. They're spending it to live now and let the future take care of itself. That's what all of us everywhere are doing with the earth. We're using it up for ourselves with no thought of the future. Does anyone think oil prices are going to keep going down the next ten years? The next fifty years? There won't be any oil in one hundred years but you'd never believe it if you were from another planet watching what the people on earth are doing with what oil they have left. Those Arabs giving gold watches and hundred-dollar bills as tips to the help in the London hotels where they're staying, will have nothing but sand in abundance within the lifetime of almost all of us.

It's strange that the word ''conservative'' is so often applied to people who don't believe in conserving anything but money. Their environmental philosophy is consistent with their economic beliefs. They honestly believe that everything works out for the best if you let everyone get all they can for themselves. They believe this is what produces the most for all of us.

Whatever else it produces, it sure produces a lot of garbage.

VIII:

SEASONS

The Fourth of July

THE Fourth of July is the second-best holiday. Christmas is first, hands down, but the Fourth is way ahead of anything else. After them come Thanksgiving, New Year's Day, Labor Day, Memorial Day, Washington's Birthday, Easter and the late starter, Columbus Day. I hope no one will be offended if I put Martin Luther King Day last.

Christmas is heavy with tradition and sentiment. It's a joyous time but it's often sad, too. You get thinking at Christmas so it has more depth. The Fourth is a mindless holiday. We celebrate our independence and we mean it and appreciate it but mostly July Fourth is a time to go out and have a good time.

The Fourth is nothing *but* relaxing. You don't have to give presents, you don't have to send cards, you don't have to do anything if you don't want to.

I remember the Fourth with great fondness because I'm old enough to have been a kid when it was legal to buy real fireworks. Just offhand, I don't recall ever having had more fun in my life than I had setting off fireworks. I know they're dangerous and I'd have been awfully nervous if my own children had shot them off but some of the best money my father ever spent giving me a good time was on the two dollars he put out every year on a bag of fireworks. Watching the professionals set off a display of rockets from the park or the town mall is fun but it doesn't compare with having a few four-inchers of your own.

July Fourth is the beginning of the serious goof-off time in America. The people who take their vacations in August don't break their backs working in July, either.

Along about Thursdays at noon at this time of year, people are beginning to say, "Have a nice weekend" to me. These are the same people who see me in the elevator Tuesday morning and say, "How was your weekend?"

There's no doubt about it, it takes the week longer to end in July. People who have never been sick a day in their lives often don't feel too good on Fridays in July so they don't come to work. Whatever they have lasts until Monday noon, when they show up again for work with a sunburn.

I haven't checked recently but I've been wondering what the statistics are in Detroit these days when it comes to auto workers calling in sick. It used to amount to as much as twenty percent of the work force in summer and again in the fall when thousands of suddenly sick auto workers went hunting in upper Michigan.

I don't want to be negative about long weekends. They're nice if the economy can afford them. Most companies give their workers long vacations now in addition to ten "sick" days. Calling in sick is standard procedure in many businesses and you can understand it. We all have personal problems to take care of. You certainly can't handle any personal business problem on Saturday or Sunday, so if you have personal business to conduct, there's not much to do but call in and lie by saying you're sick. There are good companies that recognize this and allow several "personal" days every year. I like that better than "sick" days. Sick days should be reserved for the days when you're sick and if you aren't sick, you shouldn't have to say you are.

The Japanese are using robots in their factories now and we have some in this country. Robots do the work that assembly-line workers used to do and I suppose the time will come in another hundred years when the robots will be getting five weeks' vacation plus ten sick days a year. Their union, the URW, the United Robot Workers, will insist on it.

The actual "Fourth" is inconvenient when it falls on a Sunday. Because that's a normal day off, we compensate for it by taking Monday. You can't plan on transacting any important business on Friday, either. Office phones don't answer.

The people I feel sorriest for on these long summer weekends are not the employers. They know where their next million is coming from. I feel sorry for people looking for work in July. How can you look for work if there's no one in at the place you go to, to look for work?

Summer—First the Good News

THERE are good things and bad things about summer and you can just about divide them in half. I've made a list.

GOOD THINGS ABOUT SUMMER: It's nice and warm.

BAD THINGS ABOUT SUMMER: It's too hot.

GOOD: If you're working, there aren't many people around the office. The boss is usually away and it's relaxing.

BAD: If you're working, there's no one around to make decisions and you can't get anything done.

GOOD: Packing up, going away and leaving all your problems behind at the office.

BAD: Having the nervous feeling while you're on vacation that you're missing something important back at work. Someone's getting ahead of you.

GOOD: Having a drink in the backyard in the evening.

BAD: Mosquitoes.

GOOD: Corn on the cob and real, ripe, red tomatoes.

BAD: Disappointingly hard peaches and tasteless melons.

GOOD: A swim in water that feels too cold when you first get in and so good after you've been in awhile that you don't want to get out.

BAD: So many people at the lake or the beach that going in the water is no fun.

GOOD: Waking up on vacation and realizing you don't have to go to work.

BAD: Waking up on vacation and realizing you only have four days of vacation left.

GOOD: Visiting places you've always wanted to go to.

BAD: Driving forever to get someplace you didn't want to go to anyway.

GOOD: An air-conditioned car on a hot day.

BAD: Getting into a car that's been closed up and parked in the sun.

GOOD: Being out in the sun and getting a tan that makes you look great.

BAD: The nervous feeling you ought not be out in the sun so much because it's bad for your skin and will make you look old sooner.

GOOD: The long hours of sunlight in July.

BAD: The realization in August that the days are getting shorter and it'll be all downhill from now on.

GOOD: Friends you don't see any other time of year.

BAD: People you can't avoid because everything's so open in summer.

GOOD: The satisfying feeling mowing the lawn can give you.

BAD: Realizing the grass is so long you have to mow it even though you don't feel like mowing the lawn today.

GOOD: Going someplace on vacation that's a complete change from home.

BAD: Leaving a perfectly good, comfortable home to stay at some resort that's too expensive and not as pleasant as what you left behind.

GOOD: An old pair of sneaks, a short-sleeve cotton shirt and cool khaki slacks.

BAD: Having to wear a hot suit and tie to work because that's how people dress at work.

GOOD: Not having to drive to work in heavy traffic during your vacation.

BAD: Leaving for a weekend in heavy traffic Friday afternoon and coming home in it Sunday evening.

GOOD: The peace and quiet and comforting sounds of crickets, bullfrogs and birds in the morning.

BAD: The blare of rock music from some kid's car radio as he drives past with his windows open and the noise of your neighbor's lawn mower.

GOOD: Cooking outdoors. It can make tough meat taste good.

BAD: Cooking outdoors. It can make good meat taste tough.

GOOD: No snow.

BAD: No snow.

August

THE last two weeks of August are the dregs of the fifty-two weeks of the year. If we ever have to drop two weeks out of the year, we should drop these.

Everything about the end of August is depressing. There's that foreboding of the death of a season in the air. There are reminders all around us that this is the end of something good and none of us likes to see a good thing end.

From the middle of August on, the threat of Labor Day looms big in our minds. We know it's coming. We count the days. The summer is dwindling down to nothing. The grass is turning brown and the plants and flowers are just holding on. They are no longer blooming. Blooming suggests robust good health and flowers are no longer like that.

The little streams and creeks that are so attractive when they're running their merry way downhill are all but dried up at this time of year and the rocks in the bottom of the streambed that like to be covered with water are baking in the hot sun. They're nowhere near as attractive as they are when magnified by a foot of water running over them.

There is no other time of year when we all become so aware of how quickly time passes and how soon the seasons go. At New Year's we cover the passing of time with the false gaiety of New Year's Eve but at the end of August with school and work and winter facing us, we can't hide from the fact that it's the definite end to another time of our lives. It is not a question of age. I have had this very same feeling about the end of August since I was eight years old.

"Never return in August to what you love."

That's a line from a poem by Bernice Kenyon. I often think of it when I go back to that place where I spent my summers as a kid. It's almost too sad to contemplate those times I had back then. August is such a sad time for remembering past good times and friends long gone out of your life. Funny thing is, I go back there in July sometimes and never feel depressed at all.

It's tough on all of us, though. Getting up in the morning is even harder. During June and July the sun shines in the bedroom window and you can jump out of bed with some enthusiasm for life. In August we begin to drag a little. It's been hot for too long. It's a little darker out because the sun isn't really up yet and we're more apt to lie in bed thinking bad thoughts or turn over and go back to sleep after the clock radio goes off. The birds aren't chirping the way they were earlier in the summer and all of nature seems to be tired. The birds have all found mates. They've made their nests, hatched their eggs and flown the coop. The plants and the birds and the bees and the bugs all know Labor Day's coming too and they don't like the prospects either. They have no more enthusiasm for the waning days of summer than I do.

The trouble with the last two weeks of August may be that we've gotten in the habit of looking ahead too much instead of enjoying what we've got at the moment. The end of August would be okay if we didn't keep thinking about summer being almost over but everything reminds us of its imminent ending. The stores are having half-off sales and the advertisements in the papers are for fall clothes. It's too hot for football but they're playing it and reminding us of fall. The economic news is all about "after Labor Day." How can we ignore the fact that summer is almost over? It's all this looking ahead that makes the last weeks of August so depressing.

It's not August's fault, it's our own.

Cannibals and Nuns

WELL, finally. It's over. I don't have to anticipate its ending with dread any longer. It's been just one damn summer weekend after another. If summer had lasted another month I might have died from all that relaxation.

I can stand a little vacation but things are getting ridiculous. Our vacation period in America lasts from Memorial Day at the end of May until the Tuesday after Labor Day in September now.

Don't tell me you only get three weeks. That's just your *real* vacation. I'm talking about all the days off and long weekends we all take in addition to our vacation.

It hardly matters anymore which three weeks or months anyone takes off. You can't find them at work when they aren't on vacation in the summer either.

The necessity of having fun in the summer is one of the most tiring things of the whole year for me. My idea of a good restful week is to get up at the same time every morning, eat breakfast with the newspaper, go to work, work, come home tired, have dinner, read, watch television and go to bed by eleven. That's what I call relaxing.

The tiring part of a vacation is planning to go somewhere, getting ready to go there, getting everyone else organized to go there and then getting there. Just as soon as you get there, you have to start planning how to get back.

I'll bet I could add ten years to my life if I didn't have to take all these summer vacations. When I'm on vacation I don't get enough sleep, I worry because I spend too much money, I do too much driving, I eat too much and drink too much. Sometimes it's two weeks after I return from a vacation or a long weekend before I feel rested again.

There used to be a game we played when I was a kid

called Missionaries and Cannibals. I forget the exact rules but the situation was this:

There are three missionaries or nuns on one side of the river and two cannibals on the other. There is only one canoe and you can only carry two people in the canoe at one time. You have to get the three nuns to one side of the river and the two cannibals to the other without ever having a cannibal and a nun in the canoe together.

I'm always reminded of that game by the family logistics of a summer weekend. My wife and I go to a country house we have and often several of our children join us there. They come from different places at different times using different modes of transportation.

The problems are always these:

"What time can you leave?"

"Do you want to go with us or should Emily wait and pick you up?"

"If they're driving from Boston they can meet you at the railroad station when you come in from New York."

My wife leaves from home in her car and I leave from the office in mine. The operation is complicated by the fact that our home is an hour from my office but my office and our home are equal distances from the summer house. Every weekend we have a problem getting the nuns across the river without being eaten by the cannibals.

There are so many things about the summer that are tiring. Someone's always suggesting a picnic, for example. You have a nice house with a table to eat from and chairs to sit on and an icebox to go to, but people aren't satisfied in the summer unless they're breaking their backs having a good time. They want to rough it and go on a picnic. What you do is, you put all the food except what you forget in a basket and take it somewhere uncomfortable. Then you sit on the ground or perhaps on a hard rock and share lunch with an ant.

It feels great to have Labor Day over with. I've only been back to work a couple of days now but already I'm beginning to feel relaxed and rested.

The Best Snowstorm of the Decade

WHEN you read about a terrible storm in some other part of the country, you feel a little smug. You feel sorry for people you see on television being flooded out or blown away but you also feel superior to them. At least you were smart enough not to live in a house that could be washed away by the sea or floated downstream by a river.

Last weekend it was our turn in the Northeast to be shown to the rest of the country because of twenty inches of snow we got. Businesses shut down, roads were closed, cars abandoned on highways and the government in Washington was brought to a standstill by Friday noon. It couldn't happen to a nicer government.

Meteorologists were calling it "one of the worst snowstorms of the decade." That's what they usually call snowstorms.

Well, if you live someplace else and got any satisfaction from thinking we were having it bad, I don't want to take it away from you but I thought it was the *best* snowstorm of the decade. I loved every minute of it. Let me tell you about it.

The storm moved up the coast from Virginia and hit New York and Connecticut Friday night after most people were home from work. We had dinner and watched Robert Mitchum fight World War II for a while but I kept getting up to check the snowfall against the streetlight on the corner. It was still coming. There were none of those big, feathery, infrequent flakes that portend the end of a snow. These were those serious little ones in a hurry to get to the ground.

We live in Connecticut and by midafternoon the state weather bureau had called off the snowstorm warning it had issued earlier. That was a good sign. We all know how weather predicting has been going this year.

When I finally got up and turned off the television set—I know how World War II comes out—there was the kind of absolute silence I've only heard a few times in my life. (You do hear silence.) No car lights flashed from the street into our windows and if there were any sounds from the highway a mile away, they were muffled by a billion trillion of those magic, fluffy white geometric wonders piled ten inches deep now, outside our door. All the people who usually have to go someplace in their cars in the middle of the night, suddenly didn't have to go anyplace. Nothing moved except the snowflakes.

In the morning I went into the bathroom and looked out the window through the plants on the window shelves. The telephone wires leading into the house had three inches of snow balanced in a precarious parabola on them. Down below, the backyard looked perfect. If I ever wanted to sell the house, I'd have it look that way for a prospective buyer. Every flaw was hidden . . . the crabgrass, the old boards I'd left by the driveway, the bare spots . . . all were painted over with snow.

We had breakfast at the kitchen table looking out the window on the backyard. We had orange juice, good coffee, homemade bread toasted, with peach jam and black currant jelly. It was the same breakfast we have every Saturday but it never tasted so good.

After breakfast I pulled on my boots, put on a heavy wool shirt, a down vest and my good leather gloves. I couldn't find my old ones. I waxed the aluminum snow shovel with something I'd used on the car (I was very pleased with myself over this because the snow slid off it so quickly). My wife didn't like her shovel but you can't worry about someone else's tools.

By 5:30 we were dog-tired. We had a drink, broiled chicken, rice and broccoli. After a nap in the living room I fell into bed by nine P.M.

Every day in my life should be so satisfying and trouble-free as the day "one of the worst storms of the decade" hit us.

'Tis the Season to Be Worried

It's still early to start worrying about Christmas presents but this is the time I start to worry about them. I worry from now until somewhere around the twentieth of December before I buy anything.

First I make a list of the people I want to give presents to. There are twelve this year. Margie buys the one for my sister so that leaves me with eleven. I buy more than one for several people on my list though, so it's a lot of purchases, a lot of boxes. I take Christmas seriously.

Let me talk to you about seven categories of Christmas presents:

Jewelry—Some of the people on my list like it but it makes me nervous to buy. If it's junk jewelry with no real value except for decoration, it has to strike the person you buy it for just right. I don't think you can predict what kind of jewelry a woman will like. Real jewelry is nice to own but if it's really real, it costs more than I spend. I don't know who has money enough to buy rubies, diamonds, emeralds and pearls. I have had some success with small gold or silver jewelry.

Books—People like to get books. A book is a flattering present and so expensive now that people don't often buy them for themselves. A book suited to the person is a perfect present. In past years members of my family have given me a lot of woodworking books and I love getting them. Anyone with a hobby likes getting a good book devoted to it.

Perfume—I don't know a woman to whom I'd give perfume. I don't know a man I would either, for that matter. I remember giving perfume years ago but I guess I've changed. I don't like perfume on a woman any better than I like sitting next to a man who is smoking a cigar in a restaurant.

Cameras and electronics—I'm mildly embarrassed to tell you that in the years I've had money to spend, I've spent more of it on these things than anything else. I've given cameras, lenses, tape recorders, television sets and assorted electronic gadgets. There's no doubt what the biggest mistake in gift giving is. We always give the things we like ourselves rather than giving much consideration to what the gift getter would like. I suppose I've got to see if there's a computer I can afford to give anyone this year.

Toys—Ever since the kids passed the age of seventeen, I've been out of the toy market. I've looked in the windows of several toy stores and I don't know what I'm going to do when I have toy-age grandchildren. So many of the toys today look like junk I'd hate to waste my money on them.

Clothes—I consider my wife and my three daughters good-looking and I always think of them in some of the good-looking clothes I see in stores. The family is reluctant to hurt my feelings so they usually say the clothes I've bought them don't fit but I suspect they take them back because they don't like what I picked out. I don't know why I think I can do it. I don't recall ever getting a piece of clothing as a gift that *I* liked. As a kid, I was always disappointed to open a package and find clothes. The last thing a kid wants for Christmas is something practical.

Cooking utensils or food—These are dependable fall-back gifts when you can't think of anything else. Over the years friends have sent us oranges and grapefruit, nuts or cheese from those specialty catalogues and those items are always good to get. You have to think of those things in advance though, so I don't give fruit or nuts from catalogues. I almost always find a pot, a pan, a knife or an electric kitchen gadget to give.

As a general rule, I buy books in bookstores, hardware in hardware stores, jewelry in jewelry stores. I also buy presents from big, dependable, non-cut-rate department stores. I know I don't get any bargains from the department stores but I don't get cheated, either.

Christmas Shopping

JIM hates buying anything," Ruth said when the four of us were having dinner a few weeks ago.

Jim was sitting right there and he didn't deny it, so I assumed it was true.

Ruth wasn't suggesting Jim was cheap—although Jim may be a little cheap. She was simply saying that he doesn't like the whole process of buying something.

I do. I like buying things. It's a flaw in my character.

This Christmas I've really been buying things and it hasn't always been a wonderful experience.

Stores are incredibly different from what they were a relatively short time ago. You used to go into a store, ask the clerk for what you wanted and he or she would get it down off a shelf for you.

I wasn't talking about grocery stores when I started this but grocery stores are the most dramatic examples of change. When I was little, my mother would often send me to the grocery store. I'd stand in front of the counter, looking up at Mr. Evans, and tell him what I wanted. He'd get it off the shelf behind him, put it in a bag on the counter and hand it to me.

People never touched anything in a grocery store. If someone else came in while Mr. Evans was getting my order, they waited until he was finished.

That's the way most stores operated. It didn't matter whether they were selling clothes, hardware or candy. Everything was behind the counter and the customers didn't mingle with the merchandise.

You were waited on.

These days, and especially at this time of year, you're lucky if you can find someone in a store to take your money. It must lead to some shoplifting by people who didn't go there intending to steal.

There are at least a dozen truly great department stores in the United States and I like to do business with them. I hesitate to mention them for fear of missing some but you know which they are. In New York City, Bloomingdale's is one. It's a trend-setter among stores. Even though I don't always like the trends it sets, I love the store and often go there.

If Bloomingdale's charged admission, I'd go there just to look. There are hundreds of theaters I've paid to get into that weren't as good shows as Bloomingdale's is any day of the week.

At this time of year, I still go there but I don't always buy something. I would if I could but there's a limited amount of time I'm willing to spend finding a salesperson to push my money on and I don't have infinite patience with the store's paperwork. There are a lot of security people Bloomingdale's has hired to keep shoplifting down and it leads to a lot of protective pieces of paper.

The day is gone when you can get what you want, put the money down and leave. Sometimes it must cost the store more for the clerk's time in wages than the item itself costs.

Today I went to a store that is not one of the great ones. You'd know it. I was after a toolbox to give as a gift. In the hardware area I saw a huge sign over one with ten drawers.

"SAVE $100! REGULARLY $199. TODAY ONLY $99."

It was, typically for the store, an adequate but not first-class piece of merchandise. When I collared a clerk, I said quickly, so he wouldn't leave, "I'll take one of these."

"We'll have to see if we have one," he said.

"What do you mean 'See if we have one'?" I said. "If you don't have one in stock, I'll take this one."

"We can't sell the floor sample," he said.

"Well, you can't advertise it for sale either, then," I said, noticing that my voice was rising.

Christmas shopping hasn't been easy for any of us this year. The only thing worse than not being able to get anyone to wait on you at Christmas is having the clerks all over you at other times of the year when they aren't busy.

"Can I show you something?" they ask. Ten feet further along the aisle, the next clerk says, "May we help you?"

Sometimes I can understand why Jim feels the way he does about shopping.

No Room at the Inn

MAKING room for things in a house is never easy, but at Christmas it becomes even more difficult.

The other day I came in with some packages and looked for an easy place to put them down. There was none and I realized that even the telephone book takes up more space than it ought to. If it had a stiff cover, you could stand it up and there'd be more room on the telephone table.

When I look around the house and think about the problem, it becomes apparent to me that a lot of household items take up too much room.

The chief offender and probably the worst space hog is the vacuum cleaner. I could hide six Christmas presents in the space the vacuum cleaner takes up.

The importance of the vacuum cleaner has been exaggerated in America. A lot of people use it more from nervous habit than because anything needs vacuuming. The vacuum makes so much noise it gives them the feeling they're doing something important. It certainly takes up more space than it's worth. It doesn't take it up in a nice way, either.

The vacuum cleaner is clumsy and impossible to store in a tidy way. It comes with a lot of little attachments you don't want and several lengths of hose you don't need. You can't pack it away, so you just have to shove it in a closet where it occupies valuable space all its life.

What the world needs is a folding vacuum cleaner that fits into a shoebox.

The second biggest space hog in the average house is the chair, often antique, that no one sits on. They don't sit on it because they know that if they do, it will break. They also know it's uncomfortable.

I like to hide small Christmas presents under some things in my dresser drawers. The problem there is shirts. I have about eight good shirts but I have eight more that are too good to throw away and not good enough to wear out in public. These are Saturday morning shirts. They prevent me from burying anything but the thinnest Christmas presents among them.

There's no room for anything extra in the garage at Christmas. Over the years I've put up various hooks and hangers along the side walls but the snow shovel sticks out so far the car door bangs against it when you try to climb out carrying packages. The leaf rake and the garbage cans are no help, either.

As a result of this seasonal storage emergency, I take special measures. I put presents and other items I have to get out of sight for a few weeks in emergency storage areas.

The prime emergency storage area in anyone's house is under the bed. I put a lot of stuff under the bed at Christmas. We have six beds in our house and we could use six more. We have enough for people to sleep in but we could use more for storing things under.

In the winter I don't use the trunk of the car as much as in the summer so I end up leaving things in the car that I should bring into the house. I don't empty out the trunk of the car until Christmas Eve.

The basement and the attic of the house are about full, so the last place where there's a little emergency room is up the back stairway. If you have a back stairway, don't overlook it as a place to put some things temporarily. We don't ordinarily use the back stairway although we try to keep it clear of debris for most of the year. It has thirteen steps going up to the landing and at this time of year I turn those thirteen steps into thirteen little shelves on which I keep things. I leave about six inches on the side of each step as a place to step so I can still use them.

One warning: Keep careful track of the emergency storage areas you use for Christmas presents. A few days after July Fourth this year, I dropped a quarter under the bed and when I got down on my knees to look for it, I discovered a Christmas present I'd forgotten to give my sister in 1974.

Struck by the Christmas Lull

A STRANGE lull sets in sometime during the afternoon of Christmas Day in our house.

The early-morning excitement is over, the tension is gone and dinner isn't ready yet. One of our problems may be that we don't have Christmas dinner until about six. We plan it for four but we have it at six.

The first evidence of any non-Christmas spirit usually comes about one o'clock. We've had a big, late breakfast that didn't end until 9:30 or 10:00 and the dishes for that aren't done until after we open our presents.

Washing the breakfast dishes runs into getting Christmas dinner. The first little flare-up comes when someone wanders into the kitchen and starts poking around looking for lunch. With dinner planned for four o'clock, there's no lunch on the schedule. Margie's busy trying to get the cranberry jelly out of the molds and she isn't interested in serving lunch or having anyone get their own. To her, at this point, food means dirty dishes.

It isn't easy to organize the meals over a Christmas weekend. Everyone is always complaining about eating too much one minute and out in the kitchen looking for food the next. We might be able to get away with just two meals if we had Christmas dinner at two. I forget why we don't but we don't.

We have thirteen people this year. The lull will strike them all but each will handle it differently.

A few will sit around the living room. Someone will decide to tidy up the place by putting all the wrapping paper and ribbons in a big, empty box that held a Christmas present a few hours earlier.

I don't do any of this because I love the mess. As soon as you clean up the living room, Christmas is over.

At one end of the couch, someone will be reading the newspaper. It's usually pretty thin. There isn't much news and very little advertising. One of the editors has had a reporter do the story about what the homeless will be having for Christmas dinner at the Salvation Army kitchen, but it's slim pickin's in the paper.

My sister Nancy sits there reading out Christmas cards and looking at presents given to other people which she missed when they were being opened.

There are usually a few nappers. Someone will hog the whole couch by stretching out and falling asleep on it. The smart, serious nappers will disappear into an upstairs bedroom.

One of the kids will be working on or putting together a present he or she got. Someone will be reading a new book. (No one watches television in our house on Christmas Day.)

At some point there's a flurry of phone calls, in and out. We'll start making calls to other members of the family who can't be there or who are close but not in our inner circle. Usually one of the twins' classmates will call to see if they can get together during the few days they're both in town.

There's always someone who wants to know if the drugstore is open. They don't really want anything, they're just looking for some excuse to get out of the house.

If I've been given some new tool, I go down to the basement and try it out on a piece of wood. That's usually interrupted by a call from the head of the stairs asking if I want to go over to the indoor courts and play tennis. I'm always touched by the fact the kids want me to play tennis with them. It wouldn't be because I pay for the courts, would it?

By about four o'clock the Christmas Day lull is over. We all congregate in the living room again to have a drink. Nancy has slow-baked almonds and pecans which have been kept hidden from Brian and Ellen all day.

Everyone's relaxed again now. Dinner's ready but a Christmas dinner can be put on hold, so there's no rush. A turkey is better left at least half an hour after it comes out of the oven before it's carved. Mashed potatoes, creamed onions and squash are all easy to keep warm. The peppermint candy cane ice cream stays frozen.

I hate to have Christmas end.

Reverse Resolutions

THOSE of us who hate New Year's Eve and the necessity it brings with it to have fun, look forward to New Year's Day, when New Year's Eve is over.

For years I've been fighting a losing battle to make September first New Year's Day but no one will listen. If we had changed the date on which the new year starts, August thirty-first would be our next New Year's Eve and we wouldn't be faced with this unpleasantness on the last day of December. We always go to a good party but I don't even like good parties on New Year's Eve. I just want to be alone that night feeling miserable about all I didn't get done in the year past and all the hard jobs I have ahead of me in the following year.

Inevitably you think of any new year as a beginning . . . even if it comes at the wrong time of year.

Beginnings are exciting because we never learn. Every time we start something new, we think it's going to be better than it was last time. Fortunately, we're all optimists. We forget everything that can go wrong and concentrate on how it will be if everything goes right. We look forward to a pleasant experience.

Our optimism makes beginnings a happy time. If we knew how long it was going to take us and all the trouble we were going to have with ninety-nine percent of the jobs we start, we'd never start them. This ability we have to put past difficulties out of our minds is one of the wonders of the human brain.

Several years ago I listed some resolutions I resolved not to make. I have more this year.

—I'm not going to stop eating coffee ice cream. I resolved not to eat it two years ago and it made me miserable. This year I'm not promising myself anything in regard to ice cream. Maybe I will and maybe I won't.

—I'm not going to smoke cigarettes this year. This is the best kind of resolution for me. I can absolutely promise this is a resolution I'll keep. I've never smoked cigarettes and it isn't likely I'll start now.

—I'm not going to try to exercise very much this year. Last winter I played twice a week with Cronkite and felt terrible. Walter's so busy since he retired that he isn't playing either. I saw him last week and he looks in great shape. Not playing tennis must agree with him, too.

—I'm not going to try to save all the pennies I take out of my pockets every night. Three weeks ago I spent several hours one night counting the pennies I'd saved. Have you any idea how much room 2,437 pennies takes up in boxes, cans and dresser drawers? All this time I've been thinking of myself as rich because of my pennies. After counting them, I realized I had exactly $24.37.

—I'm not going to be as loyal to the company. Every

time I'm loyal to the company, management changes and whatever I was being loyal to is gone. I'm left holding my loyalty.

—I'm not going to try to keep from being cynical if the situation calls for cynicism.

So, Happy New Year. If you drink, don't drive and if you drink and drive, don't do it near me.

IX:

A TIME TO WRITE

Ecclesiastes

I AM sitting, at the moment, in a hotel room in Beverly Hills. It is late but I don't feel sleepy. I have nothing to read and there's nothing on television I want to watch.

I have found the Gideon Bible in a dresser drawer next to the bed and I've opened it to Ecclesiastes. I only read parts of the Bible I already know. I've always found the Bible difficult to read and I've never started from the beginning and read it through. I don't know anyone else who has, either.

When you read the Bible in its old-fashioned, stilted English, you get the impression that you're reading the actual words as they were written or spoken so long ago. Ecclesiastes was written in Hebrew not English, of course, and I suppose this version I have in front of me represents the work of hundreds of editors and rewriters through the ages. Even so, it has a wonderful rhythm to it:

"To every thing there is a season, and a time to every purpose under the heaven:

—A time to be born, and a time to die; a time to plant, and a time to pluck up that which has been planted;

—A time to kill, and a time to heal; a time to break down, and a time to build up;

—A time to weep and a time to laugh; a time to mourn and a time to dance;

—A time to cast away stones, and a time to gather stones together; a time to embrace, and a time to refrain from embracing.''

Some of that is just great but some of it needs rewriting. It has obviously been updated many times and probably should be modernized again now. ''A time to cast away stones'' doesn't mean much to us and there might be a better way to put ''A time to kill, and a time to heal.''

The world needs the wisdom the Bible has to offer but it has to be readable or not many people are going to read it. It has to pertain to our lives today as we live them and not to some ancient time we don't understand. There are biblical scholars working on revising the Bible right now in both England and the United States and I respectfully suggest there's some work to be done on Ecclesiastes.

Here are some additions I'd like future editors of the Bible to consider including in Ecclesiastes:

—There is a time to travel and a time to stay home and not go anywhere at all.

—A time to play basketball which shall be in the wintertime and a time to knock it off with basketball which shall be as the wintertime comes to an end and not in June.

—A time to play the radio too loud and a time to turn the radio and television set off and let silence pervade all the house.

—A time to gather together wordly goods and a time to throw stuff away.

—A time to make telephone calls and a time to get off the telephone and go to work.

—There is a time to get up in the morning even if you don't feel like getting up and a time to go to bed at night even if you don't feel like going to bed.

—There is a time for exercise and a time for lying down and taking a little nap.

—A time for putting chocolate sauce on vanilla ice cream and a time for eating vanilla ice cream without chocolate sauce.

—A time to go to the movies and a time to watch the movies on television and a time not to watch movies at all.

—A time to read the sports pages and a time to turn away from the sports pages and read what's really going on in the world.

—There is a time to have a dog and a time not to have a dog.

—A time to walk, a time to run, a time to take a train or a plane and a time to let your fingers do the walking.

—A time to start writing and a time to finish writing.

An Interview with Andy Rooney

ANYONE attracted to the rugged features of his handsome countenance might at first glance fail to observe the piercing intelligence of Andy Rooney's steel-blue eyes.''

That's the way I'd like to have an article about me

begin. In the past year I've been interviewed twenty times by reporters and none of them has started a piece that way. The articles have been friendly and many of them well done but no one who reads anything about himself is ever totally satisfied. Do they have to point out I'm grumpy? Must the reporter mention that my clothes are unpressed? Is it necessary to say that I'm overweight and getting gray?

What follows are some guidelines for reporters who wish to interview me in the future. I'd like to have the report go more like this:

"Rooney, who wears his expensive but tasteful clothes with a casual grace that conceals his position as one of the style setters in the men's fashion world, talked to this reporter in his hotel suite where he draped his taut, muscular frame over an easy chair.

"Considered by critics to be the leading essayist in print and broadcasting, Andy was disarmingly diffident when this reporter compared his work with that of Mark Twain, Hemingway, Robert Benchley, E. B. White, Walter Lippmann and Art Buchwald.

" 'Shucks,' he said modestly as he dug his toe into the deep pile rug of the carpet in his penthouse suite, 'I don't know about that.'

"Although it is not widely publicized," this article about me would continue if I had my way, "Andy Rooney might well be known as a modern-day Chippendale, were his mastery of the cabinetmaker's art not overshadowed by his genius with the English language.

"On the tennis court, Andy's serve has often been compared to that of John McEnroe. He moves with a catlike quickness that belies his age.

" 'Andy is wonderful to work with,' says his wife, Marguerite. 'He's always good-natured and a joy to have around the house. I can't recall an argument we've had in all the years of our marriage.'

"Rooney's four children, Ellen, Martha, Emily and Brian, are all perfect, too.

"On the average day, Andy rises at 4:30 A.M. By 6:00 A.M., because of his unusual ability to read 600 words a minute, he has finished two newspapers and *Time* magazine. His photographic memory enables him to store anything he has read for long periods of time and it is partly this ability that makes it easy for him to turn out three interesting, accurate, informative and perceptive essays each week.

"Of his friend, Harry Reasoner says, 'I only wish I could write as well as Andy does.'

"During our interview, Rooney got several telephone calls. William Buckley called to ask his advice on a point of grammar. There was a call from someone identified only as 'Ron' asking for advice on the economy. A third call came from E. F. Hutton asking Andy how he thought the stock market would behave in the days ahead."

I'm going to clip this out of the newspaper now and carry it with me wherever I go. If a young reporter wishes to interview me, I'll show it to him, just to give him some idea how I think his report should read. There's no sense having reporters waste a lot of time getting the facts.

Graduationese

THE headline reads, GRADUATES TO FIND JOBS SCARCE.

How many times have you read that story?

I don't offhand recall any year that wasn't the most difficult there ever was for graduating seniors to find jobs.

Each of us, at one time or another in our lives, has had a tough time finding a job, so we're sympathetic. We want to help. We don't want to give them a job, but we want to help.

The speakers at high school and college graduation ceremonies want to help by giving advice. I've been reading excerpts from some of the speeches.

For some reason, giving a commencement address brings out the worst in a speaker. Otherwise bright, normal, nice people turn themselves into pompous asses for the day. Years ago I spoke to the graduating class at the high school I attended, and I shudder to think what I told them and what my attitude was while I did it.

Pompous speeches are not necessarily the speaker's fault. That's what a commencement speech is supposed to be. The speaker is there to give the ceremony some importance so he or she has to say some important-sounding things.

(I don't know who makes the decision about whether to call it "graduation" or "commencement."

There's a big difference in attitude between the two words. "Graduation" suggests students have finished with something and "commencement" suggests they're just starting.)

President A. Bartlett Giamatti of Yale University gave one of the speeches I read. Except for the fact that he uses the "A." that way for his name, Dr. Giamatti is a brilliant, down-to-earth scholar. Normally what I see of his writing is so much smarter than I am that I'm discouraged by it, so naturally I was happy to note that he's only human. When he wrote this, he fell into the rhythm of the traditional graduation speech cliché, proving he's mortal.

There are some easily identifiable clues by which a graduation address can be detected.

First, the speaker starts with some light, often deprecating remark about either himself or commencement speeches in general. Dr. Giamatti did that:

"Commencement speeches are often as difficult to endure as to deliver," he said, "and you are, I trust, relieved that Yale doesn't have one."

That's a good remark for its kind but it is of a kind. And, of course, Yale *does* have a commencement address and he was giving it.

"Commencement speakers who have mastered the genre," he said, "manage to be at once condescending and conspiratorial . . ."

The key cliché there is the phrase "at once." You'll find it several times in most graduation speeches. Dr. Giamatti went for it again a few lines later when he referred to something as "at once satisfying and singular." That's perfect graduation speech language, too, because it's a little obscure and sounds at once important and euphonious.

Look for the word "indeed." This indicates that the speaker has had another idea for padding out his talk.

"Indeed to blend pomp and independence . . ." Dr. Giamatti said.

"Indeed I think a healthy family . . ."

He also told the Yale graduates that "no small challenge lies ahead."

This must mean he thinks there's more of a challenge than if he'd said simply, "A big challenge lies ahead."

No matter how the speaker says it, challenges always lie ahead in graduation addresses.

The meat of Dr. Giamatti's speech, though, came toward the end of it:

"I do not bring you any easy answers," he said.

I was frankly disappointed with that. It costs $50,000 to put a kid through Yale. For that much money, the least their president could do when they graduate is give them a few easy answers.

Numbers, Numbers, Numbers

It's never been clear to me whether the brain clogs up or not when you put too much in it.

Would I be able to think better about other things if I hadn't filled my head with a lot of information I never use?

For instance, I've inadvertently memorized a lot of

numbers I don't need. If I did need them, it would be almost as quick to look them up or work them out. The multiplication table is handy to have in your head, and I even wish my teacher hadn't stopped at 12 × 12, but there are too many numbers I know that aren't any help at all. I was thinking of some of the numbers I know:

There must be at least twenty-five telephone numbers rattling around in my brain, taking up space.

I know our street address and the street addresses of at least ten friends and family members. I've memorized some ZIP codes and even a few telephone area codes. As a good example of mind clutter, I realize I know that the area code for Indianapolis is 317.

What am I doing storing numerical garbage like that in my brain? I haven't made more than three phone calls to Indianapolis in my life, I don't plan to make another soon and it would be better out of my head. But there it is, taking up valuable space that could just as well be occupied by the names of people I forget when I meet them on the street.

There are numbers in everyone's life that stand out as landmarks. The number 204 is a big one for me. When I was a kid we lived at 204 Partridge St. I suppose 204 has more meaning for me than any other number between 100 and 1,000 although I no longer have any use for it. For the past thirty years I've lived at number 254 on another street but 254 has never assumed the same prominence in my memory as 204.

Most people who served in the Armed Forces know their Army serial number. I remember mine but I've never memorized my Social Security number. That comes up often and my Army serial number never does.

Not knowing my Social Security number is something I've put my mind to. I'm a little perverse about it. I don't want to be numbered by the government. They can make me take a number but I'll be damned if they can make me memorize it. I think we all owe it to ourselves to keep from memorizing as many numbers as we can. Facts and ideas are what our heads should be filled with.

It isn't easy rejecting a number. I remember Frank Gifford was No. 16 although he hasn't played for twenty years. I know Joe DiMaggio was No. 5 and I don't even like baseball.

Which numbers you remember and which you forget, don't seem to make any sense. I don't know the license plate number on my car but I remember that the battery in my watch was put in last January 9th. I keep the combination numbers to the lock on my locker at the indoor tennis court on a little slip of paper because I can't ever remember it, but the combination on my Dudley lock in high school in 1938 was 23-8-13. Why can't I delete that from my brain and replace it with the combination I'm using now?

It's difficult to understand why we don't have more control over what we recall and what we forget. It's a shortcoming our brains have. Each of us ought to be able to make a conscious effort to remember or to forget something and have that decision stick.

The computer salesmen talk about storage capacity. I'm not so interested in storage. It's that "erase" or "delete" feature a computer has that I like. My brain runneth over with numbers I no longer use. I keep remembering things I'd rather forget and forgetting things I'm trying to remember.

Intelligence

IF you are not the smartest person in the world, you usually find some way to be satisfied most of the time with the brain you've got. I was thinking about all this in bed last night because I made a dumb mistake yesterday and I was looking for some way to excuse myself for it so I could go to sleep.

The thing that saves most of us from feeling terrible about our limited intellect is some small part of our personality or character that makes us different. Being uniquely ourselves makes us feel better about not being smart. It's those little differences we have that keep us from committing suicide when we realize, early in life, that a lot of people have more brains than we have.

There are two kinds of intelligence, too. One can be measured in numbers from tests but the other and better kind of intelligence is something no one has ever been able to measure. The second kind is a sort of understanding of life that some of the people with the most intelligence of the first type, don't have any of. They may have scored 145 in the I.Q. tests they took in school but they're idiots out in the real world. This is also a great consolation to those of us who did *not* score 145 in our I.Q. tests.

It almost seems as though the second type of intelligence comes from somewhere other than the brain. A poet would say it comes from the heart. I'm not a poet

293

and I wouldn't say that but it does appear as though some of the best decisions we make spring spontaneously to our minds from somewhere else in our bodies.

How do you otherwise account for love, tears or the quickened heartbeat that comes with fear? All these things strike us independently of any real thought process. We don't think things through and decide to fall in love or decide to cry or have our heart beat faster.

There is so much evidence that there's more than one kind of intelligence that we can relax, believing that we have a lot of the less obvious kind. I prefer to ignore the possibility that someone with a higher I.Q. than mine might also have more of the second kind of intelligence. One person should not be so lucky as to have intelligence of both the brain and the heart.

I wish there was some way to decide who the five smartest people are in the world because I've always wanted to ask them the five hardest questions. I haven't decided who the five smartest people are and I haven't settled on all five questions, either.

One question I've considered for my list is this:

"Are people smarter than they were a thousand years ago?"

It's a hard one. Athletes are running faster, jumping farther and lifting heavier weights. This suggests our brains must also be performing better.

On the other hand, are our eyes and ears any better than the eyes and ears of the Romans who watched the lions eat the Christians in the year 200 A.D.? Probably not. My guess would be that our eyes and our ears haven't changed for better or for worse except as we abuse them through misuse.

If our eyes and ears haven't changed in size or improved in performance, the chances are our brains haven't either. I forget when they invented the wheel but did it take any less intelligence to invent the wheel centuries ago than it took this century to invent the windshield wiper, the ballpoint pen or the toaster oven?

It must have been 2:30 before I finally fell asleep.

Of Sports and Men

Iᴛ's hard to guess what sports will be like in fifty or a hundred years. Two race car drivers were killed recently, one of them hit a wall head-on in a car going 187 miles an hour. The car disintegrated and the driver was killed instantly.

At Indianapolis this year, several drivers have qualified for the Indianapolis 500 at speeds of more than 200 miles an hour. Where are we going with records? The average qualifying speed for the Indianapolis 500 this year was 197 miles an hour. In 1970 the average qualifying was 167. In 1960 it was 144 and in 1950 it was 131.

My question is this: What will it be in the year 2032? Will it be 300 miles an hour? 400? And if it is, how many drivers will be killed hitting walls head-on?

For automobile racing the solution is easy: put a limit on engine size so that racing becomes a contest solely of drivers and mechanics, not cars. But what's going to happen to records in other sports and how are average young athletes going to compete against the supermen we seem to be breeding?

Twenty years ago, Wilt Chamberlain was one of the few seven-foot basketball players around. Today there are fourteen National Basketball Association players at least that tall. A couple of them are heading for eight feet. Every high school has a few players six foot three inches and in college the short fellows who are only six feet tall don't have any better chance of making the team than the Indianapolis driver who only averages 175 miles an hour. The six-footer today isn't tall enough and the 175-mile-an-hour driver is too slow.

My father took me to a track meet at Madison Square Garden when I was young and I watched a man set the world's record in the pole vault at 14'4". Today the record is 19'2".

The sports page of my newspaper last week carried a small-type listing of the results of a high school track meet and I noticed that the boy who finished third in the high jump, cleared the bar at 6'6". Fifty years ago that was the world's record. Today a jumper doesn't win anything if he can't clear 7' and the record is 7'8¾".

If the record keeps going up at that rate, approximately one foot every fifty years, does that mean some athlete will be jumping ten feet high in 2082?

The question is: Is there any limit to human capacity and if there is a limit, what is it? If an athlete can jump ten feet high in a hundred years, will athletes be jumping twenty feet high in five hundred years?

In track and field some of the records can be attributed to better equipment but the basic improvement in every case has been in the athletes themselves. They're bigger, stronger, faster and have more endurance. Football players have gotten heavier and stronger the way basketball players have gotten taller. When a defensive lineman from a good college team gets to the pros weighing only 235 pounds these days, he's made into a linebacker because he's too small to play end or tackle.

One of the most encouraging things about all this is that while the human race has never been subjected to any kind of selective breeding, it seems to be improving physically and mentally.

On the other hand, horses have been bred selectively for hundreds of years in an attempt to produce ones that run faster but horses aren't much faster than they ever were. The horse race records at various distances haven't improved anywhere near as dramatically as human records have.

In 1882 the world's record for a man running a mile was 4:21. In 1942 it was 4:04. Today it is down under 3:50.

In 1941 Whirlaway won the Kentucky Derby, a distance of a mile and a quarter, in 2:01. In the past five years it has been run in 2:02 or more.

This is perhaps the strongest case that can be made against racism and Adolf Hitler's kind of superrace theories. It seems the kind of random breeding the human race does, produces a better strain than that produced by scientists or dictators deciding, as horse breeders do, who should breed with whom and who shouldn't breed at all.

If the human race continues to improve as sports records indicate it has, someone in the year 2100 will run the mile in a minute, swim 100 yards in 30 seconds and basketball players will all be ten feet tall.

I'd love to be around to watch but I was probably born a little too early to live to be 180.

A Penny Saved Is a Waste of Time

WHAT follows is some advice I forgot to give our kids before they left home:
—There is a Santa Claus but he doesn't always come.
—Being well dressed is like being six feet tall. You either are or you aren't and there isn't much you can do about it.
—Learn to drink coffee without sugar.
—Throw away the can of paint after you've finished painting something, no matter how much there is left in the can.
—Don't keep your watch five minutes fast.
—Go to bed. Whatever you're staying up late for isn't worth it.
—Don't expect too much from the company you work for even if it's a good company.
—You're almost always better off keeping your mouth shut, but don't let that stop you from popping off.
—There are few satisfactions in life better than holding a grudge. Pick them carefully but hold them.
—Don't fuss a whole lot with your hair.

—You're better off missing a bus or an airplane once in a while than you are getting there too early all the time.

—Don't save string. If you need string, buy it.

—Don't save pennies, either. They don't add up to anything.

—If you can't find comfortable shoes that are good-looking, buy comfortable shoes that aren't, but don't buy good-looking shoes that are uncomfortable.

—Don't call in sick except when you're sick.

—You aren't the only one who doesn't understand the situation in the Middle East.

—Nothing important is ever said in a conversation that lasts more than three minutes.

—Very few things you buy will be the answer to the problem you bought them to solve.

—There's seldom any good reason for blowing the horn on your car.

—If you work moderately hard you'll find a lot of people aren't working as hard as you are.

—It is unlikely that you'll have any success gluing a broken chair together.

—If you buy a book and feel like making marks in it with a pen or pencil, make them. It's your book and it doesn't ruin it for anyone else anyway.

—Be careful but don't be too careful.

—In a conversation, keep in mind that you're more interested in what you have to say than anyone else is.

—If nothing else works, take a hot shower.

—Don't keep saying, "I don't know where the time goes." It goes the same place it's always gone and no one has ever known where that is.

—If you own something useless which you like, don't

throw it away just because someone keeps asking what you're keeping it for.

—The fewer, the merrier.

—Don't believe everything you read in the newspaper but keep in mind almost all of it is true.

—Keep the volume down on everything. It's like salt. You can get used to less of it.

—Money shouldn't be saved for a rainy day. It should be saved and spent for a beautiful day.

—Language is more important than numbers.

—Don't make a date for anything more than a month in advance.

—It's *i* before *e* except in the following words: "Neither leisure foreigner seized the weird height."

—Travel just for the sake of going somewhere is usually a disappointment.

—Use profanity sparingly and don't use any obscenities at all.

—If you can't afford the expensive one, don't buy it.

—Try to be aware of how you're being.

—You'll be better off in the long run making decisions quickly even if a lot of them are wrong. They probably won't be wrong any more often than if you took a lot of time making them.

—When you cross a street, look both ways . . . even on a one-way street.

The Power of Negative Thinking

THIS is It, Readers! I think I've found the secret for eternal optimism. I've discovered how to keep from getting down on myself and I'm going to pass it along to you. I may even expand this article and write a book called *The Power of Negative Thinking!*

—All my life I've suffered from periods of depression because I got thinking about how much better a lot of people do things than I do. All that's behind me now. Today I'm concentrating on the negative. When I do something badly, all I'm going to think about is the great number of people who probably would have done it even worse. Concentrate on other people's shortcomings. Compare yourself with the worst and forget about the best.

When I reread something I've written in the past, I often feel terrible about it. It isn't as profound as Walter Lippmann. It isn't as well phrased as E. B. White. It isn't as funny as Art Buchwald or Russell Baker.

Well, I'm not going to compare myself with those masters any longer. I read the other day where twenty percent of all Americans can't read or write. Now when I get worrying about how inadequate my writing often is, I'm going to think of them. Twenty percent must be almost fifty million people and I certainly write better than they do.

—I enjoy cooking and often entertain the notion that I do it well. When people come to my house for dinner they tend to flatter me about my cooking but when I go to France or eat in a good restaurant or even at the home of a few friends who are truly good cooks, I'm ready to quit the kitchen. I'm a mediocre cook with high ambitions and no real talent.

Well, I'm through comparing myself with gourmets and master chefs. Yesterday I came through the turnstile at our supermarket and I looked at what other people had in their shopping carts. I saw precooked frozen cherry tarts, boxes of sugar-coated cereal, Brand X hot dogs made of who-knows-what and packaged TV dinners. By comparison to these people, I'm Julia Child in the kitchen.

—On the tennis court I start thinking I'm playing better and then someone in the family comes along with a camera and takes a picture of me serving. A week later they show me the picture and it gets a good laugh all around. My tennis is obviously a joke. I watch Jimmy Connors on television and his tennis is to mine what Einstein's mathematics is to my arithmetic.

With my new theory of negative thinking, I'm going to stop watching Jimmy Connors and concentrate on the people who play tennis *worse* than I do. There are some. If I watch the people playing in a public park, I can always spot players I could beat. I'm through worrying about my tennis. As a matter of fact, if there was a National Ranking for men over sixty years old, under five foot nine and weighing more than two hundred pounds, I bet I'd be in the top one hundred.

—Looking in the mirror mornings can be a disheartening experience for most of us. The trouble is we're comparing ourselves to the models in the store windows. I'm forgetting the beautiful people. From now on I'm checking my features, my form and my manner of dress against the people I see with the frozen TV dinners at the checkout counter in the supermarket.

—I don't read fast and when I'm reading over someone's shoulder, they finish before I do but I'm through worrying about it. When I was in the Army at Fort Bragg it took half the guys five minutes to read a twenty-word note on the bulletin board from the First Sergeant. I read faster than most of them. And I write better than my First Sergeant did, too.

Each one of us has got to start thinking about all the people who do things worse than we do. The United States is full of people who aren't doing things very well at all. These are the people against whom we should measure our own achievements if we want to feel good. (If we don't want to feel good, we shouldn't of course, but that's another book.)

A Rich Writer

Wʜᴀᴛ does your husband do?'' I asked a young woman I met at a wedding last weekend.

''He's a writer,'' she told me.

''What does he write?'' I asked and I noticed that as I did, the tone of my voice turned ever so slightly away from conversational to reportorial.

''All sorts of things,'' she said. ''Novels, short stories and . . . you know.''

One of the surprising things about being a writer is

that a person need not actually write anything to be one.

On further gentle prodding, it turned out that in addition to being a writer, the young woman's husband had also inherited a lot of money. That's the kind of writer I've always wanted to be.

If there is one thing I know a lot about, it's how to keep from writing. For those of you who want to call yourselves writers, here are some tips on how to be a writer without the drudgery of actually putting words on paper.

1—Only write when your mind is free and clear of any other responsibility. Don't try to write if there's something else you could be doing. Finish all your chores first. Sweep out the garage, clean out your bottom drawer and file those papers and old checks.

2—Work in comfortable surroundings. There should be a couch in your office. If you're sleepy or want more time to think through your idea, relax on the couch for a while. Have yourself a little nap if you think it will help.

3—If, after you awake from your little nap, you find that it's almost lunch or dinner time, close up shop. There's no sense trying to write on an empty stomach. And don't try to write on a full stomach, either.

4—Don't try to write with equipment that is anything less than perfect. Nothing physically wrong with your typewriter, paper supply, pencils, pens or paper clips should come between you and the clear flow of an idea. If, just for example, the holes in the *o*'s, *e*'s or *a*'s on your typewriter are clogged with dried ink from your ribbon and are producing a shaded area there on paper instead of a clean blank spot, bend out the end of a paperclip and pick out the clot of ink embedded in the keys.

5—If there's a telephone call you ought to make, make it before you write anything. If you think of an old friend you might call, call him. Make all your calls before you write.

6—There is nothing more distracting for a writer than for him to have the feeling that he's missing out on something good. If you hear the television set on in some other part of the house, go see what it is

7—A writer ought to have a work area that is free of other materials. If there are letters you haven't read on your desk or copies of old Sunday newspaper sections, *Harper's* magazine, *Playboy* or last week's issue of *TV Guide*, read them and throw them away before you start to write.

8—Smoking can be a big help in not writing. Cigarettes are good but the pipe is far and away the favorite smoke for the writer who isn't going to actually write anything. A pipe can keep a writer busy all morning just cleaning, packing, lighting and relighting it.

9—Don't write unless the temperature is right. You can fuss with the thermostat and if that doesn't work, change your clothes for more or less warmth.

10—All of us need plenty of time to worry. There simply are not enough hours in the day for each of us to do all the worrying there is to be done. If you have a lot of worrying to do, put off writing until you've done some of it.

By following these simple rules, and inheriting a million dollars, you too can be a rich writer.

Swimsuits

THERE are a lot of sexy bathing suit advertisements in the newspapers and magazines and you have to admit they add a little to the printed page that advertisements for computers and specials on mayonnaise do not. I have never understood some things about advertising though. How do pictures of suntanned male models sitting on horseback help sell cigarettes? How do pictures of beautiful young women with great figures in teeny-weeny brief bikinis help a store sell bathing suits to the average woman?

You can never underestimate mankind's ability to fool itself and I suppose that's what the advertisers know that the rest of us don't. They know that even though the average woman *knows* she isn't going to look like the girl in the ad wearing the bikini, there still remains the faint, faraway dream that she might look a *little* like her.

I imagine there are a lot of bathing suits in dresser drawers across the country that have never been worn in the water or anywhere near it. A woman buys the suit but in the cold light of the mirror in her own bedroom, she realizes she doesn't dare go out in public wearing it. I have a few pieces of clothing of my own that fall in that category. They seemed like a good idea when I bought them but I've never worn them.

Last Sunday I saw an ad for a bikini and another item they called "the barest cover-up" for it. The woman who wanted to appear modest on the way to the water could wear this fishnet garment over her bikini. From what I could see in the add—and I could see just about everything—the cover-up garment didn't really cover anything except, perhaps, the manufacturer's overhead.

Modesty or lack of it is an interesting subject. A great many women who modestly cover their knees when they sit down and cross their legs while wearing a skirt, pantyhose and underpants, have no hesitation about going to the beach or pool in two pieces of cloth no bigger than one small handkerchief.

Modesty is mostly what any civilization says it is. On many of the beaches in France, it is common practice for women to go topless. They wouldn't dream of wearing a skirt without a top on the street but on the beach they seem perfectly at ease wearing just the bare bottom of a bikini. They're a lot more at ease wearing so little than I am watching them wear it.

I don't really know why women have traditionally covered their breasts in our society. It hasn't been so long since men used to, too. My first five bathing suits covered me from thigh to chest and the shoulder straps always made swimming more difficult. Even in championship swim meets, men were required to wear full bathing suits. Johnny Weissmuller set all his records in one.

When men started wearing just swim trunks, a lot of people didn't think it was any more acceptable than the average person would think topless women were acceptable at the beach today. Many clubs with pools and beach committees posted signs in the 1930s and

1940s saying that men were expected to wear full bathing suits.

It's strange that bare-chested men are accepted now and bare-breasted women are not. There really isn't that big an anatomical difference. Men's breasts look about the same as women's except they don't protrude as much and are not considered sex objects.

I can't make much of a logical case against nudity or near-nudity and yet I have the feeling women's bathing suits have gone too far with revelation. I've been following the trend closely with a purely academic interest for years now and it seems to me that the advertisers and the people selling these minimal bathing suits are headed for trouble. There is just so much design a top designer can give a piece of cloth the size of a handkerchief and if they get any smaller, the designers are going to find they don't have room on them to put their names. ''Cole of California'' must be in trouble already. And the next step for women would, of course, put all of them out of business.

Dogs

THERE are forty million dogs in the United States. That's probably too many but don't suggest to anyone who has one that he or she ought to get rid of it. Most dog owners are very loyal. The dog may be man's best friend but very often man is dog's, too.

For almost no reason at all except that she felt sad and wanted to write someone, a woman in Orlando,

Florida, wrote me a touching letter about the death of her boxer, Maximilian. She describes him as a wonderful dog and says that she still cries when she thinks of him.

"I can't even bring myself to make Jello anymore," she says, "because whenever I made it Maximilian stood around waiting for his share."

Anyone who has ever lost a dog knows exactly how this woman feels even though they may have reservations about Jello. We all say the same thing. "He was like a member of the family."

I've lost two dogs in my lifetime and it was so sad that I don't think I'll ever lose another because I'll never have another. Spike and Gifford were both English bulldogs. I grew up with Spike and my children grew up with Gifford. They were some dogs. Like most owners—although I don't like to use that word— we thought our kind of dog was best. I don't think there is another dog in the world so kind, so gentle and with as much personality to love as an English bulldog. I'm glad most people with dogs feel the same about their breed. It's good that we're loyal. If the dog is a mixed-breed mutt, the owner usually thinks mixed-breed mutts are best.

It is in memory of Spike and Gifford that I almost always speak to a dog on the street. I may ignore the person he's with but I speak to the dog. With the exception of a chow, an Airedale named Bim, several German shepherds and the bad-mannered dog of a good friend I don't want to offend by naming, I've never met a dog I didn't like.

I wouldn't want a Chihuahua, a Pomeranian or a Doberman pinscher but that's probably because I've never really known one. I didn't like poodles, either, until I got to know several and then I realized what the people who have them are always raving about.

Big dogs appeal to me the most but it would probably be better if there were fewer big dogs. Big dogs need more exercise than any of us have time to give them and unless you live on a farm, there aren't many places a dog can be free to roam and run. Next to the bulldog my favorites are golden retrievers and Labradors but I hate to see people walking them early in the morning in New York City. You just know the dog has been sleeping all night and at seven or eight in the morning he'll get a five-minute walk because the owner is in a hurry to get to work. For the rest of the day these real outdoor dogs will be in an apartment waiting for another five-minute walk in the evening.

You often see people acting foolishly with their dogs but I suppose other people would have thought I was foolish with Gifford. In the evening I'd often get down on the living room floor and lie there with him, watching television. He'd paw at me or chew on my hand affectionately and I'd roll him over and pat his stomach.

We only had a couple of rules for Giffy. We didn't feed him from the table and we didn't let him up on the furniture. Sometimes, in a moment of wild exuberance, in the morning, he'd leap up on the bed and start biting at me through the blankets. He knew he was wrong but he was having such good fun I never said much to him about it.

Some dogs are so cruelly treated that we don't even like to think about them but, for the most part, dogs and people provide as much happiness and friendship as Maximilian and the lady in Orlando provided for each other. Our behavior with dogs isn't always very adult but we express an affection for them that we often withhold from our human companions. It's nice.

Photography

As someone who has taken a lot of bad pictures I feel experienced enough to give some advice and make some observations on photography:

—The great World War II *Life* magazine photographer Bob Capa gave the best advice I ever heard. He said, "If your pictures are no good, you weren't close enough." Ironically, Bob was killed getting too close, but it doesn't alter the truth of his statement.

—It's a great temptation to take pretty pictures, but try to resist it. The only pictures that interest you a year after you take them are those of people. If you travel, don't bother with the familiar landmarks. People have already taken better pictures than you'll ever get of Rockefeller Center, the Eiffel Tower, the Taj Mahal, Notre Dame cathedral, the pyramids, Stonehenge and the Grand Canyon. If you want pictures of those, buy postcards.

—Try to remember that it is unlikely anyone but you will ever be interested in looking at your pictures, unless they're in them. Only take pictures you'll want to look at more than once.

—Don't take pictures you hope will impress people with where you've been. They don't care where you've been or what pictures you took while you were there.

—Most pretty good cameras come with a 50mm lens. This refers to the width of a picture. The smaller-numbered lenses such as a 28mm lens take a wider view but make things look more distant from the camera. The higher-numbered lenses are called telescopic lenses. They bring objects closer but cover a smaller field. You need one wide-angle lens and one medium-long lens. You don't need the all-purpose lens that comes with the camera.

—The second-best advice I ever heard was a general rule about lens openings of *f*-stops, as they're called. The rule is "sunny day, small hole, cloudy day, big hole." (If you don't know anything at all about a camera, that's not a joke.)

—Professional photographers have a difficult time. There are so many people who own good cameras and are at least reasonably competent with them, that they often get as good pictures by accident as the professionals do on purpose.

—There are some pretty good inexpensive cameras made in the United States but we have never made one that could compete with the best made in Germany or Japan. Why is that?

—When you get your pictures back, throw half of them away. If you have two almost the same, pick the best one and discard the other. Be tough on yourself when you edit your pictures.

—If you're taking pictures of people, get to know enough about your camera so you can take them quickly. Pictures of people waiting to have their pictures taken are usually poor.

—Write names and dates on the back of the pictures you keep. You're so sure who everyone is the day you get your pictures back, that it's hard to believe you'll forget some of their names a year from then. You will though, and in ten years you'll be lucky to remember half of them.

—When you see a man taking a picture of the woman he's with on vacation, offer to take a picture of both of them standing together. It's one of the small, nice things to do in life.

—Don't put pictures in an album. Put them in a box. Albums don't hold enough.

—If you're showing pictures to people, don't hand the pictures over one at a time with a speech. Give them the whole batch and let them go through the pictures like a deck of cards. This way they can decide how long they want to look at each one. Don't do too much explaining about where you were or what was happening at the time. Remember, everyone has a low tolerance for anyone else's pictures.

—When you go on a trip, don't make the decision about whether to take a camera along lightly. Having a camera and taking pictures is a very intrusive element on a trip. Make sure it's worth it. There's a lot to be said for leaving a camera home sometimes.

Letters Not Sent

FOLLOWING are some letters I wish I'd mailed.

Mr. Michael Vishniac
Acme Plumbing Co.
Dear Mr. Vishniac:

I know what a busy man you are and I hate to bother you but I am writing in the hopes of being able to make an appointment with you to fix the faucet in our downstairs bathroom. It has been dripping for five months. I have called your plumbing company but all I get is an answering service. I understand you have been wintering in the Bahamas.

If it isn't convenient for you to make a house call to fix the faucet, would it be possible to make an appointment for me to bring the sink over to you to be fixed?

Sincerely, Andrew A. Rooney

Leslie Cartwright
Abraham Lincoln Grade School
Dear Mrs. Cartwright:

How wonderful it was of you to ask all thirty-one students in your fourth grade English class to write me individually for details on how I got started writing, how I get my ideas, who has influenced me most as a writer and what a young person who wants to be a writer should study.

I was so touched that I'm going to set aside the other

work I had planned to do in the next three or four days and answer all thirty-one of your students.

I have to go now because many of the students told me to please get my answers back to them quickly as you told them their assignment was due next Thursday.

Ethel Washoure
Wentzville, Missouri
Dear Ethel:

Thank you for writing but I don't seem to remember you from the sixth grade. My father's name was not Arthur. It was Walter. I did not have a brother named Terrence who became an Eagle Scout. Obviously you have me mixed up with some other Andrew Rooney because I've only been to St. Louis twice in my life and I didn't get out to Wentzville either time.

Lester Grantham, Chairman
Whiteville, Section B,
Bowling League Speakers Selection Committee
Dear Mr. Grantham:

Thank you for your invitation to address the annual banquet and dinner dance of the Whiteville, Section B, Bowling League on October 4, 1987. I will be unable to accept your invitation because of a previous engagement on that date. I promised my wife I'd have dinner with her in the kitchen that night.

Mrs. Franklin Z. Welles
Glenmont Library Charity Assn.
Dear Mrs. Welles:

I would like to contribute an article of old clothing

for your auction to raise money for the new sidewalk in front of the Glenmont Library but am unable to do so. I wear my old clothes.

William Wilson
Orlando, Fla.
Dear Mr. Wilson:

It was kind of you to write to say how much you dislike me and my column and that you are canceling your subscription to the newspaper and will never read it again. It is independent Americans like you who have made this country great, Mr. Wilson. May I also say that it made me feel good to know you sent a copy of your letter to the editor of the newspaper. I like an editor to know how readers feel about me. If you're ever in New York, look me up.

Sincerely, Andy Rooney

X:

THE SWEET SPOT
IN TIME

The Sweet Spot in Time

I'M lukewarm on both yesterday and tomorrow. Neither science fiction nor nostalgia interests me as much as today. I am tempted by the promise of all the great things coming up tomorrow, of course, and I do enjoy all the good memories and the graceful, simple and efficient artifacts of yesterday, the antiques, but this moment is the moment I like best.

These thoughts inevitably come at Christmas time. It's easy to get sentimental about the memories of Christmases past and years past and the people you spent them with. The advertising for gifts with which to commemorate the season, on the other hand, often emphasizes the new technology. "Buy her a computer, the tool of the future!"

So I feel a certain ambivalence toward both the past and the future. I dislike retyping a piece to correct mistakes or rearrange paragraphs. My son, Brian, said that if I got with it and bought myself a word processor, I wouldn't have to do those things. He said that if I tried one for just a few days, I'd never go back to my ancient Underwood #5.

Well, I did buy a word processor and I've tried it for a year but I still write primarily on my old machine. There are times when it's best for all of us to close our eyes to the future. There's just so much progress we have time for in our lives. Mostly we are too busy doing it the old way to take time to learn a new way. I do close my eyes to progress when it comes to typewriters. This may spring, in part, from a deep feeling I have that it's wrong to try to impose efficiency on a writer.

My antipathy for too much nostalgia can probably be traced to several hundred little antique shops where I have stopped to talk with conniving antiquaries. It seems as though every time people find out there's money in something, they ruin it. The good antique shops are outnumbered by the bad ones.

The revival of the style of the 1920s and 1930s has helped turn me off nostalgia. They call it Art Deco but to me it was the ugliest era that progress ever took us through. It's all phony frou-frou. Its ashtray art and gilded replicas of the Empire State Building put me off. The emphasis was on how it looked and not much on how it worked. Except for being old it has no virtue and it isn't even very old. Being old isn't reason enough to originate a revival of anything anyway. Age is no guarantee of quality in objects or people.

Too many of the revivals in art forms are fads based more on commercial enterprise than artistic worth. Someone stumbles across an obscure style in architecture, painting or furniture practiced by an appropriately unknown artist and they revive that style because they know where they can lay their hands on fifty examples of it and make themselves a quick buck. Art doesn't enter into it and nostalgia works as well for the dealer as fear does for the insurance salesman.

It isn't easy to live in the present. The temptation to

sit thinking about the past or dreaming of the future is always there because it's easier than getting up off your tail and doing something today.

I love the electronic gadgets that promise a magic future in which we can do the hardest jobs with the touch of a button. It's just that experience has taught me that the promise usually precedes the product by so many years that it's better to put off anticipating it until it's actually in the store window.

I like old movies, old music, old furniture and old books but if I had to choose between spending the day with dreams of the future or memories of the past or this day I have at hand, I think I'd take pot luck with today.

Reunion

THERE's just so much sentimental baggage you can carry through life. I'm not much for reunions. Anyone who has reached the age of sixty could easily spend the rest of his days just sitting around, remembering.

I've returned to an old U.S. Eighth Air Force Base near Bedford, England, though, because members of the 306th Bomb Group were having a reunion and I flew with them on the first U.S. bombing raid on Nazi Germany in February 1943. It's sentimental baggage I carry easily and with great pride.

It's been forty years now since these men flew their four-engined B-17 Flying Fortresses out of here. They're the kind of men Americans like to think are typical Americans but they're better than typical. They're special. A lot of World War II Air Force men were.

It was a terrible war for them, although during this reunion they're managing to recall a lot of the good things about it. It would be too sad if they didn't. It was terrible because so many of them were killed. One evening they'd be sitting around their huts talking, worrying, playing cards and writing letters home. The next evening, if there had been a bombing mission that day, the bed next to theirs or the one next to that—and maybe both—might be empty, its former occupant, their pal, dead. Perhaps he had come down in a parachute that caught fire. "Who burned Bailey?" MacKinlay Kantor wrote. "Was it you?"

It was a great and terrible war for me because as a young reporter for the Army newspaper, *The Stars and Stripes*, I was in a strange position. I came to this base often when the bombers went out and when they returned—if they returned—I talked to the crews about what had happened. Then I'd return to London and write my story. I often felt ashamed of myself for not being one of them. I was having the time of my life as a newspaperman and they were fighting and dying. That's how I came to fly with them to Wilhelmshaven. It made me feel better about myself.

Looking out at the crumbling remains of the old runways at the airfield, I'm haunted by flashes of memory. Often the bombers came back badly damaged and with crew members dead or dying. In April of 1943 I was here when they came back from a raid deep in Germany and one of the pilots radioed in that he was going to have to make an emergency landing. He had only two engines left and his hydraulic system was gone. He couldn't let the wheels down and there was something even worse. The ball-turret gunner was trapped in the plastic bubble that hung beneath the belly of the bomber.

Later I talked with the crewmen who survived that landing. Their friend in the ball turret had been calm, they said. They had talked to him. He knew what they had to do. He understood. The B-17 slammed down on its belly . . . and on the ball turret with their comrade trapped inside it.

There are funny stories, too. Everyone here remembers the eccentric gunner Snuffy Smith, Sergeant Maynard Smith. He was an oddball kind of guy but he did his job well in the air. The Air Force loved to give medals and they had good reason in Snuffy Smith's case. On one occasion, Henry Stimson, then called Secretary of War, came to England and officials, thinking this would be a good time for publicity for the Air Force and the Secretary, arranged to give Snuffy Smith the Medal of Honor. The whole entourage came to this base with the Secretary and a dozen generals but the hero was nowhere to be found. It turned out he was in the kitchen washing dishes. He was on KP being disciplined for some minor infraction of the base rules.

Any reunion is a bittersweet experience. Last evening I had a drink at a bar where there was a gathering and a strong-looking weatherbeaten man came over and quietly said he'd like to buy me a drink. He's a Nebraska farmer now. He had been the tail gunner on the *Banshee*, the B-17 I flew in over Wilhelmshaven. We'd been hit that day and it was a terrifying trip but it made a good story for me. We laughed and talked together and he paid for the drink. As we lifted our glasses in a mutual toast, I noticed that two fingers on his right hand were missing. It often happened to crewmen who stuck by their guns while their hands froze.

And he was buying *me* a drink.

Friendship: Handle with Care

Six months ago I was talking to a friend on the telephone. We used to talk two or three times a week and we often had lunch. For about the fiftieth time he started telling me about some money he was trying to get from his father's estate. (After his mother had died, his father remarried a schoolteacher. Later his father died and the schoolteacher took up with another man and my friend thinks this fellow is after the money.)

I didn't really know or care about all the details and finally I said, "Charley, if you'd spent as much time working in the past years as you've spent trying to get that money, you'd be rich."

It seemed like half a joke and half a sharp remark that I could make to my old friend but I was wrong.

"Who needs a friend like you," he said, and slammed down the receiver. I haven't talked to Charley since and may never. I made one attempt to call him but he was out and I haven't tried again.

I suspect I violated the first rule of a friendship. To stay friends with anyone you have to avoid saying anything unforgivable and in Charley's mind, what I said was unforgivable. I embarrassed him.

The funny thing is that real differences of opinion about important matters like religion, money or politics don't damage a good friendship. It's those little things that come up that kill one. I've often thought I should have remembered that old quotation when I was talking to Charley: "Instead of loving your enemies, try treating your friends a little better."

We all know old friends are the best friends but we don't knock new friends. We need them. We have to replace all the Charleys we lose as we go along.

This year I've been to three reunions and that's two too many. I went to a high school reunion, a college reunion and the bomber crew reunion. In each case there were about a hundred people present. I could reminisce with all of them but I really only enjoyed seeing three or four in each group. I noticed that the ones I liked seeing most were the ones I did the least old-time talking with. We talked about what we were doing now.

There's no way to figure out why you make friends with some people and not with others. I meet as many people I dislike as I meet people I like. There can be something equally hard to define that puts you off.

There seems to be some little trick of mind each of us has that matches up with some people and not with others. Something goes on between friends that doesn't go on between acquaintances even when neither person is saying anything. You don't have to say everything to a friend for both of you to understand what you mean.

The funny thing about your good friends is that

sometimes you don't enjoy being with them. One of my best and dearest old friends is about the most cantankerous, aggravating, negative SOB I ever met. I don't know why I've put up with him all these years but if someone had me make out a list of my best friends, he'd be right up there near the top.

Politicians abuse the words "good friend" by using them to describe someone they met once for thirty seconds at a cocktail party in Washington. I object to that but I concede that it's possible to consider someone a good friend whom you've never spent much time with. It depends on the intensity of the time you did spend. There are people I've known for twenty-five years that I don't really know at all. On the other hand, there are people I don't see more than once every ten years whom I consider good friends.

Maybe I ought to try calling Charley again.

Wally

I SEE a lot of my friend Wally in the summer. Wally is the best old friend I ever had. I haven't known him for long but he's eighty-two. That's an old friend. My relationship with most people I've known who were that age has been distant. I felt separated from them. I've loved some, admired many and felt sorry for quite a few older people but I never had a pal eighty years old until I met Wally.

Wally and his wife have a place in the little village where we spend much of our time in the summer. Our house is on top of the hill about a mile out of town. What Wally and I have in common, in addition to that indefinable sense of understanding one another that friends have, is an interest in woodworking. We travel around the countryside together looking for good pieces of cherry or walnut in some of the little sawmills and we swap tools and exchange problems. Wally's idea of a good time is to drive into the city and buy a new tool. That's my idea of a good time, too. Each of us has more wood and more tools than we know what to do with.

Wally's real name is Wellington and he has the stature to handle that kind of a name, although no one ever calls him by it. Wally is six foot five, a giant of a man and still strong. When I go down to his workshop with a problem, he'll dig out one of his cabinetmaker's books that explains what to do in detail. He goes to the book more often than I do. He'll come out of his workshop and put the book on top of his car parked in the driveway at the side of the house and start looking for the answer to my problem. He points to some page in the book. The problem is, he's eight inches taller than I am so my eyes are only on a level with the top of his car. He's looking down on the book. Last week, for instance, I was trying to find out how to bend a piece of oak by steaming it and Wally read me how to do it from his book on top of the car.

Later in the day I came by again and Wally was worried because he couldn't remember where he'd put the cabinetmaking book we'd been looking at. He was afraid he might have absentmindedly left it on top of the car and that his wife had driven off with it up there. Wally's very aware of his age and he thinks he's more absentminded and forgetful than he used to be. I don't know, of course, but I suspect he's always been about the way he is now. Forgetfulness seems to come very naturally to him.

"There are three things bad about getting old," he says. "One, you can't remember anything . . . and I forget the other two." He laughs. Wally likes old jokes.

Early in the summer when we first came here, I went down to greet Wally. We talked about our winters and then he said, "Hey, come in here a minute."

We went to his crowded workshop and he pointed to a pile of pieces of cherry on his workbench. There were four carefully turned and fluted legs, several small pieces that had been dovetailed or rabbited and one wide board that looked like the top of something.

"Look at this stuff," Wally said. "I did this at the end of last summer and left it here and now I can't remember what the hell I was making."

Wally has better tools than I have but his workshop is just as much of a mess. He says he waits until the sawdust reaches his knees before he cleans it out. Last week I loaded up my station wagon with scraps of wood and two barrels of sawdust to take to the dump. Wally went with me but when we got there the people in the little office at the entrance to the dump said I had to have a sticker on my car to prove we were residents.

I filled in a form but I had to go outside to look at my license plate number. "Hey, Eddie," I heard one of the men say to another. "How about that. He don't even know his license plate number."

Wally decided he ought to get a dump sticker too so

he came back into the office with me. He started filling out the form and when he came to the license plate question he looked up at the dump man and said, "I don't know my license plate number." The man shook his head and gave a knowing look at Eddie. To him it was evidence that we were two dumb city slickers, neither of whom knew his license number. To me it helped explain why Wally and I are such good friends.

When Wally was known as Wellington, he was vice-president of a very big corporation. He must have been good at his work to have been so successful but I suspect Wally never did anything better in his life than he does being eighty-two years old.

The Art of Conversation

THE best conversationalists are people whose stories or ideas have a definite beginning and a definite ending. The bores are the ones who talk on and on without ever making a point.

The other night we had Pranas Lape, an old friend, to dinner and I got thinking afterwards that he's one of the best conversationalists I know. He has original ideas, serious thoughts and usually punctuates them with a twist that makes everyone laugh.

Pranas lives a monastic existence on the coast of Maine, painting huge canvases of abstract art and living off the fish he catches, the vegetables he grows and the mushrooms he finds in the woods. He buys an occasional bottle of ketchup toward the end of winter when the things he froze don't taste as good as they did when they were fresh. He can live, he says, on three thousand dollars a year.

Pranas left Lithuania as a young man thirty years ago and he still speaks with a heavy accent. He uses the English language with great directness but with very little regard for traditional grammar. When he speaks there's no doubt about what he means although the words are never arranged the way I would have arranged them.

"He is already going for long time with this program," Pranas will say of President Reagan. "Ven vill it do something except bad?"

I have never liked Pranas's paintings but I think that's more my shortcoming than his. I simply don't understand the ideas he's trying to express with his shapes and colors. I've never dismissed him as a painter, though, because I assume he has as many good ideas when he's painting as when he's talking.

"Put all the MX missiles together in one six-pack on a remote island in the Pacific Ocean," he says. "Make them so they could be shot off by remote control from someplace else. Tell the Russians exactly where the island is. Keep a few nuclear weapons on board submarines and heavy bombers. If the Russians ever declare war on us, they'd first have to destroy that island with all our missiles six-packed on it.

"Our missiles would be destroyed but no American would be killed and no city would be destroyed but at the instant the island was destroyed, we'd know we were at war with Russia and we could strike with our other weapons."

Everything at dinner reminds Pranas Lape of a

story. He has a Lithuanian friend who exchanges letters with her family in her Russian-dominated homeland. The letters are often censored so the woman arranged a code with her family. They include pictures with their letters. If the picture shows the family standing, things are going well. If the family is sitting, things are not so good.

"Last time she get letter," Pranas says, "they are lying on floor."

We had wine with dinner and even that reminded Pranas of a story. A summer neighbor of his, Roger Fessaguet, is one of the fine chefs in America and owner of La Caravelle restaurant in New York. Roger invited several other chefs to Maine for a weekend and Pranas was asked to dinner. One of the chefs, a renowned wine expert, had brought several rare old bottles of Bordeaux. When the first bottle was opened, each guest tasted it. Some expressed doubt about the wine. Others, not wishing to offend their friend who had brought it, withheld their opinion.

When the chef who had brought the wine tasted it, he quickly spit it out.

"Undrinkable vinegar!" he declared.

A second bottle was opened. Each chef tasted it and their reaction was good this time. Then the expert who brought it swished it around in his mouth.

"Magnificent," he said. "One of the best I have ever tasted."

"So," Pranas said at our dinner table, "I taste both wines. I try first one, then other. I cannot tell difference. Both same!" He roars with laughter.

If every table had a conversationalist like Pranas, we wouldn't need television.

"You Aren't Going to Tell That Old Story Again?"

No one ever said married life was easy and if anyone ever did say it and I missed it, they were wrong. Young people getting married listen to the for-richer-for-poorer-in-sickness-and-in-health talk but not many of them understand the real pitfalls in sharing a whole life with someone else.

Over the weekend I was thinking about one cause for divorce that wouldn't occur to a young couple just starting married life. I think they ought to be warned about it in the wedding ceremony. If you're going to be married to someone for a long time, you have to be prepared to listen to them repeat the same stories over and over again hundreds of times during your life. You'll find from experience that every time a husband or a wife is in a conversation with a few people around, they'll find a way to be reminded of one of their favorite stories.

Telling an old story is taking a calculated risk. If there are eight people listening to you at the dinner table, for instance, and your wife and two other people at the table have heard it before, it's probably a wise idea not to tell the story again. If, on the other hand, your husband or wife is the only one who has heard it, you sacrifice whatever respect you may lose from your spouse and go ahead with it.

The wedding ceremony ought to be rewritten to make certain both parties understand that they are not only "to love, honor and obey" but also "to listen, laugh and approve." It isn't easy to laugh at a story you've heard 183 times before but a good wife or husband should put her or his mind to it and try.

This comes to my mind now because we had some good friends at the house for dinner last weekend. The subject of speeding tickets came up because someone at the table got one on the way to our house.

"I'll never forget a ticket I got years ago," another good old friend said.

"Dear," his wife said looking at him with a pained expression, "you aren't going to tell that story again, are you?"

There were eight people at dinner and three of them admitted they'd heard my friend, Bill, tell the story before. Several of the others who hadn't heard it or didn't remember hearing it before, urged him to continue with it. One of the three who had heard it several times before is always nice to everyone. He said, "Oh, that's a great story. Go ahead. Tell Brian what happened when the cop pulled you over when you were on your way to give a speech at the dinner for the Police Commissioner."

"It was way back when I was doing a radio show," Bill began.

Bill's wife dropped her eyes to her plate and toyed with a few pieces of lettuce.

Bill is a great storyteller and he's had so much practice with this one that he really tells it well.

"And so," he concluded after five minutes, "this cop says to me, 'Well, holy mackerel then, you better get over there in a hurry. Here, give me your license and registration. This won't take a minute.' "

Everyone laughed, and when the laughter subsided I didn't want the conversation to die so I said, "That reminds me of the time I was driving through this little town in Georgia."

"You told that story last time Bill told that story," my wife said.

"I haven't told it as often as you've told the one about what happened in the shooting gallery on board the ship when your parents took you to Europe when you were seventeen," I said.

"Tell us what happened on the ship, Marge," the friend who is always nice to everyone said.

I decided to clear some of the dishes off the table. If I couldn't tell my story about being arrested in the little town in Georgia, I wasn't going to sit through that story about the shooting gallery on the ship again.

The Wedding

THE beautiful daughter of good friends of ours was being married last Saturday in a local church. Her father is the most successful businessman among our old friends and her mother is one of the most attractive and charming people we know. If you were invited, it was a wedding with reception party afterwards that you didn't miss. I missed part of it.

At five A.M. Saturday morning I awoke and rushed for the bathroom. I knew I was ill. Having just recovered from the flu, I couldn't believe I had it again. The day before I'd had lunch with a camera crew at a big, sloppy Italian restaurant. The food tasted good at the time but I noticed that when I thought about the eggplant parmigiana, my stomach turned over. This is usually a clue.

By nine Saturday morning, I talked myself into thinking I felt better and went downstairs to do some odd jobs. By noon I knew I was kidding myself. I had something. Not going to the wedding was unthinkable and I put that out of my mind. One way or another I had to go. Usually you can take a shower, pull yourself together and do something if you really have to, even when you're sick.

The wedding was a formal affair. My wife had bought a new dress and I was to wear a tuxedo. I went upstairs to lie down but first decided to see if my tuxedo was pressed. I could not find my tuxedo. My wife could not find my tuxedo. She called the cleaners and the cleaners could not find my tuxedo.

Because my tuxedo was twenty-five years old, worn and ill-fitting anyway, I decided to buy a new one. It is not easy to buy a tuxedo at two P.M. Saturday and wear it that evening, particularly if you are somewhat misshapen, as I am.

I need a tuxedo two or three times a year and I hate to pay twenty-five dollars to rent one so, still feeling absolutely terrible, I drove twelve miles to a good men's store. I am ill at ease with clothing store salesmen. They are always so nice they make me suspicious. The salesman was not only nice to me, he found a tuxedo that practically fit. The sleeves were a little long but I was in no position to look for a perfect fit. The tailor agreed to shorten the pants then and there and I walked out with a $250 tuxedo thirty minutes later. You can see I wasn't taking this wedding lightly.

The wedding was at 6:30. The thought of the church ceremony was torture but my wife has always made it clear to me that you don't go to the party afterwards if you don't go to the wedding itself. It was then about five P.M. and I had to lie down. I spent the next hour between the bed and the bathroom. Then I gritted my teeth, took the shower, dressed and left for the church. I kept thinking how different my situation was from the bride's.

We didn't arrive at the church until 6:25 and the bride's mother was already standing in the back of the church with her entourage. She greeted me and I had a terrible decision to make. As affectionate old friends, we usually kiss. I didn't have time to say, nor would she have been interested in knowing, that I had either food poisoning or the flu. "She'll be kissed by a hundred people today," I thought to myself, "and one more won't hurt. I'll stay way up on her cheek, away from her mouth and my germs will never get to her." I kissed her.

Until Saturday I had never realized how much you sit and stand during the standard wedding ceremony, which, incidentally, is in serious need of being rewritten. It seemed as though the minister had us bobbing up and down for hours when all I wanted to do was ask the people next to me to move over so I could lie down in the pew.

After the ceremony, we walked back to the car. It was obvious I couldn't make it to the country club for the party. We don't have a bathroom in our car. All I wanted to do was go home to bed. My wife agreed I should. It's okay, I guess, to go to the wedding and not the party.

Every time you go any place where there's a crowd, I suppose someone is in the condition I was. I sure hope the bride's mother noticed my new tuxedo and that I didn't give her anything.

Trust

ONE day I was driving in a city I don't know very well. I came to a major crossroads where I wanted to turn right but the light was red so I stopped.

I'm still not totally comfortable with the law that lets you turn right on red, and there are so many exceptions that when I'm on a street I'm not familiar with, I'm never sure whether I can go or not.

A car pulled up behind me with its right blinker on, and as I looked up into my rearview mirror, my eyes met the eyes of the driver. He quickly took his right hand off the wheel, raised it with his palm toward his face as though his hand were a Stop sign and nodded twice.

The motion wasn't any standard form of sign language but I understood perfectly what he meant. There was no suggestion of irritation on his part. He simply understood my confusion and was indicating to me that it was okay to make the turn.

It wasn't much but it struck me as very nice and I

had a brief sensation of warm, friendly fellow feeling. Two strangers had understood and trusted each other. We had exchanged a little moment of understanding. He had helped me and thus himself and then we'd each gone our own way, never to meet again.

There are more people in the world than all of us can be friends with but friendliness seems to be a disappearing quality of life. Friendliness and trust go together and while I suppose we can do without friendliness, we can't do without trust. We have to have some confidence in each other or everyone is going to end up living in a fenced-off world of his or her own.

The most valuable thing the bad guys have stolen from the rest of us is not money but trust. We're suspicious of everyone.

We're suspicious of strangers because we know they might steal or attack us.

We're suspicious of government because we've read about the dishonest politicians and know they may be cheating us.

We're suspicious of products because we know that what some dishonest companies say about them in their advertisements is not true.

In the building where I've worked for twenty years, there's a guard desk at the door and everyone is asked to show an identification card. It's common now in most offices and factories.

I detest the new distrust. The basic assumption is that people are no damn good.

In many stores in big cities, you're expected to check the bags you have with you. Before you've even been in the place, you're suspected of being a thief.

I know there are shoplifters but I don't go in stores

that make you check your bags. If they don't trust me,
I don't trust them. I don't like wandering through a
store knowing the management thinks I'm trying to
steal. Civilization rests on trust. Without friendliness
and the understanding that we're all in this thing together, one of us is going to drop the bomb.

In the parking lot of the supermarket my attention is
often attracted to a person locking a car door. I know it
may be the sensible thing to do but I never feel friendly
toward the people doing it.

Last week I was reading the paper and feeling pretty
bad about all the devious, dishonest work our Central
Intelligence Agency feels it's necessary for it to do in
Central America. After I read the paper I drove over to
a hardware store and lumberyard in a nearby town and
then I felt better.

I went into a back room where they keep small
pieces of hardware and picked out a selection of
screws and carriage bolts and took them to the front
desk.

"How many carriage bolts you got here?" Lou, the
man at the desk, asked.

"Twenty," I said.

"Twenty times thirty-three . . . that'll be six sixty," Lou said.

He didn't count the carriage bolts. Lou trusts me and
I suspect he has less stolen from him at the hardware
store than they have at those places in the city where
they make you check your shopping bags at the door.

Letting the Experts Decide:
What Could Go Wrong?

RECENT Presidents have hit on an interesting new way to deal with the problems of government. When faced with an issue so difficult that it seems to have no solution, they appoint a committee to look into the matter and report back to them with a recommendation. I'm so impressed with this presidential method that I'd like to apply it to my own life.

Today I'd like to appoint a committee of experts to come up with the answer on what to do with my old station wagon. Just as Central America is too much for a President to figure out, that station wagon problem is too much for me. Should I keep it another year? Should I spend a lot of money getting it fixed? Should I bother to have the dent taken out of the right rear fender where I mashed it in against the side of the garage door?

I'm going to let the committee decide.

For the committee on station wagons, I think I'll appoint Lee Iacocca as chairman. He's with Chrysler, and the station wagon's a Ford, but he won't let that interfere with his judgment. He'll be fair as presidential committees always are.

Just as soon as the Iacocca Commission gets back to me, I'll take action. In the meantime, I'm just going to drive the car, as always. Of course, I may just drive it as always after the commission gets back to me, too, no matter what their recommendation is.

I'm going to appoint another commission to study my financial condition. The commission will be headed by the economic expert Alan Greenspan and will have such members as Milton Friedman and Paul Volcker. It will report back to me within ninety days on whether or not I can afford to buy the new power saw I have my eyes on.

In addition to the question of the saw, it will explain to me things like the money market, tax-free municipal bonds and whether it really matters to me what the price of gold is in Zurich.

We're having some people in for dinner Saturday night and I'm going to appoint another commission to come back within three days with a fair, honest and bipartisan report on what we ought to serve. Once that report is made, no one else will have any grounds on which to complain. The decision on the food will have been made, not by me, but by the experts.

The Saturday Night Dinner Commission will be headed by the great executive chef Pierre Franey. He will have on his commission André Soltner, chef at America's best restaurant, Lutèce, and food writers Mimi Sheraton and Craig Claiborne. Craig and Mimi don't speak to each other but I'm sure they can put aside their differences for the good of our dinner party on this important occasion, just as members of the President's commissions have.

If the food commission advises anything for dinner Saturday night that's too expensive, I'm going to turn over its recommendation to the financial committee and let the two committees argue it out between them.

I'm tired of making decisions. The answer obviously is to appoint a committee.

In the event that there are any disagreements between two committees, I'll appoint an Arbitration Committee whose sole job will be to decide which of the two committees is right.

I'm going to appoint a commission on overweight to study the problem of why I can't eat ice cream and still get thin. For this committee, I'm going to look through *Family Circle*, the *Reader's Digest*, *Redbook*, the *National Enquirer*, the *Ladies' Home Journal* and all the book best-seller lists and find the best diet writers.

I anticipate that once these committees report back to me, I'll have my life as well organized as any of our Presidents have organized the country.

Self-Improvement Week

I THINK I'll improve myself this week.

I ought to do more reading. Maybe I'll buy an important book tomorrow and read that and learn something I didn't know. As a matter of fact, why don't I decide to do that every week. I'll read one good book a week. That would improve me.

It wouldn't do any harm if I stopped eating so much, either. I'll cut down on butter and stop eating so much ice cream. For breakfast I'll just have half a grapefruit and some dry toast.

If I cut down on what I eat and start jogging in the morning before I go to work, I could lose some weight and really get into shape. My tennis would improve if I was in better shape. Maybe I'll start jogging a half mile at first and work up to two miles. That's what I'll do. I'll do two miles every morning, take a shower, read a chapter or two of a good book and have half a grapefruit before going to work.

I'm going to stop wasting so much time watching television, too. Half of what I watch is junk and I'm only watching because I'm sitting there and it comes on. I'm going to start turning off the television set. I'll go to bed earlier and get more sleep. That'll be good for me, more sleep.

There are a lot of exercise books on the market. I'll get one of those. It wouldn't hurt if I tightened up my stomach muscles. They say you can do some of those exercises anywhere. I heard a man on radio say it's a good idea to get used to tensing and then relaxing muscles wherever you are. He said you could even stretch some muscles while you were brushing your teeth. That sounds easy and I haven't been brushing my teeth enough anyway. I'll start brushing my teeth for longer and tensing up some muscles while I do it.

My fingernails don't look too good. I ought to be more careful cutting them and then I ought to file them a little. My toenails are much too long and I've got to start cutting them more often so they don't keep poking holes in my socks.

Speaking of my fingers, I'm going to learn a new skill with them. I've always thought it would be great to know how to take notes in shorthand so I'll enroll in a secretarial school for an hour at noon instead of eating a big lunch or maybe I'll go evenings, instead of watching television. If I can find a simple course in accounting, I'll take that too. It'll make it quicker and easier to pay bills and keep track of bank accounts. If they have a computer course, I might as well take that while I'm at it.

I ought to be more careful about my clothes. I have a reputation for not being very neat. It would be a good idea if I got my pants pressed more often. I don't even change a shoelace when it breaks. I pull the lace through so it's level again and just tie the short ends in a regular knot instead of a bow. It looks terrible and I'm determined to stop doing that. If my pants are pressed and the rest of my clothes are neat and tidy, I ought to get a haircut more often. There's nothing that looks worse than someone who needs a haircut. I've got to stop letting my hair come over my collar in back the way it does now.

What I ought to do is organize my time better so that I can do more in a day. I'll set aside one hour in which to read the newspaper, for instance. Instead of this hit-or-miss way I read the paper now, I'll start on page one and go right through the paper until I've read the whole thing.

After I jog and eat my grapefruit and do my exercises and brush my teeth and read the newspaper, press my pants and cut my fingernails, I'm going to take a few minutes to relax, meditate and plan my day. I read somewhere that everyone should plan his day in advance and not just start out willy-nilly in the morning so that's what I'll do.

I'm just sick and tired of myself the way I am. In the near future, if I follow these plans I'm making to improve myself, I'm going to be smart, efficient, muscular and in beautiful shape. I can hardly wait to see myself in the mirror.

I Did It Again—Nothing

PROBABLY I'll learn this week but why has it taken me so long? Perhaps, if not this week, next week? Or by the year 2000 at the latest?

I know I haven't learned yet because I did it again this year. I went away on vacation, took along a lot of paperwork and didn't do any of it. I did the same thing last year, the year before that and for as many years back as I can remember. I took mail to be answered, bills to be paid and notes on things I wanted to write. Nothing. I took two boxes of papers and a full briefcase this year and haven't opened any of them except to get out a pen I left in the briefcase.

In the middle of my vacation I had to go to Chicago for two days and I took the briefcase with me because I thought I'd have some extra time at night. I returned from Chicago with the briefcase unopened. I didn't even look for another pen in there. Now, when I go back to the office shortly, I'll take the briefcase and the two boxes of papers with me in the exact condition they were in when I left, without the pen, of course.

That I've never learned is one of the first rules of life. Everything takes longer than you think it's going to. Even vacations take longer and are harder work than you thought they were going to be.

If I did all the work I've taken home with me nights

or taken on vacation with me, I might be President. I'd be rich, relaxed and without a worry in the world. I wouldn't have that nagging feeling all the time that there were things I should have done and didn't. My life and everything in it would be organized and up to date.

If I'd done all my homework I'd have written the letter to my aunt with a little gift in plenty of time for her to have received it before her birthday, not three days after it. I'd have personally answered hundreds of good letters I've received. No one would think I was rude or that I considered myself a big shot too busy to respond to a nice letter. My loans would be all paid up and my dues would be paid to the Writers' Guild, the Directors' Guild and AFTRA, the American Federation of Television and Radio Artists and the Authors' League. I'd have checked my bank balance against my canceled checks and I'd have found a new, cheaper insurance company for my car. I'd have filled in all the forms you have to send in to get your guarantee for the things you buy. I'd be some great person.

I can understand just plain not doing something but what I don't understand is how I can so consistently fool myself into thinking I'm *going* to do something when life's experience should remind me that there isn't a chance in the world I'll do it. I remember when I was in high school, I took five or six books home with me every night. I had briefcases to carry them in, I had special bags sometimes and one year I had a thick strap. I always worried about how to carry my books home. I should have worried more about doing something with them when I got them there. Tonight was always going to be different. Finally I'd get at doing all my homework. I never did and it was a habit I carried over with me into college. I must have carried a cumulative total of ten tons of books home from school over the years without ever having read more than a few pounds of them.

My genius for thinking I'll do more than I can do is nowhere more apparent than with the reading I plan to do and don't. I buy books, magazines, newspapers and I save all the good Sunday supplements and put them aside for when I have more time. I have never once in my whole life had more time and I don't know why I think I ever will. If I did read all the books on our shelves, all the magazines I've subscribed to and all the newspapers I've put aside for a rainy day, I'd be one of the best-informed people in the world. If it ever rains for long enough for me to get all my rainy-day reading done, I'll be reading on board an ark.

Safe at Last

DID you ever have one of those days when nothing goes right? It sounds like the beginning of a joke but it's no joke, and the thing that worries me is that I'm running into the second day.

Yesterday I was in Hershey, Pa., talking to 2,500 school kids who had gathered in an auditorium. The people running the event flattered me by pointing out how many kids had come to hear me. But I'm not that old. When you're in school and you get a chance to break the regular classroom routine, you'll do anything different that's offered to you.

As I was leaving, someone who runs an inn near Hershey presented me with a little wicker hamper of delicacies they thought I might eat for lunch on my way back to New York. They thought I was driving, but I flew. At the airport I ate a delicious little shrimp salad in the basket and a piece of apple tart. There was a bottle of sparkling cider which was too good to leave but I couldn't drink it all so I decided to take it home with me. I carried it on board the plane and put it in the overhead rack with my coat.

I was dozing on the flight to New York when there was a sudden commotion from the seats ahead of me and as I awakened something started dripping into my lap from above. The cabin of the small commuter plane was poorly pressurized and the cork had popped out of my sparkling cider, spraying the passengers in front of me.

It was embarrassing and there was no sense trying to convince them it was cider, not champagne. I turned the bottle over to the stewardess and she poured what was left into cups and gave them to the wet passengers as a consolation prize.

My car was in the parking lot at La Guardia Airport in New York. When I got to the booth where they take the money, I couldn't find the parking ticket. They're used to that but still it took almost half an hour to fill out the forms they demanded before they'd let me leave with my car.

On the highway home I pass through two toll gates. The exact-change lanes are much quicker than the manned gates. I fished change out of the ashtray where

I keep it and drove up. I stopped and reached out to flip the quarter into the basket. My hand hit the edge of the window which I hadn't rolled down all the way and the quarter fell to the pavement. There were no more quarters in the ashtray and as I reached in my pocket to look for another, the horns behind me started blowing.

I got out and started looking under the car for my quarter. The exasperated driver behind me finally gave me one. It wasn't kindness, it was impatience but I thanked him profusely.

It was 11:00 when I got to bed last night. My clock radio is set to go on early, 5:37 A.M. When I finally awoke without its assistance this morning, it seemed lighter than usual. I looked at my watch on the table next to the bed. It was 6:20 A.M. and I'd already missed my regular train.

"I meant to tell you," my wife said. "The power went off for a little while yesterday." That's why the clock radio didn't go on.

I dressed hurriedly and as I yanked on my right shoelace, I got the end of it in my hand. Threading a frayed, broken shoelace through a small eyelet is not a job to be done in a hurry.

When I finally boarded a later commuter train, I thought my troubles were over. I got a seat and opened my newspaper, safe at last.

Ten miles down the track, the train ground to an ominous halt. After about fifteen minutes the conductor's voice came over the intercom.

"We're having trouble with the braking system, ladies and gentlemen. They're going to pull another train up alongside us and you'll get off and board that."

The train that came alongside was already filled. By the time perhaps 1,500 people from our train were loaded on it, there wasn't room for anyone who might have fainted to fall down. Reading the paper was out of the question.

I'm at the office now, two hours late, typing and waiting expectantly for my typewriter to break down. It's been dependable for forty years but if it's ever going to go, this'll be the day.

Florence Nightingale Never Would Have Said That

ON the last day of my vacation I was fixing the roof, standing on the top rung of a ten-foot ladder, when the rung broke.

The only good thing to say about the fall is that it was a better way to end a vacation than it would have been to begin one.

I came down through the uprights of the ladder and caught my ribs on the second rung from the top. My ribs broke the second and third rungs of the ladder. The ladder broke my seventh and eighth ribs. If this column isn't as clear as usual today, it's because I'm hitting the keys of my typewriter lightly in order not to jar my frame.

It happened quickly, like an auto accident. I didn't slide off the roof, I dropped like a stone. My wind was knocked out when my ribs hit the oak rung which, for an instant, delayed my plunge to the ground. The rung caught me under my left arm toward my back and temporarily paralyzed my breathing muscles. As I lay there, stunned and gasping, a lot of things went through my mind.

"I think I'm hurt," I remember grunting to myself. I even remember thinking how strange it was I'd taken time to think that. I wondered, too, whether I'd get any air into my lungs before I suffocated.

After three or four minutes I got my wind back and pulled myself up. My elbow was bleeding and I could tell my left leg was bruised from ankle to hip but the only thing that really hurt was my ribs.

I hobbled to the kitchen and called upstairs.

Margie came down and because I was such a sorry-looking sight and in obvious pain, she was instantly tender and solicitous.

She got me to lie down on the kitchen floor, pulled my shirt off and put a dish towel filled with ice on my ribs. Florence Nightingale couldn't have done more . . . for five minutes.

When I finally got myself up off the floor and onto a kitchen chair, it must have appeared to her as though I was going to survive because her attitude changed abruptly.

"What were you doing up on the ladder anyway?" she asked, critically. There wasn't a tender inflection in her mouth.

"I had one of those caulking guns," I said. "I was trying to fix the leak."

"You're too heavy to be standing on the top rung of a ladder at your age," she said, stabbing me twice in one sentence. Tender people can be so cruel when they aren't being tender. Florence Nightingale never would have said that to a person as wounded as I was.

That night I hurt so much that there was no part of my body I could lie on and I spent much of the time sitting in a chair.

The following morning it seemed likely that I was more than scraped and bruised so we drove thirty miles to the hospital for X-rays.

You never know for sure whether you're making more of a fuss about pain than you ought to, so naturally I was pleased when the doctor came back with the pictures a few minutes later and announced that I had two broken ribs. Not that knowing your ribs are broken does you any good.

"The woman over there at the cashier's desk will take care of you," the young doctor said next.

"Isn't there anything you do?" I asked.

"We don't strap ribs anymore," he said. "I'll give you some pills for pain. You'll be uncomfortable for about a month."

I paid for the diagnosis and left.

When I got home I'd traveled sixty miles, spent two hours in the emergency room and a fair amount of money, and I hurt exactly as much as before I'd gone to the hospital.

In the days following that first five minutes on the kitchen floor, I've sought consolation from people other than my wife. I haven't gotten much. For one thing, I haven't run into a single person who hasn't interfered with me telling them about my broken ribs by them telling me about theirs. Everyone, it seems, has broken a rib.

Three days later, all I'm getting is advice on how

not to fall off ladders, or pessimistic talk about how long it takes ribs to heal. All I want is for them to kiss it and make it better and they're giving me advice.

I don't feel like doing much work these days but at least I'm not on vacation. I'm at the office where I don't have to.

Jenny Kissed Me

TEACHERS are no longer making pupils memorize things as much as they used to. Those in favor of making kids memorize things, hold up your hands. Those against?

When I had to memorize things, I thought it was stupid. It didn't seem to me as though learning something by heart had anything to do with an education. The phrase "to learn by heart" suggests that memorizing has nothing to do with the part of the brain we think with, and yet today I'm not so opposed to memorizing a few things as I used to be.

It may be idiocy to learn something by heart but there's a great comfort in knowing all the words to a long, well-written passage. Like an old friend, familiar words are nice to have around sometimes. It was probably true that the worst teachers made you do the most memorizing but once you've done it you have something that stays with you. Maybe it's only to laugh about with your classmates when you meet twenty years out of school, but you have it.

Nothing in the world could convince me that the

quality of mercy is strained, for example. I learned that the quality of mercy is *not* strained when I was about fourteen and I've never forgotten it. Furthermore, it droppeth as the gentle rain from heaven, upon the place beneath. I could no more forget that than forget my name.

If you start thinking about it, you'll be surprised at how many things you learned by rote. In my school we started with the alphabet and the multiplication tables. Sometimes now I have to stop and think for a minute whether nine times seven is fifty-six or sixty-three but I can always start from the beginning and get the right answer. I'm told that some schools aren't even making kids learn the multiplication tables anymore. They all have computers!

I hate myself for having turned so conservative about some things but I don't think it's a bad idea to make kids memorize a little good literature. I don't know as Henry Wadsworth Longfellow does much for them but the preamble to the Constitution is pretty good stuff to have permanently in your head.

"We, the People of the United States, in order to form a more perfect union . . ." are magnificent words expressing a profoundly important idea and we shouldn't forget them.

Most of us have in our heads hundreds of fragments of poems and long segments of prose. We don't use them much but they're nice to have up there. They're like the chairs in a room you don't sit in very often. They're good for special occasions.

In my high school poetry book there were two poems on one page written by Leigh Hunt. We had to memorize "Abou Ben Adhem" (may his tribe increase), and I hated it. The second poem on the same page is one I loved and have never forgotten.

> Jenny kissed me when we met,
> Jumping from the chair she sat in;
> Time, you thief, who love to get
> Sweets into your list, put that in!
> Say I'm weary, say I'm sad,
> Say that health and wealth have missed me,
> Say I'm growing old, but add,
> Jenny kissed me.

The things you memorize inadvertently, as I memorized that, are probably better than the things you have to memorize.

One of the things in my repertoire now is Lincoln's Gettysburg Address. I learned it not in school but working with Harry Reasoner. When you're filming something, the sound man asks the person doing the talking for a voice level so that he can adjust the dials on his recorder. Some people, when asked to do this by the sound technician, merely count off: "Testing, one, two three . . . testing, testing, one, two, three."

Harry always gave the sound man Lincoln's Gettysburg Address. "Fourscore and seven years ago our fathers brought forth . . ." he'd say. Sometimes he'd only get through a few lines before the technician stopped him and said, "That's fine." Sometimes, though, he'd go the whole way through it and after listening to Harry recite it several hundred times, I learned the whole thing myself.

If you're ever over to my house for dinner, I'll give you the Gettysburg Address, Lewis Carroll's "Jabberwocky," half a dozen short poems by Robert Browning and "Jack and Jill" in Latin.

"Jack et Jill quaerentes fontem/Ascendebant parvum montem" is the way it begins.

Tarawa

WHEN the President spoke at a luncheon for 125 Medal of Honor winners, my thoughts turned to war and to one Marine who never got a medal.

The year was 1943. No one knows who he was. He came wading into the beach at Tarawa with a rifle held high over his head. When he hit the beach, he was one of only four left from the group of twenty Marines who had been dumped off the small blue Higgins invasion boat, 600 yards out on the coral reef beyond the shallow lagoon.

A Japanese machine gun had dropped all but those four men into the lagoon, dead or so badly wounded that they drowned with the seventy-five pounds of equipment on their backs.

The Marine lay still for five minutes. His khaki started to dry out and turn light again, except where the blood oozed out near the shoulder.

Finally he raised his head. He could make out the Japanese machine-gun position concealed in a nest 100 feet to his right. It was four feet above him, behind a line of coconut logs that formed a barricade the length of the beach.

The Marine looked back. He saw men pile out of

other landing boats off the atoll. He knew they were going to get it from the same machine gunner who got the men who started in with him. As the Marines waded closer, he could see bullets kicking up the water around them. The bullets came from the position just up the beach from where he lay.

Some Marines were hit. First he saw their helmets, then their rifles, sink below the surface.

Marines on the beach with him who told the story saw him get to his knees. They knew what he was going to do even though they could see a sticky splotch of red where blood still flowed from the wound on his shoulder.

He quickly pulled himself up over the log barrier so that he was on the sandy plateau above the beach, on a level with the Japanese gunners.

The others lost sight of him as he moved inland a little, behind a tangle of brush.

Suddenly there were wild shouts in English mixed with Japanese. Then there was a short burst of machine-gun fire and, almost simultaneously, an explosion. Then, silence.

When the other Marines made their way to the scene, there were pieces of two Japanese machine gunners blown apart by the Marine's grenade. In front of them, there lay the Marine, cut in two through the middle by the last burst of machine-gun fire as he hurled his grenade.

Out in the lagoon, Marine reinforcements waded in safely. They never knew why the machine-gun fire had stopped. The men who knew never had time to tell them. That's the way the battle for Tarawa began forty years ago.

During the fight for one square mile of coral in the Pacific, 4,690 Japanese soldiers were killed. Seventeen were taken prisoner. None escaped.

There were 1,026 Marines killed, 2,296 wounded.

It was war at its disgusting worst and not all the Marines were heroes, either. There were huge pyramid-shaped cement barriers that the Japanese had built in the shallow waters to prevent landing craft from getting to shore. Some of the wading Marines stopped and hid behind the barriers while the braver among them waded onto the beach in the face of enemy fire. It's always that way and who among us is certain what he'd do under the circumstances.

There were other horrors. One live Japanese soldier would often lie among a pile of his own dead, wait until the Marines had passed by and then rise and attack them from behind. It led to the unpleasant Marine habit of firing their automatic weapons into any pile of dead Japanese they passed.

There should be better ways to settle differences among us.

XI:

PASSING

The War Correspondent

HE was Hollywood's idea of what a war correspondent should be when I first met him, a kind of James Bond of journalism. He was quick, bright, tough and good-looking in his belted trench coat. To me, he was one of the Big Guys. He knew the story he was after and when he'd written it, he'd sell it for a lot of money to the *Saturday Evening Post, Collier's* or the *Reader's Digest*.

His name doesn't add anything to the tragedy and I'm not going to use it. The last time I heard from him he needed money. He always needed money. We all have friends who have borrowed and we may have done some of it ourselves but this man was an all-time, world-class borrower. He'd borrowed money from everyone he'd ever heard of and he'd touched the best—men like Budd Schulberg and Walter Cronkite.

He had different ways of asking for money from different people and he never suggested you were giving him anything. He was going to pay you back next Thursday. He had sold an article to the *Reader's Digest* and they'd told him the check was in the mail so it was just a matter of a few days to tide him over, he'd say.

His name appears in more than one hundred entries

in the *Reader's Guide to Periodical Literature* for articles he wrote for America's most prestigious magazines . . . but the last entry is one he wrote for *Coronet* magazine in 1958. It had been downhill ever since.

In the beginning this peerless borrower did things in a big way. He ran up tabs of hundreds of dollars at the best drinking places in New York. When he was poor, he didn't mingle with the poor. He went to the 21 Club and mingled with the rich. In the beginning he'd ask for loans of a thousand or fifteen hundred dollars, but in recent years he reduced his demands to a hundred dollars or less. The last time he called me was just six weeks ago. He was suffering from a rare blood disease, he told me, and desperately needed thirty dollars for medicine. It was so like him to make it thirty dollars instead of twenty-five because it sounded more believable.

I didn't give it to him.

Still fresh in my memory was the time ten years ago when he'd come to my office with tears streaming down his cheeks. His son, he'd told me, had a rare eye disease and would I loan him two hundred and fifty dollars so he could take his son to Boston where there was a doctor who knew how to treat the problem. Too late, I'd found out that the story of the ailing son was pure fiction.

Yesterday I was sitting in the back seat of a car with Walter Cronkite and he pulled a letter out of his pocket.

"Dear Walter," the letter began, "your friend is dead." The letter mentioned his name. "He died December first in the library at 11 East 40th Street or just outside in the cold. Positive identification was made at the City Morgue.

"I've known him for the past five years," the letter continued. "I'm a bartender at McAnn's on Third Avenue.

"Over the past five years he would speak about his World War II days with you. He was quite good at telling anecdotes. We spent many hours talking about many subjects under the sun. He brightened up many days which would have been otherwise boring for me. I thought you would want to know."

The bartender's letter to Walter was a warmer and more sincere obituary than anyone else could have written.

"I consider it a privilege to have known him," he wrote. "Unfortunately I met him in the twilight of his life. He died of a rare disease, the name of which I can't even pronounce."

Henry Fonda

I'D never met Henry Fonda before and I never saw him again but in the late spring of 1975 I spent five intense hours with him while he read a script of mine for a television show. Until that day I had considered Henry Fonda's success an accident of birth that had given him a special and charming way of being. From that day on I understood that Fonda's success came to him mostly because he was a talented and hardworking professional actor.

When television has a documentary to which it hopes to attract a large audience, it often asks some famous person to lend his name to it by reading the script. I've never approved of the system and I didn't like the idea of hiring Henry Fonda to read my script on Franklin Roosevelt called FDR: *The Man Who Changed America.*

It was out of my hands, though, and the date was made for Fonda to narrate the film on camera. About three minutes before his appointed hour, Henry Fonda walked into a barnlike New York television studio carrying a suitcase not much bigger than a briefcase. Three or four of us introduced ourselves and Fonda immediately asked to see the director.

Vernon Diamond, one of television's top news directors, identified himself and Fonda put his little suitcase on a bare table on stage and opened it to reveal four new shirts and eight neckties.

"I didn't know what your background or lighting would be so I brought a selection," Fonda said to the director. "What do you want me to wear here?" he said, pointing to the open suitcase.

It was a small thing but it was the beginning of one of the most pleasant, low-key, professional performances I have ever seen.

Fonda said very little but he made several small jokes about his pacemaker and about the fact that he was hard of hearing. He seemed at ease with himself and with us. He gave us no impression that he felt he was among strangers. He assumed we were as professional as he was, which was giving most of us a break.

What I really recall is how malleable he was. I realized then that unless an actor is a one-part player who goes around being himself in every role he plays, he must be able to adjust to how others want him to be or think he ought to be for the part.

He had been given my script several days earlier and I was curious about whether he would have bothered to read it in advance. He had not only read it, he had marked it throughout with heavy pen lines. I was nervous about whether he liked it or not and I never got any satisfaction from him in this regard. It did not seem to enter his mind to make any judgment about whether my script was good or bad. That was not his business. His business was to make what I had written sound as good and as much like the way I intended it to sound as he was able.

Vern Diamond sat Fonda on a stool in the middle of a barren stage with a circle of light on him.

"If you are fifty years old," Fonda started to read, "Franklin Delano Roosevelt was President for almost a quarter of your life. If you were born after 1945, he was already gone when you got here."

I was sitting to the side and Fonda stopped and turned toward me. He knew my name now.

"How do you want me to read that, Andy? Do you want it like that or like this?" He read it again, changing the rhythm and emphasis of his voice to give it another nuance of meaning.

For the rest of those five hours Henry Fonda kept turning to me to ask how I wanted something read and what I had in mind when I wrote this or that.

It was the last time I ever thought of Henry Fonda's art as an accident of birth. I have never seen anyone so thoroughly professional work so hard to do a good job.

"I'm going over to the hospital now," he said as he

left the studio. "Need a new battery for my pace-maker."

Jud

It's strange about friends. You don't even like some of them, you just have them.

Jud was my friend and I liked him. He was fifteen when we first met, sitting on the bench just outside the locker room, lacing up our football shoes. Jud's parents were moving to our city and Jud was transferring to our school. He was the new kid. We'd heard he was already six feet tall and weighted 185 pounds, so we had high hopes he could help us beat Albany High School.

Fifteen-year-old kids don't talk much under those circumstances. We just laced up our shoes, but even so, I remember liking him.

Jud and I played next to each other on the football team for three years. He was a tackle and I was a guard and we had an understanding between us about the moves we'd make that no one else would have understood. It was just between us.

We shared all kinds of good times growing up and we've had fun remembering them ever since. Remembering can be pleasant if you don't do too much of it. A few days ago Jud was remembering the telephone number of a girl named Peggy he was in love with for two months in 1937. He had a great memory for trivia like that.

It was a pretty, blue dress that finally came between him and Peggy. She came to dancing class wearing it one night. She looked beautiful, but Jud said he realized right then that she was the only girl who wore a brand-new dress to dancing class every week. That worried him about her, and things were never the same.

Summers, Jud's family went to Speculator, a small town near Lake Placid, where he had a horse. The horse was well along in years but Jud loved it. To help pay to feed the animal, he let other people ride it for a dollar an hour.

One summer Max Baer, the World Heavyweight Champion, and his younger brother, Buddy, were training in Speculator. Buddy weighed 240 pounds and he liked to ride horses. One day he rented Jud's horse. The next morning the horse was so tired he could hardly stand up and Jud felt terrible. After that when Jud saw Buddy Baer coming down the road, he'd run in and take his horse out the back door of the barn and hide him in the woods until Buddy left.

Now it's forty-seven years later. We've stayed as close as we were when we played football together. We never played the same games again but we always understood each other's moves.

Jud became a B-17 pilot during World War II. He had the kind of coordinated grace it took to fly a four-engined bomber. Learning how to fly came more easily to him than the irregular verbs we'd tried to master sitting side by side in Mr. Sharp's French class.

After the war, nothing came easily to Jud for a while. He got a job selling Cadillacs on commission and we used to laugh about it. In 1945 the dealer he worked for had back orders for fifty cars, but General Motors was still switching over to peacetime production and Jud's dealer was only getting two Cadillacs a month. There were four salesmen who had seniority.

I don't know why we remained such close friends. We had little in common but memories and understanding. Jud ended up owning a liquor store in New York and I knew as little about his work as he knew of mine. We called each other two or three times a week and said almost nothing.

On Christmas Eve, Jud had a heart attack. On the day he was to be released from the hospital, doctors discovered what they referred to as "a spot on his lung." He recovered from his heart attack and went back to work. A month ago they operated on Jud's lung. It was not a spot. The malignancy was pervasive and surgery was a mistake. He had nine of what were to have been twenty-one cobalt treatments and Friday he went home to have lamb chops.

Sylvia called me this morning at 6:25. Our phone does not ring at 6:25 with good news.

"Jud's dead," she said.